Diana Souhami

is the author of *Gluck, Gertrude and Alice* and *Greta and Cecil* (also in Flamingo). She lives in London.

D0064166

DIANA SOUHAMI

Mrs Keppel and Her Daughter

Flamingo
An Imprint of HarperCollinsPublishers

Flamingo
An Imprint of HarperCollins*Publishers*
77–85 Fulham Palace Road,
Hammersmith, London W6 8JB

Published by Flamingo 1997
9 8 7 6 5

First published in Great Britain by
HarperCollins*Publishers* 1996

Author photograph by Peter Campbell

ISBN 0 00 638714 4

Set in Linotron Spectrum

Printed and bound in Great Britain by
Caledonian International Book Manufacturing Ltd, Glasgow

Contents

List of Illustrations

Major Denys Trefusis, Royal Horse Guards: Private Collection

The Sackvilles' family home, Knole, Sevenoaks, Kent: Mary Evans Picture Library

Vita Sackville-West: Lenare, National Portrait Gallery

Sketch by Violet of her as Eve and Vita as Julian, 1918: Beinicke Library, Yale University

Mrs Keppel in 1932: Private Collection

Pat Dansey: B.O. Hoppé, Private Collection

The Princess de Polignac: Piaz, Paris, National Portrait Gallery

Violet in 1932: Private Collection

Violet at the Ombrellino circa 1937: Private Collection

The Ombrellino, Florence, with views over the River Arno, the Duomo, Ponte Vecchio and Palazzo Pitti: Cecil Beaton and Private Collection

Violet in 1919: B.O. Hoppé, Mansell Collection

A Personal Note

Violet Trefusis's letters to Vita Sackville-West suggested this book to me. Written between 1910 and 1920, immediate, unedited, passionate, they are a cry from the heart quite unlike the polished style she contrived for her novels. Most are collected in the volume *Violet to Vita* published in 1989, others are at the Beinecke Library, Yale. They give Violet's version of her affair with Vita. Romantic, overstated, eloquent, they testify to the destruction of love.

Behind these letters lies a story of more than thwarted love. Its essence is hypocrisy and double standards, of high social standing for Violet's mother, Alice Keppel, and of silence and exile for Violet.

Mrs Keppel loved profitably. 'La Favorita' of Edwardian high society, she was the mistress of Queen Victoria's son Bertie, when he was Prince of Wales then King Edward VII. It was an affair that brought her social splendour and great riches. Memoirs, diaries and her own letters give evidence of her style. Those old enough to remember her — her niece Lady Cecilia McKenna, the Contessa Visconti who knew her in Florence — told me I could not imagine the scale of her entertaining, the lavishness of her houses, the silver, the servants, the dinners for seventy.

Violet saw her mother as 'luminous', 'resplendent', 'dazzling', a paragon of romance. But her mother had impressive practicality. Confident, assertive, determined, she was not going to stand by while her daughter became declassé and a social pariah and tarnished the family name.

Mrs Keppel and the King conducted their extra-marital relationship with discretion, propriety and unwavering confidence. Violet described herself as struggling with frightening emotions in uncharted waters. There were no rules for her sort of love, no discussion of it.

The law neither condoned nor condemned. A move to legislate was made in 1921. A Tory MP, Frederick Macquister, proposed a clause 'Acts of Gross Indecency by Females' to the Criminal Law Amendment Act. In the House of Commons he deplored the decline in female morality, averred that lesbianism induced neurasthenia and insanity, debauched young girls, threatened the birth rate and was due to an abnormality of the brain. His clause was passed. Pat Dansey, Violet's go-between, wrote to Vita:

> One thing I did urgently want to call your attention to was 'The Criminal Law Amendment Bill' and the clause that was inserted in the Bill at the third reading. It only makes me *implore* you to be *careful* for your own sake as well as Violet's.

She need not have feared. The debate moved to the House of Lords. Their lordships speculated on the effect of breaking silence. Lord Desart of Desart Court, Kilkenny, former Director of Public Prosecutions, said:

> You are going to tell the whole world there is such an offence, to bring it to the notice of women who have never heard of it, never thought of it, never dreamed of it. I think this is a very great mischief.

Lord Birkenhead, Lord Chancellor, concurred:

> I am bold enough to say that of every thousand women, taken as a whole, 999 have never even heard a whisper of these practices. Among all these, in the homes of this country, the taint of this noxious and horrible suspicion is to be imparted.

It was not a crisp debate. The clause was rejected. The underlying directive 'don't talk about it' prevailed.

Vita Sackville-West in 1920 wrote her account of her affair with Violet Trefusis, then locked her 'confession' away in a leather bag. Neither wrote openly about it after it reached its stormy end. They talked of together writing 'a better *Well of Loneliness*' but this did not happen. Both wrote *roman à clefs* about their love for each other but coded these in heterosexual show for the sake of their mothers, husbands and reputations.

Vita died in 1962, Violet ten years later. Some months after Violet's death, Nigel Nicolson, Vita's son and executor, published his mother's confession, her *De Profundis* as he called it. In a decade of knowing about the manuscript he had not shown it to his father, Harold Nicolson, who died in 1968, or to Violet. It was not, in his judgement, a story to be aired while either was alive.

He interpolated his mother's account of 20,000 words, with 50,000 words of his perspective on it and gave his book the title *Portrait of a Marriage*, not *Portrait of a Lesbian Relationship* which was how she had written her story. He set her affair with Violet into the context of the subsequent years of her long, peaceable and supportive marriage to Harold Nicolson. He offered the book as a 'panegyric' to his parents' marriage and called the story, in his introduction to the 1992 reissue, the triumph of love over infatuation. 'It is a love story, not the love between Vita Sackville-West and Violet Trefusis, as many people assumed, but between Vita and my father Harold.' The hero of the story is his father, whom he described as rock-like and angelic and whose determination and understanding saved the marriage.

Violet is the 'villainess'. 'Remember that Violet was evil' he said to me when I visited him at Sissinghurst Castle in Kent in 1993 to talk about this book. In his introduction to a collection of his parents' letters to each other he wrote of Violet's 'pernicious influence' and 'cynical wickedness'. In letters to Violet's executor, John Phillips, he wrote of her 'intolerable conduct' and 'abominable character'. His dislike of her was not personal, for all he remembered of her were her French clothes and perfume when once or twice, in her later life, she visited his mother at Sissinghurst. It stemmed from his deep regard for his father. 'I wish Violet was dead,' Harold wrote to Vita in September 1918, 'she has poisoned one of the most sunny things that ever happened.' He compared her to 'some fierce orchid, glimmering and stinking in the recesses of life.' She was, he said, tortuous, erotic, irresponsible, 'absolutely unscrupulous', irremediable and a reptile.

In December 1972, three months before *Portrait* went to press, Nigel Nicolson wrote to John Phillips warning him that quotation in the book from his father's letters and mother's diaries would 'certainly put the reader against Violet':

> I cannot help that because I believe it to be true. Let her be a devil in a scarlet cloak for those two years, and think that a devil is more interesting and dramatic than a saint in wings.

Those who see through different eyes draw different portraits. I do not see Violet for those years as a devil in a scarlet cloak. And though Vita may well have been a successful wife as vouched for by her son and executor, her sexual prescription in *Portrait of a Marriage* was of little use to her women lovers who did not want to be marginalized or abandoned.

Violet wanted a context for her love. 'I HATE,' she wrote to Vita in 1920,

> the furtiveness and dissimulation, the petty hypocrisies and deceits, the carefully planned assignations, letters that must be 'given' not posted. It revolts and nauseates me.

She wanted an open relationship with Vita, which was not a villainous desire. Context, for Vita and Harold was their property, gardens, work, friends, marriage, family. They each took same-sex lovers but made it a rule that these affairs were always on their own terms. They talked about their marriage in a BBC broadcast in 1929 – a year after *The Well of Loneliness* was judged obscene and banned – and said it was the greatest of human benefits, guided by a common sense of values, respect and give and take.

Portrait of a Marriage does not dwell on the litter of hurt lives left by Vita. She was magnificent and proprietorial but unavailable. Lovers wrecked existing relationships in the vain hope of being with her. Harold referred to the wreckage as her 'muddles'.

Violet moved to France after her affair with Vita ended. Few people there knew about her past. Her husband Denys Trefusis, and Mrs Keppel's husband George, in anger burned Vita's letters to her, written between 1910 and 1920. Violet herself tore up those she considered indiscreet. She did not have the same eye to posterity as Vita and Harold. She was not methodical, calculating or even organized. But later letters from Vita to her have survived, written during the Second World War, and numerous references by her to Vita's earlier letters make their content clear.

I hope I vindicate Violet in this story of adultery, royal and aristocratic families, dominant mothers and how not to conduct a lesbian relationship. Ironies unfurl in it, and a gulf between private life and public display. Mrs Keppel was 'much toadied to' by peers of the realm when she was with the King. Violet and Vita, when they partnered each other at a tea dance, were asked to leave the hotel. By way of bias I question why *Portrait of a Marriage* should be an acceptable story and *Portrait of a Lesbian Relationship* not.

It is a tribute to Nigel Nicolson's generosity that he made material available to me and allowed me to quote freely from family papers, both published and unpublished. Most of these papers, in particular the letters and diaries of Vita Sackville-West, Harold Nicolson and Lady Sackville, are at the Lilly Library at the University of Indiana.

I offer special thanks to Violet Trefusis's executor, John Phillips. He helped me at every stage, answered the endless questions I put to him, suggested contacts and made unpublished material available to me, including letters from Alice Keppel to her husband George and to Violet. Most of Violet's unpublished letters and papers are now at the Beinecke Library, Yale.

I thank Ian Anstruther for information about Pat Dansey; Félicité Potter and Phyllida Ellis for letters, papers and photographs of Denys Trefusis and the Trefusis family; Ann Ravenscroft-Hulme for facts and photographs I would not otherwise have found; Lady Cecilia and David McKenna, the Ducessa Franca Visconti, the Duc d'Harcourt, Cécile

Wajsbrot, the Marquise de Chabannes La Pelice, Bernard Minoret, Anthony Allfrey, the Honourable Lady Mosley, Maggs Bros, the Earl of Listowel.

I acknowledge the gracious permission of Her Majesty The Queen to quote from material in the Royal Archives and for the republication of material which is subject to copyright. I also acknowledge the permission of the Trustees of the Broadlands Archives Trust to quote from papers in the Cassel archive housed at the Hartley Library, Southampton University.

I am grateful to my agent Georgina Capel, to Michael Fishwick and Rebecca Lloyd at HarperCollins and to Terence Pepper at the National Portrait Gallery.

To avoid cluttering the text, references, including specific copyright credits, are at the end of the book by page number and opening phrase. Bibliographic sources are in these references too.

PART ONE

Queens and Heirs Apparent

ONE

At Christmas 1900 the Honourable Mrs George Keppel gave a Fabergé cigarette case to her lover Bertie, Prince of Wales and heir to the English throne. Made from three kinds of gold, enamelled in royal blue, over its cover front and back coiled a serpent contrived from diamonds. The head and tail of the serpent formed a knot. It was a symbolic gift from the Prince's temptress, 'La Favorita', his 'little Mrs George'.

Ten years later when Bertie – King Edward VII – died, his widow Queen Alexandra, mindful of the sexual link between her husband and Mrs Keppel, returned the cigarette case to her. In 1936, Mrs Keppel asked Bertie's daughter-in-law Queen Mary to accept it as a gift. It is now in the permanent royal collection of pieces by Fabergé. A fanciful equivalent, had times not changed, would have been for Mrs Keppel's great-granddaughter Camilla Parker-Bowles to have given cufflinks to her lover, the Prince of Wales, engraved with their entwined initials, for his wife Diana, had she become a widowed queen, to have returned these to Mrs Parker-Bowles at the time of King Charles's death, for Camilla at some later date to have given them to the wife of William, Charles's and Diana's son, to be kept in the royal trove.

But niceties are now scrutinized for what they conceal. In 1992 Princess Diana and her husband separated. She found it unacceptable for him, however exalted his rank, to be the lover of another woman while married to her. 'There were three of us in this marriage and it was a bit crowded,' she told the world. The triangle gave her 'rampant bulimia'. Mrs Keppel would not have sympathized. For her it was not how things were that mattered but how they appeared. Her precepts were those of Society: discretion, manners, charm. The appearance of civilized marriage was as imperative as a hat at Ascot, pearls and furs. It was her art to be Bertie's *boudoir belle* while he was Prince of Wales then King and, if not a pillar of the Establishment, then at least a cornice or an architrave.

She served the Crown and did not allow jealousy and sexual possession to blur her manners or her style. On 10 December 1936 Bertie's grandson, Edward VIII, abdicated the throne to marry Wallis Simpson, a divorcee. Mrs Keppel dining at the Ritz was heard to declare, 'Things were done much better in my day.'

In her day she both shared a bed with the King and advised him on presents for his wife. Queen Alexandra collected pieces by Fabergé. At Mrs Keppel's suggestion Bertie commissioned jewelled, gold models of all the Sandringham animals for his Queen. Artists sent from St Petersburg made wax maquettes for the stonecutters. The Fabergé workshops produced a glittering farmyard of heifers, goats, cocks, pigs. Persimmon — Bertie's Derby-winning horse — was there and Caesar, his Norfolk terrier, with rubies for eyes, a gold bell and a collar inscribed 'I belong to the King'.

In her turn Mrs Keppel's daughter, Violet, gave her lover, Vita Sackville-West, a symbolic present, a token of their tryst. It was a Venetian ring of red lava, carved with a woman's head. It had belonged to a fifteenth-century doge. Violet acquired it on a visit with her mother to the art dealer Sir Joseph Duveen of Bond Street. He supplied the Prince of Wales with paintings for Sandringham, Buckingham Palace and Marlborough House. (Bertie liked pictures of yachting scenes, battles and pretty women without much on.) Sir Joseph invited Violet to choose a present. She was six at the time, had a precocious heart and cried when her mother tried to make her put the ring back and choose a Victorian doll.

Seven years later, in 1908, Violet and Vita, accompanied by governesses, went to Florence for the summer to learn Italian. Violet cried again when they parted for home, told Vita she loved her and gave her the doge's ring. By 1919 this love had become passionate and volatile. As a pledge to each other, and in sexual rejection of their husbands, they took off their wedding rings. The following year Vita wrote of the doge's ring, 'I have it now, of course I have it, just as I have *her*.' In her will she decreed that it be returned to Violet. When she died in August 1962 her husband Harold Nicolson duly sent it with a circumspect letter. And when Violet died a decade later the ring was returned to her nephew so that it might form part of the Keppel memorabilia.

But the doge's ring was a memento of unacceptable love. Private devotions were one thing, social conformity another. A myriad of hypocrisies preserved the relationship between Mrs Keppel and the King. Marriage vows and even the Coronation Oath were rituals and semblances that preserved the *status quo*. An indiscretion of dress or etiquette mattered more than adultery. *Noblesse oblige* was the rule. Divorce was unthinkable because of loss of status, however compromised the relationship between husband and wife. When Violet in 1920 tried to extricate herself from a marriage that was worse than a sham her mother warned, 'You'll be a laughing stock, becoming Miss Keppel again.'

Group photographs of huge shooting parties commemorate Mrs Keppel's weekends with Bertie. He sits at the centre, portly and assured, Homburg tilted, hands folded on his walking stick, flanked by ladies in ankle-length gowns, their hats like nesting birds. All look inscrutably at the camera. Nothing is revealed of the secret relationships between other women's husbands and other men's wives, of the elaborate games of adultery decorously conducted at these country-house weekends.

These were Edwardian heydays for Bertie, Alice and their set. Taxation was low, servants cheap:

Money was freely spent and wealth was everywhere in evidence. Moreover it was possessed largely by the nicest people, who entertained both in London and in the country ... The champagne vintages from 'eighty to 'eighty-seven were infinitely superior to anything since produced.

Strict ceremony regulated their lives. Mrs Keppel, as the King's Lady, would change four times a day. She required two maids to iron and lay out her clothes, curl her hair, scent her bathwater, wind her watches.

It was a good hostess's duty to attend to the 'disposition of bedrooms', Vita Sackville-West wrote in her satirical novel, *The Edwardians*:

> It was so necessary to be tactful and at the same time discreet
> ... the name of each guest would be neatly written on a card
> slipped into a tiny brass frame on the bedroom door ... Lord
> Robert Gore was in the Red Silk Room; Mrs Levison just across
> the passage. That was as it should be.

The housekeeper, maids and valets understood the careful coding of the cards that hung beside the bell indicator outside the pantry and 'the recurrence of certain adjustments and coincidences'. At times scandal surfaced – to do with jealousy, betrayal, broken hearts. The Prince of Wales was twice threatened with the law by angry husbands. But these elite gatherings were untroubled by intrusion from zoom-angle lenses through the windows of the Tapestry Room, the tapping of cellular phones or bugging devices in the chandeliers.

Mrs Keppel turned adultery into an art. Her demeanour and poise countered 'whispers, taints and horrible noxious suspicions'. Clear as to what she wanted – prosperity and status – she challenged none of the proprieties of her class. She knew, said Consuelo Vanderbilt, the Duchess of Marlborough, who lived in Blenheim Palace in unhappy proximity to the Duke, 'how to choose her friends with shrewd appraisal'.

Even her enemies – and they were few – she treated kindly which, considering the influence she wielded with the Prince, indicated a generous nature. She invariably knew the choicest scandal, the price of stocks, the latest political move; no one could better amuse the Prince during the tedium of the long dinners etiquette decreed.

Bertie when King asked Margot Asquith* if she had ever known a woman with a kinder and sweeter nature than Alice's: 'I could truthfully answer that I had not.'

In her later years, Mrs Keppel displayed a large signed photograph of Queen Alexandra in her drawing room to show how far approval reigned. The Queen, too, had to appear not to mind her husband carrying on with a woman twenty-four years younger than herself. An extant letter from her to Mrs Keppel expresses formal concern at the illness of Alice's husband:

Dear Mrs Keppel

I am so sorry to hear of yr husband's illness in New York & that you should have this terrible long journey before you in addition to all the great anxiety . . . I do hope that on your arrival you should find the attack of typhoid less severe than you should fear.

Yrs sincerely

Alexandra

Less formal concerns were not recorded, though one year her daughter-in-law the Duchess of York wrote to her husband George when Mrs Keppel arrived at Cowes, 'What a pity Mrs G.K. is again to the fore! How annoyed Mama will be.' And on another occasion the Queen called her lady-in-waiting, Charlotte Knollys, to share the view from a window at Sandringham of Bertie and Alice looking fat and comic in a carriage in the grounds.

Dressed in gowns by Worth, with collars of diamonds and ropes of pearls, Mrs Keppel was there at the King's left hand for racing at Ascot, sailing at Cowes, grouse shoots at Sandringham, sea air and casinos at Biarritz and Monte Carlo. She dazzled and seduced. Her daughters were enthralled. 'As a child', Violet wrote in an unpublished piece, 'I saw Mama in a blaze of glory, resplendent in a perpetual tiara.' Her

---

* Wife of the Prime Minister from 1908–19: 'She is stone white with the brown veiled eyes of an aged falcon', Virginia Woolf wrote of her (4 June 1923).

mother, more than the crowned queen, was the Queen of Hearts, the stuff of fairy tales. Her alabaster skin, blue eyes, chestnut hair, large breasts, kindness and charm so overwhelmed the King that he gave her love and great riches. 'I adore the unparalleled romance of her life,' Violet wrote to her own lover:

> My dear our respective mothers take some beating! I wonder if I shall ever squeeze as much romance into my life as she has had in hers; anyhow I mean to have a jolly good try!

Mrs Keppel eclipsed her daughters. 'We are not', Violet wrote of herself and her sister Sonia, 'as lovable, or as good looking, or as successful as our mother. We do not equal, still less surpass her. We make do and mend.' Sonia concurred: 'From my earliest childhood,' she wrote in her autobiography, *Edwardian Daughter*,

> she was invested for me with a brilliant, goddess-like quality . . . she could have decreed that her particular pedestal should have been made by Fabergé. I can picture her as she lay back among her lace pillows, her beautiful chestnut hair unbound around her shoulders . . .
>
> And I can see the flowers sent as oblations to this goddess, the orchids, the malmaisons, the lilies. Great beribboned baskets of them, delivered in horse-drawn vans by a coachman and attendant in livery. They would have been banked in tall, cut-glass vases about her bed.

The great beribboned baskets were not from Mrs Keppel's husband George, who had very little money or imagination. In Sonia's memory her mother's bedroom was always scented by flowers 'and a certain elusive smell, like fresh green sap, that came from herself'. In such a bower, mother seemed a touch unreal: 'My mother began as an atmosphere,' Violet wrote,

> luminous, resplendent . . . She not only had a gift of happiness, but she excelled in making others happy. She resembled a Christmas tree laden with presents for everyone.

She particularly excelled in making King Edward VII happy. He for his part excelled in making her very rich. They were lovers for the last twelve years of his life and fêted as principal guests by most of the owners of the great Edwardian country houses. Mrs Keppel was not welcomed by the Duke of Portland at Welbeck Abbey near Sherwood Forest where life, said the Duchess of Marlborough, was 'enshrined in a hyper-aristocratic niche', nor by the Duke of Norfolk at Arundel, nor the Marquess of Salisbury at Hatfield House in Hertfordshire where segregated prayers were said in the private chapel every morning before breakfast and every evening after tea. And Vita's mother, Lady Sackville, in deference to Bertie's wife excluded her from a party at Knole on 10 July 1898:

> The Prince had wanted to invite Lady Warwick and also his new friend Mrs Keppel, but I told him that I preferred to ask some of the County ladies . . . especially as the Princess was coming. He acquiesced and was very nice about it.

Such rebuffs were few. Little Mrs George was openly escorted by the King at Chatsworth and Sandringham, where tea was a full-dress meal − ladies in gowns, lords and gentlemen in short black jackets and black ties − and dinner a banquet − the guests bedecked in tiaras, ribands and Orders of the Empire. Both were friends of Lord and Lady Alington of Crichel, Lord and Lady Howe of Gopsall, Lord and Lady Iveagh of Elvedon, Ronald and Maggie Greville of Polesden Lacey. Mrs Keppel took holidays with Bertie in Paris, Marienbad, Biarritz, sailed with him on the Royal Yacht, dined with him at Buckingham Palace, entertained him for 'tea' at her house at 30 Portman Square.

In her autobiography Margot Asquith described her first weekend party as the prime minister's wife at Windsor Castle in June 1908. At prayers the King, Queen and their daughter Princess Victoria sat in a box, Alice Keppel sat below:

We heard a fine sermon upon men who justify their actions, have no self-knowledge and never face life squarely, but I do not think many people listened to it.

For tea all motored to Virginia Water. The King was in a filthy temper. The Queen, 'with her amazing grace and in her charming way', tapped his arm, pointed to his car and invited Mrs Keppel to accompany him. At dinner, 'at 15 to 9', Mrs Keppel, the Asquiths and others assembled, standing, in a room awaiting the entrance of the King and Queen. The Queen 'looked divine in a raven's wing dress, contrasting with the beautiful blue of the Garter ribbon and her little head a blaze of diamonds'. After dinner, at adjacent tables, Henry Asquith played bridge with the Queen and 'the King made a four with Alice Keppel, Lady Savile and the Turkish Ambassador.'

'For mama', Violet wrote, 'lack of self-confidence was unthinkable.' Mrs Keppel's confidence rested in her body, 'my mother's ripe curves', wrote Sonia, 'were much admired', her clothes and jewellery, blue eyes 'large, humorous, kindly and discerning', her conversation, 'bold, amusing and frank', her aptitude for bridge, her social status. She was the Honourable Mrs George Keppel, daughter of Admiral Sir William Edmonstone, wife of the third son of the seventh Earl of Albemarle and mistress of the King.

She was thought to manage her regal lover with political shrewdness and wifely concern. Sir Charles Hardinge, aide to the King, Permanent Under-Secretary of State for the Foreign Office and Viceroy of India, wrote of the 'excellent influence' she always exercised:

There were one or two occasions when the King was in disagreement with the Foreign Office and I was able, through her, to advise the King with a view to the policy of Government being accepted. She was very loyal to the King and patriotic at the same time.

It would have been difficult to find any other lady who would have filled the part of friend to King Edward with the same loyalty and discretion.

Friend was an acceptable euphemism. Rules of precedence were disregarded in deference to her charms. Bertie placed her next to the Archbishop of Canterbury at dinner which, the Earl of Crawford and Balcarres wrongly surmised, 'he would never have done if she had been, as generally supposed, his mistress – it would have been an insult to the Church and utterly unlike him'.

At a dinner at Crichel Down in December 1907, not attended by Bertie, she was placed next to his nephew and enemy Kaiser William II of Germany so 'she might have the opportunity of talking to him'. The Austrian Ambassador, Count Mensdorff, a second cousin of Bertie's, wondered 'what sort of report she sent back to Sandringham'. Alice got on well enough with the Kaiser to send him, care of the German Embassy in Carlton House Terrace, a photograph of a new portrait of herself. It showed her with plunging neckline, flicking at her pearls. 'Dear Mrs Keppel,' the Kaiser replied, 'Will you kindly allow me to thank you most warmly for the splendid photograph you sent me. It is very artistic & also very like you, & shows that the picture must be very well painted.'

Mrs Keppel pleased Bertie in bed, influenced his judgement, partnered him at bridge, pandered to his little ways, fussed over his welfare. The King's Assistant Private Secretary Sir Frederick Ponsonby – pronounced 'Punsonby' – described in *Recollections of Three Reigns* a *déjeuner* in a restaurant garden at St-Cloud in Paris. Mrs Keppel insisted that a man at an adjacent table be vetted. She said he had criminal features:

> She was convinced I had given the police the wrong name of the restaurant and that there we were at the mercy of any apache who fancied robbery and any anarchist who loved assassination.

The man, apparently, was 'one of the best and most trusted detectives in the force'.

And, in 1905, she wrote with her customary tact and discretion to the King's *alter ego*, his boon companion the rakish Marquis Luis de Soveral, Portuguese Ambassador, nicknamed 'the Blue Monkey' for his shadowy growth of beard and mischievous way with the ladies:

I want you to try to get the King to see a proper doctor about his knee. Perhaps the Queen would make him do so. He writes that it is very painful and stiff and that massage does it no good or rather harm as there is a slight 'effusion' on it. This I know ought to be seen at once for it he gets water on the knee this might mean a stiff knee for life.

    Cher Soveral
       From your affectionate old friend
          Alice Keppel

(Bertie had trouble with this knee after breaking it in July 1898. He fell down the spiral staircase at Waddesdon Manor, home of Baron Ferdinand de Rothschild. Things were made worse when the carrying chair, used to get him to the Windsor train, broke on the passenger bridge at Aylesbury station.)

In a memoir, *Customs and Characters*, Peter Quennell wrote of Mrs Keppel that in a *tableau vivant* of her time she should have played Britannia. Like Lady Thatcher some decades later, she seemed to personify her country, rule the waves and have her way with English men. Lady Cecilia McKenna, Alice's niece, said she had many of the characteristics of a man. 'She liked to control situations. And she was in control of her life.'

Not everyone was impressed. The American writer Henry James thought the King an 'arch vulgarian' and the relationship between him and Mrs Keppel no more than 'carrying on' in an undignified manner, ugly, vulgar and frivolous.

And Virginia Woolf in her diary was less than flattering when she met her in March 1932. Mrs Keppel, by then, was past her prime, lived most of the year in a villa in Florence and in London stayed in a furnished suite at the Ritz. 'Oh dear,' Virginia Woolf wrote,

I had lunched with Raymond [Mortimer] to meet Mrs Keppel; a swarthy thick set raddled direct (My dear she calls one) old grasper: whose fists have been in the money bags these 50 years: but with boldness: told us how her friends used to steal, in country houses in the time of Ed. 7th. One woman purloined any jewelled bag left lying. And she has a flat in the Ritz; old furniture; &c. I liked her on the surface. I mean the extensive, jolly, brazen surface of the old courtezan; who has lost all bloom; & acquired a kind of cordiality, humour, directness instead. No sensibilities as far as I could see; nor snobberies; immense superficial knowledge, & going off to Berlin to hear Hitler speak. Shabby under dress: magnificent furs: great pearls: a Rolls Royce waiting − going off to visit my old friend the tailor; & so on

Mrs Keppel was not jolly or extensive in 1918 when her daughter Violet suffered for love. Love in her view had no rights when it disrupted or confused the mores of her class. Her sort were aristocrats, political rulers with pedigree wives, owners of castles, houses, fields and forests, employers of legions of servants, makers and arbiters of the law, close to the Crown and close to God.

She intervened in her daughter's life on a startling scale to ensure that propriety and appearance prevailed. 'How can one make the best of anything,' Violet wrote to Vita, 'that revolves on lies and deception?' Her mother's way was through charm, discretion and deference to the social code. Vita as a child was taught the habit of concealment: '*toute vérité n'est pas bonne à dire*' her mother would say. Violet trailed the words in the memoirs she dedicated to her own mother and which revealed little of her life.

In 1944 − by which time Violet was plump, false and middle-aged − Cyril Connolly gave her a copy of his book, *The Unquiet Grave*. She scored in red the lines,

We love only once, for once only are we perfectly equipped for loving ... And on how that first great love-affair shapes itself depends the pattern of our lives.

From the testimony of her letters, her memoirs and her life, it is not entirely clear whether Violet's first great love affair was with her mother or with Vita, or whether, like the serpent and its segments, the diamonds and the lovers' knot, they coiled their way into one.

TWO

Violet did not know who her father was, though she was sure he was not her mother's husband George. In adult life she claimed to be the daughter of Edward VII. She shared his temper, impatience and louche appetites and looked like him and his descendants, particularly his great-granddaughter Princess Margaret and Count Raben of Denmark who was rumoured to be his illegitimate son.

She did not confront her mother on the subject — *toute vérité n'est pas bonne à dire* — but she viewed her blood as royal. It became an obsession and a joke. The assumption had a child's logic. Her mother's life revolved around the King. All her sexual charms were for him. Mama lived in a blaze of glory and perpetual tiara because of him. He was the man Violet saw coming from her mother's bedroom, not George Keppel, a shadowy figure whom she in no way resembled and with whom she had no rapport.

'Who was my father?' she wrote to Vita Sackville-West in 1919:

A faun undoubtedly! A faun who contracted a *mésalliance* with a witch, or rather the other way round! . . . ever since I was a child I have had the vague obscure terror of being 'taken away' *claimed* by someone or by something . . . that is partly why I hate being alone.

Maternity was not in doubt. Alice Frederica Edmonstone, known to her husband as Freddie, was born in 1869 at Duntreath Castle near Loch Lomond, Scotland. In aristocratic tradition her forebears acquired the castle and its land as a royal gift. It was the wedding present, in the fourteenth century, of King Robert III of Scotland to his daughter Mary, when she married Sir William Edmonstone. It was inherited, father to son, from then on.

15

Violet as a child went to Duntreath every summer with her mother. The place, she felt, reflected her mother's past. 'Here I can breathe freely and live freely — sympathetic hills surround me on all sides.' There were streams, roe deer, kestrels, a Highland train with a cinder track. The castle, set between twin hills, Dumfoyne and Dumgoyne and built round a courtyard, had four corner pepperpot towers. The courtyard bell tolled for meals. Inside were smells of cedarwood, tuberoses, gunpowder, mince. There was a medieval staircase, a gun-room, billiard room, armoury, a dungeon with stocks and thumb-screws, an Oak Room supposedly haunted by the Dumb Laird whose ghost was said to crouch over the fire making gurgling noises. 'The atmosphere of the place was complex, half medieval, half exotic.' It formed Violet's sense of what living quarters should be like.

For Alice, Duntreath was home. Violet described her as

in many ways typically Scots. Intelligent, downright ... she loved a good argument ... she was one of the most consulted women in England; she was certainly one of the funniest.

Alice's married sisters lived in Edinburgh, Perthshire, Stirlingshire. Their mother, Mary Elizabeth Parsons, was born in Ithaca, a daughter of the governor of the Ionian Islands. When she was sixteen the fourth Sir William Edmonstone, a naval officer who became an Admiral, wooed her, wed her and took her to Duntreath. 'From Ithaca to Kelvinside!' Violet wrote, 'What an odyssey. How she must have loathed and resented the indefatigable rain, the sulphurous fogs, the grim bewhiskered elders.'

Fastidious and conventional, Lady Edmonstone wore white dresses, acquiesced to her despotic husband, did drawings of imaginary birds with long comet-like tails and year after year in the castle gave birth to daughters. The required male heir died as a baby. 'At last in 1868 she was rewarded ... Archie was born to join a plethora of sisters.' Alice, ninth and last, followed eleven months later. Her father was sixty, her mother in her forties and most of her sisters as old as aunts.

One, Charlotte, married a vicar three years before Alice was born. Another, Louisa, when Alice was three, married a major employed at the Tower of London. A third, Mary Clementine, married the Lord Advocate of Scotland, lover of Queen Marie of Romania. Violet and Sonia described their aunts as diffident women, given to malapropisms, 'tiny tornadoes of tears' and to knitting stockings and shapeless mufflers. None made a remarkable marriage in terms of wealth, status or power. Alice was considered the liveliest and prettiest.

Uninterested in her sisters, she was inseparable from 'beloved Archie', called him her twin, deferred to him, ruled him and when married turned to him not her husband for advice. With her influence he too served the Crown. She secured Archie a place in the royal household. He became Groom in Waiting for the last three years of Bertie's reign. When rich, Alice provided for him and his family. 'They seemed to complete one another,' Violet wrote. 'My mother all dynamism, initiative, and, yes, virility, my uncle all gentleness, acquiescence, sensibility. They adored each other, could not bear to be long parted.' Archie disliked sport, shooting and fishing and in his studio in the castle painted shepherds and shepherdesses, saucy harlequins and wistful pierrots.

Childhood at Duntreath was privileged and feudal. The Edmonstones were Scottish aristocrats without much money but confident of status. Labour was cheap, there were cooks, valets, governesses and, at the entrance to the west drive, the Lodge and its keepers, Mr and Mrs Strachan, who supervised servants, dealt with repairs, admitted guests. There was a nursery wing with playrooms and a children's dining room. The schoolroom had views of croquet lawns, tennis courts and Ben Lomond which Alice climbed. A pen-and-ink drawing of Sir William Edmonstone hung over the fireplace. 'Characteristically it bore his signature not the artist's,' Violet wrote.

In 1888 he died. Alice, the remaining unmarried daughter, needed a husband. She found the Honourable George Keppel, a lieutenant with the Gordon Highlanders. He had blue eyes, dark hair, an aquiline nose, a waxed moustache. He was six foot four inches tall and in his

Gordon Highlander busby nearly eight feet. 'One could picture him waltzing superbly to the strains of The Merry Widow,' Harold Acton, who knew him in the 1920s, wrote in *More Memoirs of an Aesthete*. Harold Nicolson called him 'Pawpaw' and thought him like a character in a French farce.

George Keppel curled his moustache with tiny silver tongs, was methodical, scrupulously tidy, liked gadgets and labour-saving devices, had 'the hearty laugh that denotes lack of humour' and an eye for big-bosomed young women whom he called 'little cuties'. He was practical, punctilious, reliable. But he had very little money. There was no way, on his income, that his wife might come to resemble a Christmas tree laden with presents for everyone. He received scant pay from the Army, a small allowance from his father, the 7th Earl of Albemarle, and that was all. He was the third son with seven sisters. Lord Albemarle was an MP, colonel, aide-de-camp – the palace term for factotum – to Queen Victoria and married to the daughter of the Prime Minister of Canada. But he had to keep up the family estate, Quidenham Park, a rambling eighteenth-century mansion in Norfolk, leave an inheritance for Arnold, his heir, and provide dowries for his daughters.

Like Alice Edmonstone, George Keppel belonged to aristocracy that had seen its income dwindle. Neither family had business acumen like the Devonshires who owned Chatsworth, or the Cadogans, Portmans and Westminsters who owned much of London. Quidenham was acquired in 1762 by General George, 3rd Earl of Albemarle, with money awarded him by the Crown for leading a campaign to capture Havana. According to Keppel family lore this wealth was gambled away by the 'Rowdy Dow', the dowager wife of the next earl. Her creditors were said to have stripped Quidenham of its mahogany doors, engraved silver and family portraits painted by Joshua Reynolds.

Alice, twenty-two when she married in 1891, had not defined her material ambitions nor realized her assets. A photograph at the time shows the Keppel sisters in dull clothes and no jewels and Alice in furs, muff and hat. Her attire, modest compared to what was to follow, outshone her worthy minded sisters in law – one of whom became a nun.

An aunt of George's put up £5000 in trust for his marriage settlement. Archie settled £15,000 'or thereabouts or the securities representing the same'. They were comfortable sums of money, but not queenly. There was no capital or property.

To his credit George was an Honourable. His family had a history of service to the royal household and held a clutch of hereditary titles – a barony, a viscountcy, an earldom – titles bestowed in the seventeenth century for services rendered to the Crown. The Van Keppels came from Holland ('Guelderland') and lived in a castle 'considerable for its privileges and antiquity'. As a sixteen-year-old boy Arnold Joost Van Keppel was loved by William of Orange, who in 1689 became King William III of England. The King rewarded his favourite boy as lavishly as King Edward VII rewarded his 'Favorita'. He made him Baron Ashford of Ashford in Kent, Viscount Bury of Lancaster, Earl of Albemarle – a Normandy town – and left him 200,000 guilders in his will.

Harold Acton alluded to this sexual underpinning of the Keppel family status when George, seeing Acton's mother reading a biography of Oscar Wilde, muttered, 'A frightful bounder. It makes one puke to look at him.'

Fortunately Mrs Keppel had enough humour to spare. Did she ever remind him that he was descended from William III's minion who was created Earl of Albemarle for his *beaux yeux*?

Subsequent Keppels served the Crown as aides-de-camp, ladies of the bedchamber, equerries, grooms-in-waiting. George's grandfather was equerry-in-waiting to Queen Victoria on her wedding day. Arnold, George's eldest brother, who inherited Quidenham and the family titles, was aide-de-camp to Bertie. Derek, the second brother, was equerry and deputy master of the household to Bertie's son when he was Duke of York then George V.

Long before he met Alice, Bertie held the Keppel family in high esteem. His favourite Keppel, prior to her, was 'dear little Sir Harry', George's great-uncle. He was Admiral Sir Henry Keppel, son of the 4th Earl of Albemarle, author in 1899 of *A Sailor's Life Under Four Sovereigns: His Personal Journal Edited by Himself*. Five feet tall, with copper-coloured hair, in his early days he was 'hard up for tin' and had numerous creditors. Bertie and he went yachting at Cowes and to the races at Epsom and Ascot.

Bertie was a friend too of little Sir Harry's nephew, Henry Frederick Stephenson, who was also in the navy. In 1886 he asked him to teach his own son George, Duke of York:

> I feel that in entrusting my son to your care I cannot place him in safer hands, only don't *spoil* him *please*! Let him be treated like any other officer in the Ship and I hope he will become one of your smartest and most efficient Lieutenants. He is sharp and quick and I think likes the Service, but he *must* be kept up to his work, as *all* young men of the present day are inclined to be lazy.

Bertie told Henry Frederick to make sure George neither ate too much meat nor smoked too many cigarettes. He made him his equerry, knighted him, corresponded with him about little Sir Harry – 'The old Admiral went every day to Epsom with me this week,' he wrote in May 1886, 'and I *fear* lost his money. I hope mylady won't pitch *too* much into him on her return home' – and about yachts, horses, deer drives and the shooting of elks, stags, grouse, rabbits and anything that flew.

So there was a time-honoured bond between the Keppel family and the Crown, a tradition of service and reward, trust and familiarity. Which meant that when the newly married George and Alice moved to Wilton Crescent in Belgravia they were from the start 'court cards'. Life's principal domain was social. George was thought splendid in his upright military way, the perfect gentleman, and Alice had, as all averred, disarming blue eyes, charm, vivacity, humour, directness, confidence, ripe curves . . .

But the costs of smart society were huge: the hats, the furs, the jewels, the crystal, the china, the champagne. The Keppels dined in houses in Grosvenor Street, Stratford Place, Portman Square and graced the weekend parties of Lord and Lady Derby at Knowsley Hall, Prescot, Lancashire, or Lord and Lady Alington at Crichel Down, Wimborne. Even the hostess's staff expected to be tipped. 'From a really great house like Lord Derby's the guests would come away at least fifty pounds the poorer,' Rebecca West wrote in her book 1900. And hospitality must be reciprocated, menus compare, pearls equal and gowns surpass.

Mrs Keppel was ambitious and her nose for profit shrewd. She wanted more than George could give. 'Throughout her life,' her daughter Sonia wrote of her, 'mama was irresistibly attractive to bank managers.' The attraction worked both ways. Violet was born on 6 June 1894, three years into the marriage. By the time of her birth the Keppels had moved from Wilton Street to a larger eighteenth-century house at 30 Portman Square. Violet's father was said to be William Beckett, senior partner in the family bank, Beckett & Company of Leeds, member of parliament for Whitby, owner of a large villa in Ravello and heir to the Grimthorpe title. Vita Sackville-West told Violet's first biographer, Philippe Jullian, that William Beckett was probably Violet's father. And William Beckett's grandson said Violet 'undoubtedly had the Beckett nose'.

Violet was never altogether clear whose nose she had. Beckett's American wife died in 1891, the year of Alice's marriage, leaving him with three small children. Perhaps Alice consoled him for his plight. 'My mother,' as Violet was to write, 'not only had a gift of happiness, she excelled in making others happy.' Daisy, Princess of Pless, in *From My Private Diary*, expressed shock at the candour with which women guests, at one of Mrs Keppel's lunch parties, admitted to having had 'several lovers'.

Mrs Keppel viewed adultery as sound business practice, a woman's work. In 1914, on holiday in Spain with the young Winston Churchill and his wife Clementine as guests of Bertie's erstwhile financial adviser Sir Ernest Cassel, she advised Clementine to further her husband's political career by finding herself a rich and influential lover. She inferred it would be selfish to desist and offered to recruit one.

Her excellence in making others happy at times received uncharitable mention. Lady Curzon in September 1901 wrote to her husband the Viceroy of India:

> Mrs Favourite Keppel is bringing forth another questionable offspring! Either Lord Stavordale's or H. Sturt's!! Lord Stavordale is going to be married off to Birdie Stewart as Mrs Keppel made a promise to Lady Ilchester to allow him to marry at the end of the summer! Jenny said people were seriously disgusted at the goings on of the King — his pursuit of the Keppel and daily visit there in his green brougham.

There is no record of Mrs Keppel bringing forth an offspring in 1901. By then her affair with Bertie was at least three years underway. Lady Sackville, Vita's mother, said they met in 1898 at the house of Georgiana, Lady Howe, daughter of the Duke of Marlborough. The Prince of Wales, she said, told her he was struck by Mrs Keppel's witty talk. He spent the whole evening talking with her on the top landing 'which rather shocked people, especially when they sat for a short time on two steps'. Bertie went to dinner at Portman Square on 27 February 1898 and 'an understanding which arose almost overnight was unclouded until the end of his reign.' This understanding was of a sexual sort. From then on Bertie enjoyed 'a good many small Mrs George dinners'.

As for Mrs George's other lovers, Humphrey Sturt — Lord Alington and MP for Dorsetshire — was a friend of Bertie's. His maternal grandfather was the 3rd earl of Lucan (a forebear of the vanished Lucan believed to have murdered his children's nanny, supposing her to be his wife). 'The Alington household was the hub of the big wheel of Edwardian fashion.' His London home, 38 Portman Square, across the road from the Keppels, teemed with butlers and footmen. Crichel was his country estate for 'Saturday to Monday' gatherings. Elaborate shooting parties took up the day. Lady Alington, 'a billowing ocean of lace and ribbons', had her own white farm on the estate – cows, dairy, porcelain and butter all were white. At night a 'glittering cavalcade' went down to dinner. After dinner all played bridge. The neighbourhood church was in their grounds, the Alington pews upholstered in crimson velvet, with high doors to separate them from *hoi polloi*.

Humphrey Sturt liked to drive in his carriage with Mrs Keppel – to Hampton Court, Richmond Park, Kew, to picture galleries and antique shops. On one outing he drove her round the slum houses he owned in London's East End. With queenly concern for the disadvantaged she used to recount how she fingered his conscience in Hoxton: 'it was charming of you to let me see Hoxton now,' she said. 'Next time I go there I shan't recognise it.'

As for Lord Stavordale, he did, as Mary Curzon said, marry Birdie Stewart in 1902. Stavordale had black hair, large dark eyes and the family motto, Deeds without Words. He became 6th Earl of Ilchester, lived in Holland House, London, and Melbury House, Dorchester, set in vast acres with parkland, deer, lakes and woods.

As the years passed, the relationship between the Prince of Wales and Mrs Keppel found context and routine. No other contenders for sexual favours were mentioned. Mrs Keppel was twenty-nine in 1898 and Bertie fifty-eight. He was five foot seven inches tall, weighed sixteen stone, had a forty-eight-inch stomach, ate five meals a day, smoked twenty cigarettes and a dozen cigars, was irritable and bronchial. When he started coughing he could not stop:

> The parties which the King loved to attend and the large meals which he consumed, the numerous cigars which he smoked and the constant journeys in which he indulged at home as well as abroad were all symptoms of that restlessness which caused him to wage a perpetual battle against fatigue and irritability. Lacking inner resources, he depended upon external distractions, and his boredom was made manifest by an ominous drumming of his fat fingers on the table, or by an automatic tap, tap, tap, of one of his feet.

A few minutes with nothing to do proved a trial to King Edward's temper, which had to find an outlet and which vented itself at times upon his friends and occasionally upon the Queen.

His temper, with him since childhood, was entirely uncontrolled. 'At times I was perfectly terrified of him,' Frederick Ponsonby said, 'more especially when I was in unusual surroundings ... when at luncheon or staying at a country house he got cross over a matter I knew little about, he fairly scared me.' 'His angry bellow once heard,' wrote Loelia, Duchess of Westminster, 'could never be forgotten.'

But he did not bellow at Mrs Keppel. She flattered, calmed, soothed, pleased him and excited him just enough. Her jokes were wry, she dressed with flair, was as addicted to bridge and cigarettes as was he (she smoked hers through a long holder) and she had her blue eyes, alabaster skin, chestnut hair and much admired ripe curves. She also had a husband who accepted his own displacement from the bedroom so that his wife might serve the Crown. And upstairs on the nursery floor was her small daughter, who adored her and was afraid of her, and who was brought to her boudoir each morning and to her drawing room each evening where she absorbed the seductive force of her mother's charm.

THREE

When Bertie began his 'small Mrs George dinners' in 1898, his mother, Queen Victoria, had been on the throne for sixty-one years. She had two to go. Her fat and wayward son, though fifty-eight, was denied a role. She did not let him represent her. It would, she said, be 'quite irregular and improper' for him to have copies of Cabinet reports. She vetoed the proposal even that he should be President of the Society of Arts. The power was hers — crown, sceptre, orb, the lot — and she was not going to share them with her son and heir:

> no one can represent the Sovereign but Her, or Her Consort . . . Her Majesty thinks it would be most undesirable to constitute the Heir to the Crown a general representative of Herself, and particularly to bring Him forward too frequently before the people. This would necessarily place the Prince of Wales in a position of competing as it were for popularity with the Queen. Nothing should be more carefully avoided.

Victoria's relationship to her eldest son began badly. She 'suffered severely' giving birth to him. 'I don't know what I should have done but for the great comfort and support my beloved Albert was to me,' she wrote in her journal. Breast feeding filled her with 'insurmountable disgust' and she described babies as 'rather disgusting'.

Beloved Albert, the Prince Consort, was, as Victoria frequently let Bertie know, 'everything' to her — 'my father, my protector, my guide and adviser in all and everything, my mother (I might almost say) as well as my husband.' Her intention was to model Bertie on his father. To mould him into a moral and intellectual paragon. 'None of you,' she told her children, can *ever* be proud enough of being the *child* of SUCH a Father who has not his *equal* in this world – so great, so good, so faultless. Try to follow in his footsteps and don't be discouraged, for to be *really* in everything like him *none* of you I am sure will ever be. Try therefore to be like him in *some* points, and you will have *acquired a great deal.*

Prince Albert read and studied avidly, disliked the company of women, never smoked and watered down his occasional glass of wine. He and Victoria 'spent days and nights of worry and anxiety' discussing every detail of Bertie's physical, intellectual and moral training. He was to be 'imbued with the indispensable necessity of practical morality', keep company with 'those who are good and pure' and not mix with children because of 'the mischief done by bad boys'. For six hours a day, six days a week and with scant holidays he was to be taught English, geography, calculating, handwriting, drawing, religion, music, German, French, archaeology, science, history, bricklaying, housekeeping, gymnastics, drill and more.

From the start Bertie was 'markedly anti-studious' and given to tantrums of stamping, screaming and throwing things around. His governess, Lady Lyttelton, reported when he was four that he was 'uncommonly averse to learning' and required 'much patience' for 'wilful inattention' and 'constant interruptions', such as getting under the table, upsetting his books and 'sundry other anti-studious practices'.

His father responded with more demands. Male tutors worked on Bertie with a pressure that made him pathologically enraged. One, Henry Birch, was kind to him and Bertie used to leave presents and affectionate letters on his pillow. Birch, when he left, dared tell Prince Albert that Bertie's

peculiarities arise from want of contact with boys of his own age, and from his being continually in the society of older persons, and from his finding himself the centre round which everything seems to move.

He was replaced in 1852 by Frederick Waymouth Gibbs who aspired to carry out Albert's wishes in 'exact obedience and subordination'. At the end of each day Victoria and Albert were given a report on Bertie's 'conduct and employment from hour to hour'. They read his essays and the journal he was compelled to keep.

Bertie passionately hated this tutor. An excerpt from Gibbs's journal reads:

> A very bad day. The P. of W. has been like a person half silly. I could not gain his attention. He was very rude, particularly in the afternoon, throwing stones in my face. During his lesson in the morning, he was running first in one place, then in another. He made faces and spat.

When Bertie was sixteen, Albert employed a rota of middle-aged tutors instructed to remember at all times 'in deportment and dress' that they were in attendance to the eldest son of the Queen. Their task was to fashion the man to wear the crown – the King, the first person in the land. Practical jokes, card games, billiards and gossip were forbidden. Even Bertie's meals were prescribed: bread and butter and an egg for breakfast, meat, vegetables and Seltzer water for lunch and dinner. And no pudding.

Reform did not follow. Far from it. Bertie, sensing his parents and their henchmen had a nasty axe to grind, worked out a simple formula: however they exhorted him to behave he did the opposite, whatever they told him to remember he forgot. In adult life he loved practical jokes, parties, gambling, illicit sex, ten-course meals, fat cigars and claret with his cake at teatime. He liked the company of wayward men and shunned anything bookish. Even his handwriting was scarcely legible. His hedonism and philandering mirrored his parents' passion to mould and control him. Victorian values led to Edwardian rebellion.

Victoria put it down to 'tainted blood' from her uncles in his veins. She said he was living proof of her 'unregenerate Hanoverian self'. 'I am in utter despair' she wrote to her daughter Vicky in 1858 when Bertie was seventeen:

The systematic idleness, laziness — disregard of everything — is
enough to break one's heart and fills me with indignation . . .
Handsome I cannot think him, with that painfully small and
narrow head, those immense features and total want of chin.

She said there was nothing innately good in him and she feared for
the country if ever he became king. 'His only safety and the country's
is in his implicit reliance in every thing on dearest Papa that perfection
of human beings.'

Sent to Oxford in 1859 Bertie made friends with the Marquis of
Hastings, who breakfasted on claret and mackerel cooked in gin. Two
years later he went to Cambridge to learn history. In September, on
vacation from the university, he was attached to the Grenadier Guards
at Curragh Camp near Dublin. Albert wanted him, in three months,
to 'learn the duties of every grade from ensign upwards', 'be competent
to command a battalion' and 'to manoeuvre a Brigade in the Field'.

Bertie was hopeless at it, his orders indistinct, his grasp of drill
negligible. In line with his genuine preoccupations he started an affair
with Nellie Clifden, actress and camp favourite of the guardsmen. The
story reached *The Times*, the Queen and Albert. 'The agony and misery
of this day' Victoria wrote, '. . . broke my Angel's heart.'

On 16 November her Angel wrote to his fallen son 'in the greatest
pain I have yet felt in this life'. Bertie, he said, was the talk of the town
and Nellie Clifden already nicknamed the Princess of Wales. Probably
she would have a child, and claim Bertie as the father:

If you were to try to deny it she can drag you into a Court of
Law to force you to own it and there, with you in the witness
box, she will be able to give before a greedy multitude disgusting
details of your profligacy . . . Oh horrible prospect, which this
person has in her power any day to realize! and to break your
poor parents' hearts.

A week later, on 22 November, Albert got soaked to the skin
inspecting new buildings at Sandhurst. He wrote in his diary of feeling

'thoroughly unwell and full of rheumatic pains'. None the less three days later he went to Cambridge to confront his profligate son. Bertie apologized for all the grief he had caused and told him he had 'yielded to temptation' with Nellie. Albert said he forgave him but that God would not.

On 7 December Albert came out in a rash which his doctor, Sir James Clark, thought was typhoid. William Jenner, Professor of Clinical Medicine at University College, London, who was called in to confirm the diagnosis and to treat him, blamed the drains at Windsor. Victoria blamed Bertie.

On 13 December Bertie, struggling with examinations at Cambridge, received a telegram summoning him to Windsor. His father, aged forty-two, died the next day. Victoria, unhinged with grief, confirmed to her daughter Vicky that the Curragh affair had killed her Angel,

> for there must be no illusion about that – it was so; he was struck down – and I can never see B. – without a shudder! Oh! that bitterness – oh! that cross!

Albert, she said, had tried to protect her from 'the disgusting details' but she knew all. She referred to Bertie's 'fall' and 'all Papa foresaw' in terms of consequences for the country and world of a debauched heir to the throne.

She was too distraught to go to the funeral. Bertie, representing her, wept with his face in his hands.

Victoria thereafter looked forward to nothing but 'future reunion with Him [Albert]'. 'To work for Him, to honour His memory more and more, to have memorials raised in His name – here is my consolation.'

She could not set eyes on her murderous, chinless son. He was to tour Egypt and Palestine to spare her 'a constant contact which is more than ever unbearable to me'. He was told to travel incognito, avoid all society except royalty and people of superior character, listen to a sermon every Sunday, visit ancient monuments, read serious books.

Away five months, he grew a beard to hide his want of chin, enjoyed shooting crocodiles, quails and vultures and resisted pressure to visit the ruins at Thebes. 'Why,' he asked his equerry, 'should we go and see the tumbledown old Temple? There will be nothing to see when we get there.'

Back home, his sister set about finding him a wife. As he was 'too weak to keep from sin for virtue's sake', there had to be some practical prompt 'and surely a wife will be the strongest'. The Queen wanted someone young, pretty, quiet, clever, sensible and of good education, character, intellect and disposition:

> I feel it is the sacred duty he, our darling angel, left us to perform
> . . . If Bertie turns obstinate I will withdraw myself altogether
> and wash my hands of him.

Princess Alexandra, daughter of Prince Christian Schleswig-Holstein, heir to the Danish throne, was found. A share of intrigue and impecunity was accorded to the Danish royal dynasty but Alexandra herself was beyond stain. Vicky judged her diffident, humble, shy, placatory, tactful, well-educated, not very clever. She was fluent in English and German, pretty and young, 'her walk, manner and carriage are perfect, she has a lovely figure but very thin, a complexion as beautiful as possible'.

The Queen gave her the highest accolade: Albert would have approved. Bertie, polite about the prospect of marrying her, vacillated between acceptance and panic. He thought her nose too long, her forehead too low. His mother lamented to Vicky that he was probably not in love: 'I don't think he can be or that he is capable of enthusiasm about anything in the world.' Vicky wrote, 'If she fails to kindle a flame no one will ever succeed in doing so . . . I do not envy his future wife.' The Queen agreed: 'What you say about Bertie and that lovely princess is so true — so sad, and the prospect a melancholy one.' But plenty of women were to succeed in kindling Bertie's flame — prostitutes in the Jardin des Plantes in Paris, actresses, society beauties, dancers wearing two oyster shells and a five-franc piece, other men's wives.

On 8 September 1862 Bertie sought permission from her father Prince Christian to marry Alexandra. The next day he proposed. In all he had seen her for a few hours. 'I still feel as if I was in a dream,' he wrote to his mother:

I frankly avow to you that I did not think it possible to love a person as I do her . . . If only I can prove to dear Alix that I am not unworthy of her love and make her future a happy one, I think I shall have every reason to be content.

The marriage took place on 10 March 1863 at St George's Chapel, Windsor. Alexandra was eighteen, Bertie twenty-two. The nation celebrated with banners, bunting, fireworks. This was the marriage of the heir to the throne, the prospective head of state, church and the royal family. Marriage was the constitutional basis for the monarchy, the context for procreation and the family. No other sexual relationship could be ordained, authenticated or admitted, as the daughter of Bertie's most favoured mistress would, decades later, find out.

The Archbishop of Canterbury conducted the service assisted by four bishops and the Dean of Windsor. Bertie wore a general's uniform and Garter robes: symbols of rank, power and glory. He vowed to God that he would love, comfort, honour and keep her, in sickness and health, and that he would forsake all others for as long as they both lived. Alexandra wore white and silver satin garlanded with orange blossom. The Queen sat 'very low and depressed' throughout the ceremony, dressed in black in a closeted gallery of the chapel, conjuring images of Albert. She began crying when the choir sang a Handel chorale and then she could not stop.

She found it all 'far worse than a funeral to witness' and chastised her daughter for enjoying herself:

I wonder even how you can rejoice so much at witnessing what must I should think be to you, who loved Papa so dearly, so terribly sad a wedding! . . . Will you be able to rejoice when at

every step you will miss that blessed guardian angel, that one
calm great being that led all.

She avoided all celebrations, the cheering crowds, plumed horses,
gilded carriages and choirs singing the Hallelujah Chorus. She took
meals alone and commanded no 'noise and joyousness' in her presence.
Three days before the wedding she took Bertie and Alexandra to what
was left of Albert in the mausoleum at Frogmore: 'I opened the shrine
and took them in . . . I said "*He* gives you his blessing!"' She then
joined their hands.

Married, Bertie's life changed. Freed from his mother's oppressive
scrutiny, he indulged in regal style. He had £600,000 capital and an
annual income of £50,000 from rents in the Duchy of Cornwall. He
spent all this and more. By 1874 he was £600,000 in debt. From the
start his spending exceeded his income by over £40,000 a year. £100,000
went on furniture, carriages and jewellery. He bought Sandringham
and its 7000 acres for £220,000 then rebuilt it with a billiard room, a
bowling alley, a smoking room modelled on one he had seen in
Turkey, gunroom, vast gamesroom, wine cellars, kennels, stables.
Parliament voted him an additional £40,000 a year with £10,000 a
year 'pin money' for Alexandra and £60,000 to refurbish Marlborough
House in Pall Mall as his London home.

There were festivities every day for his first London season: fêtes,
receptions, processions, balls, parties. Marlborough House, designed by
Wren in 1710, became the lavish showpiece for 'the Prince of Wales's
set'. Eighty-five servants worked there — uniformed and powdered
footmen, pages, porters. The reception rooms were large enough to
entertain the whole of smart London society at a single ball. Dapper
and jaunty, Bertie constantly bought new clothes. Two valets and a
brusher cared for them. He innovated side-creases in trousers because
mother had criticized his bandy legs.

Tireless for fun he played bowls, billiards, baccarat, indulged practical jokes of the forbidden sort – like putting a dead seagull in the bed of a drunk friend, went to Evans's Music Hall in Covent Garden, on trips to Paris, horse-racing at Epsom, Doncaster, Ascot, Newmarket and Goodwood, yachting at Cowes, grouse-shooting and deerstalking in Scotland.

At Sandringham his shooting parties were elaborate affairs of pomp and pageant. His game larder was said to be the biggest in the world. Three thousand birds were shot in a single day. Parades of gamekeepers and beaters wore velveteen suits and satin smocks. Bertie held elaborate picnics in the shooting fields. Animals introduced to the area for the doubtful privilege of his shoot caused great damage to crops. Mrs Louise Cresswell left her 900-acre farm after the Prince arrived because, she wrote in *The Lady Farmer: Eighteen Years on the Sandringham Estate*:

> I could not remain unless I killed down the Prince's game from Monday morning till Saturday night and reserved Sunday for lecturing the agent.

At first, to the Queen's disdain, Alexandra partnered her husband in the social whirl. 'She never reads and I fear Bertie and she will soon be nothing but two puppets running about for show all day and night.' The Princess was not on show for long. Ten months after her marriage her first child was born, two months prematurely. The Queen chose the name – Albert Victor – without consulting Bertie or Alexandra. She felt 'thoroughly shaken' at the christening. 'Alix looked very ill,' she wrote to Vicky on 12 March 1864, 'thin and unhappy. She is sadly gone off; the *fraicheur* is gone.'

Within three years the Princess had two more children which made her *fraicheur* go off even more. Pregnant with the third, Louise, in February 1867, she had rheumatic fever, was ill for months and racked with pain. Bertie found *fraicheur* elsewhere and seldom returned before the small hours. 'The princess had another bad night,' her lady-in-waiting wrote, *chiefly* owing to the Prince promising to come in at 1 a.m. . . . refusing to take her opiate for fear she should be asleep when he came! And he never came till 3 a.m.! The Duke of Cambridge is quite *furious* at his indifference to her and his devotion to his own amusements.

In August one of Alexandra's doctors spoke out 'very forcibly' to Sir William Knollys, Bertie's Private Secretary, 'on the tone people in his own class of society now used with respect to the Prince, and on his neglect of the Princess and how one exaggeration led to another.'

Bertie was seen 'spooning with Lady Filmer' to whom he sent, via her husband, lots of photographs of himself, 'she will be quite bored possessing so many of me – but the waste paper basket is always useful . . . I hope she won't forget to send me one in her riding habit – as she promised.' At Ascot he lunched with 'fashionable female celebrities'. At night he met up with actresses. In Paris he kept a private suite at the Hotel Bristol. Knollys heard 'very unsatisfactory' accounts of 'supper after opera with some of the female Paris notorieties etc., etc.'

On 2 July 1867 the Queen visited Princess Alexandra at Marlborough House. She found her 'very lovely but *altered*.' Alexandra was in a wheelchair. Thereafter she walked with a limp. She had also partially lost her hearing. Photographs of her and Bertie show him bulging in his clothes and her like a wraith. None the less she had a fourth child, Victoria, a year later; a fifth, Maud, in November 1869; a sixth, John, who lived a day, in April 1871. 'Then the torrent of royal fertility stopped,' Rebecca West wrote in her memoir *1900*. Alexandra was twenty-six:

> She was the loveliest creature . . . But I do not think that anyone amongst the people around me in 1900, including those who must have seen her at her most moving, said, 'A terrible thing happened to that woman. She was raped of her youth.'

Alexandra did not speak of this rape. If she felt marginalized, dispirited and used, she could not say. Her role declined to that of royal dignitary, present at formal functions, excluded from the life her husband lived.

Bertie's power was hereditary. He was born to be King and to secure the royal succession. He proved his virility, lived in splendour and exacted ceremonial respect. And though his philandering became public knowledge and his rakishness a way of life, trappings were what mattered, not the inner man.

FOUR

The pursuit of sex preoccupied Bertie, whatever his marriage vows. To avoid public scrutiny he called himself Baron Renfrew or the Duke of Lancaster and used public carriages when visiting unkingly parts of town. But before he settled in late middle age for staid infidelity with Mrs Keppel, his and his friends' behaviour provoked comment in the papers and led to brushes with the law.

Soon after the royal marriage his Oxford friend the Marquis of Hastings eloped with Lady Florence Paget who was engaged to marry Henry Chaplin. Colonel Valentine Baker was sent to prison for a year for assaulting a woman in a railway carriage. 'If ever you become king' the Queen told Bertie in 1868, 'you will find all these friends *most* inconvenient and you will have to break with them *all*.' They were, she said, pleasure-seeking and immoral, the women fast and imprudent. One of his set, Lord Carrington, told her that not only was Bertie leading 'a very dissolute life, but far from concealing it his wish seems to be to earn himself the reputation of a roué'.

This dissolute life brought scandal and questions about fidelity and what being kingly meant. In February 1869 Harriet Mordaunt, wife of Sir Charles Mordaunt, Conservative MP for Warwickshire, gave birth to a son. The date of conception precluded Sir Charles as the father – he was fishing in Norway at the time. Harriet, aged twenty, eleven years younger than her husband, confessed that she had had sex 'often and in open day' with the Prince of Wales and two of his philandering friends, Lord Cole and Sir Frederick Johnstone. Sir Charles broke the lock on his wife's writing desk, found her diary and incriminating letters and sued for divorce.

The Times published Bertie's letters to Lady Harriet before the case came to court. The tone and content of these was light:

I am sorry I shall not be able to pay you a visit today, to which
I had been looking forward with so much pleasure . . . but if you
are still in town, may I come to see you about five on Sunday
afternoon?

The paper thought them uncompromising and 'not such as to entitle
the writer to a place in the next edition of *Royal and Noble Authors*'. But
they were just the sort of letters that decades later, often and in open
day, Bertie wrote to Little Mrs George. Five was the hour for his
teatime assignations. 'I am so looking forward to Monday when I shall
hope to our next meeting between 5 & 6,' he wrote to Mrs Keppel
from Sandringham. 'I shall motor over from here.'

Sir Charles's petition for divorce went before a special jury on 23
February 1870. Bertie was called as a witness. Though not obliged to
appear he feared that if he did not 'the public may suppose that I
shrink from answering these imputations which have been cast upon
me.' The Lord Chief Justice, Sir Alexander Cockburn, gave him advice
on the wisdom of testifying:

The matter appears to me to depend entirely, first on how far
Your Royal Highness can with a clear and safe conscience deny
the main fact in issue, so far as you are concerned and, secondly,
how far you may be constrained, when pressed, to admit circumstances calculated to detract from the credit which would otherwise be due to your denial . . . I would not, for the world, that
Your Royal Highness should go into the witness box and that
your evidence should fail to command the credit and respect
which ought to attach to it. I am sure that the country would
be more ready to look with indulgence on what might be thought
only a youthful transgression, especially with a lady apparently
of such fragile virtue, than on a supposed disregard of truth in
one who will one day be the fountain of justice and in whose
name the law will be administered. It must not be forgotten that
a man, no matter what his station, comes forward on such an
occasion under very disadvantageous circumstances, arising out

of the notion that one to whom a woman has given herself up, is bound, even at the cost of committing perjury, to protect her honour.

Bertie's circumstances were not entirely disadvantageous. His Private Secretary, William Knollys, recorded that Gladstone, the prime minister, 'took all the *indirect* means in his power (and *successfully*)' to prevent anything coming out in the course of the trial that might harm Bertie or the Crown. Nor was Harriet Mordaunt's fragile virtue and honour protected. Her punishment was to be declared insane. She was diagnosed as suffering from 'puerperal mania', deemed unfit to plead and put in an asylum. Far from finding her frail and fascinating, it proved expedient to call her mad and bad. The confessions her husband used as evidence were dismissed as insane ramblings. Servants from the Mordaunt household testified to her nervousness and weeping, to how she 'was hardly better than a beast of the field,' how she threatened to kill the 'poor, miserable, horrid little thing' to which she had given birth and which might or might not have had a Royal Highness for its father.

Bertie, questioned by her counsel, admitted that for anonymity he used hansom cabs when visiting her. Asked, 'Has there ever been any improper familiarity or criminal act between yourself and Lady Mordaunt?' he replied, 'No, never.' In the evening he wrote to his mother, in language perhaps chosen by his lawyers:

I trust by what I have said today that the public at large will be satisfied that the gross imputations which have been so wantonly cast upon me are now cleared up.

He then took his wife to dinner with the Gladstones.

The affair made waves, but the man destined to be the fountain of justice, in whose name the law would be administered, went on his way. Alexandra referred to him as 'my naughty little man'. *The Times* wrote, 'The Prince of Wales has learnt by painful experience how carefully he must walk.' *Reynold's News* asked the question that might, given Bertie's proclivities, have been on the minds of those in the courtroom:

> Why should a young married man be so eager to pay weekly visits to a young married woman when her husband was absent, if it was all so innocent?

It said that it was unsurprising that rumours of the Queen's ill-health caused anxiety when

> the people of England read one year in their journals of the future King appearing prominently in the divorce court and in another of his being the centre of attraction at a German gaming-table, or public hell.

Satirical pamphlets appeared about Bertie's private life. Gladstone warned that Victoria was invisible and Bertie not respected. A leading article in the *Observer* declared,

> there are not wanting those among the opponents of the mon- archical system who have ceased to regard royalty with that veneration which they have hitherto shown.

Crowds gathered in Hyde Park to listen to speeches advocating republi- canism — an occurrence Bertie deplored:

> The Government really ought to have prevented it . . . The more the Government allow the lower classes to get the upper hand, the more the democratic feeling of the present day will increase.

As Ascot approached in 1870, the Queen told Bertie to limit his visits to the races to two days at most and to keep company with 'really good, steady and distinguished people'. 'I am over twenty-eight,' he wrote back, 'and have some considerable knowledge of the world and society.' She must, he said, permit him to use his own discretion.

His own discretion permitted him to do whatever he pleased. In 1873, his Private Secretary, Francis Knollys, found him a London *pied-à- terre* where he took lady friends. In 1874 he spent two weeks in Paris.

Shadowing him in the parks and clubs kept the gendarmerie busy. In October 1875 he went to India but would not allow Alexandra to accompany him. She said she would '*never* forget or forgive him' for refusing her request to go too.

He preferred to travel with his inconvenient friends. He carped at what he considered the inadequate money allocated him for the trip: £52,000 from the Admiralty, £60,500 from the Treasury for his personal expenses, £100,000 from the Indian government. His party went pig-sticking, shot peacocks, kingfishers, tigers and elephants. 'It is the custom for the successful sportsman to cut off the animal's tail, and this the Prince did, streaming with perspiration,' wrote Alfred E. Watson, author of *King Edward VII as a Sportsman*.

The Prince was distracted from such sport by another scandal. On 20 February 1876 Lady Aylesford, wife of 'Sporting Joe' who was in the party, wrote to tell him she was going to run off with Lord Blandford. By the same post Bertie got a letter from Blandford's brother, Randolph Churchill, asking him to dissuade Sporting Joe from divorcing his wife or feuding with her lover. Lady Aylesford had, Churchill warned, given to him a packet of letters written to her by Bertie which 'if made public would greatly damage and greatly embarrass the Prince of Wales'.

Bertie wished to steer clear of the whole business. But a further letter from Lady Aylesford's brother, Lord Lansdowne, accused him of insisting that Sporting Joe go on the Indian trip, knowing this was against Lady Aylesford's wishes − she 'anticipated the danger to which she would be exposed during her husband's absence'.

Randolph Churchill claimed to friends that 'he held the Crown of England in his pocket'. With Henry Sturt − Lord Alington, father of Mrs Keppel's admirer Humphrey Sturt − he went to Marlborough House to see the Princess of Wales. He told her that

being aware of peculiar and most grave matters affecting the case he was anxious that His Royal Highness should give such advice to Lord Aylesford as to induce him not to proceed against his wife.

He warned her that if Aylesford sued for divorce Bertie would be subpoenaed to give evidence and that if Bertie's letters to Lady Aylesford were published he 'would never sit upon the throne of England'.

Bertie perceived these machinations as impugning his honour, threatening his marriage and as blackmail. He called for a duel with pistols with Randolph Churchill in the north of France. Disraeli – who succeeded Gladstone as prime minister in 1874 – and Lord Hardwicke intervened. 'Blandford,' Disraeli said, 'I always thought was a scoundrel, but this brother beats me.' Hardwicke wrote to Bertie, 'You have been scandalously used by a lady and two men passing as gentlemen. We shall know how to deal with them after the storm is passed.' Disraeli called the Prince of Wales's private affairs as troublesome as the Balkan crisis. Aylesford was persuaded not to divorce but to 'arrange his matters privately', separate from his wife and 'make proper provision for her etc.'.

'How can one make the best of anything,' Violet Keppel was to write to her lover Vita Sackville-West, 'that revolves on lies and deception?' The sexual affairs of Bertie and his set – the royal family, aristocrats, the fountains of justice, makers and administrators of laws – revolved on lies and deception: lies to ostensible partners, deception of wider society. For a few years Lady Aylesford and Blandford lived in France as Mr and Mrs Spencer. When he inherited his dukedom he left her and married Mrs Hammersly, an American widow. Lord Aylesford – Sporting Joe – went to America in 1882, bought 27,000 acres in Texas and died of alcoholism within three years. Randolph Churchill apologized to Bertie who none the less shunned his company for years.

As he grew older Bertie's context for infidelity was the long-term affair. He chose young, pretty women who were married to someone else. The implication for his wife was that he did not want her sexually or emotionally. Prior to Little Mrs George he had two equally public lovers.

Lillie Langtry, daughter of the Dean of Jersey, was an icon of beauty painted by Millais and Burne-Jones. In May 1877 Alexandra was ill and went to her brother in Greece to recuperate. As soon as she had gone Bertie asked friends to arrange for him to meet with Lillie. On 24 May at a supper party in Stratford Place given by Sir Allen Young, an Arctic explorer, he was introduced to the 'Jersey Lily' and her husband. Next day she received a note saying the Prince of Wales would like to call. Fame with a royal flavour was assured:

> It would be difficult for me to analyse my feelings at this time. To pass in a few weeks from being an absolute 'nobody' to what the Scotch so aptly describe as a 'person'; to find myself not only invited to but watched at all the great balls and parties; to hear the murmur as I entered the room, to be compelled to close the yard gates in order to avoid the curious, waiting crowd outside, before I could mount my horse for my daily canter in the Row; and to see my portrait roped round for protection at the Royal Academy — surely I thought London has gone mad, for there can be nothing about me to warrant this extraordinary excitement.

She was born Emilie Charlotte le Breton in 1853, had six brothers and when she was sixteen fell for a young man whom her father admitted was his illegitimate son. Three years before she met Bertie, when she was twenty-one, she married Edward Langtry, who owned two yachts, lived in Eaton Square and drank too much.

Bertie, enamoured, called her My Fair Lily and wanted to be seen in public with her. 'My only purpose in life,' she wrote, 'was to look nice and make myself agreeable.' He presented her to mother, took her to country-house weekends of the sort spoofed by Vita in *The Edwardians*, and to Marlborough House, Sandringham, Balmoral and Buckingham Palace. 'These balls at Buckingham Palace completely realized my girlish dreams of fairyland,' Lillie wrote in *The Days I Knew*. They went riding together in Hyde Park — 'etiquette demanded that I should ride on so long as His Royal Highness elected to do so' — and for weekend shooting parties. 'I was once persuaded to see a stag stalked. But I felt so sick and sorry for the fine beast that I have never forgotten it.' When Lillie went on the stage in 1881 – as Kate Hardcastle in *She Stoops to Conquer* at the Haymarket – Bertie patronized the theatre and ensured her success. At her first night *The Times* commented on 'the most distinguished audience ever seen in a theatre'. They went to the races, Cowes, Paris, Bournemouth. 'He always smelled so *very* strongly of cigars,' she said. Edward Langtry, like George Keppel after him, was invited too when it was seemly for him to appear: the complaisant husband, conscious that the Prince came first.

The liaison was sniped at in cartoons, caricatures and satirical verses, attention that irritated in courtly circles, but was part of public life. But in 1879 *Town Talk*, edited by Adolphus Rosenburg, ran a story claiming:

> A petition has been filed in the Divorce Court by Mr Edward Langtry. HRH The Prince of Wales and two other gentlemen whose names up to the time of going to press we have not been enabled to learn are mentioned as co-respondents.

Langtry sued for libel and told the jury there was no truth in Rosenburg's assertions, he had never contemplated divorce, he and his wife lived on the most affectionate terms. Rosenburg got eighteen months in prison and the judge, Mr Justice Hawkins, regretted he was unable to sentence him to hard labour.

So the waters closed over yet another questioning of regal sexual behaviour. It took eighteen years and several tries for Lillie to divorce her husband. He died alcoholic and destitute on 15 October 1897 in an American 'asylum for the insane'. 'He was caught in the whirlwind of London fashion,' wrote the *Daily News* by way of obituary, 'and being anything but a swimmer, and having no artificial supports in fortune, he was quickly on his way to ruin.'

Sex of the noxious sort was rumoured in 1889. Bertie's equerry, Lord Arthur Somerset, left the country to avoid prosecution in 'the Cleveland Street scandal'. For months police watched a gay brothel in Cleveland Street, London. They shadowed Lord Arthur and identified him as a client. His solicitor warned the Deputy Director of Public

Prosecutions in September that if the case was pursued 'a very distinguished person will be involved (P.A.V.)' – Prince Albert Victor, the
Duke of Clarence, Bertie's eldest son and heir to the throne. The
Prince – Eddy, nicknamed 'Collar and Cuffs' for his dandy clothes –
was, Margot Asquith wrote, 'rather afraid of his father' who let him
know he was a disappointment and perpetually gibed at him 'a form
of ill-judged chaff' which Alexandra hated.

Bertie thought Lord Arthur's involvement 'inconceivable'. Anyone
capable of such behaviour, he said, must be an 'unfortunate lunatic'
and the less heard 'of such a filthy scandal the better'. Chorus girls
were one thing, rent boys quite another. After Lord Arthur's departure
and helpful intervention with the process of law, the case was dropped
and Eddy spared such limelight.

Eddy was spared, too, the roles of marriage and kingship and the
nation was spared a perhaps homosexual king. He died of pneumonia
in January 1892 when he was twenty-eight, a month before his marriage
to Princess Mary of Teck. Two years later she married his brother
George and they became Queen and King after Bertie's death.

Harold Nicolson writing to Vita Sackville-West on 17 February 1949
recounted a conversation over dinner with Lord Goddard, Lord Chief
Justice from 1946–58. According to Goddard, a solicitor committed
perjury to clear Prince Albert Victor, was then struck off the rolls,
and later reinstated. 'It is one of God's mercies to us that that horrible
young man died,' Goddard said.

Eddy's father was unswervingly heterosexual. In 1891 Daisy Countess
of Warwick replaced the Jersey Lily as his official mistress. Twenty
years younger than he, good-looking, feisty, rich, she lived in Carlton
Gardens, London and Easton Lodge, Essex. She indulged in the usual
social round of balls, hunting, house parties, adultery. She had married
Lord Brooke ten years previously in Westminster Abbey. Bertie and
Alexandra were at her wedding.

One of her lovers, Lord Charles Beresford, had accompanied Bertie on his Indian trip in 1878. In 1891 he had sex with his wife who became pregnant. Daisy's revisionist ideas on fidelity were confounded. She wrote him a letter saying he had no right to behave in such a way, he must live with her, Daisy, on the Riviera, one of her children was his and 'more to that effect'. Lady Beresford opened the letter and took it to a solicitor. Daisy turned to Bertie for help. He invited her to Marlborough House. 'He was more than kind and suddenly I saw him looking at me in a way all women understand. I knew I had won so I asked him to tea.'

He called her 'my own darling Daisy wife', gave her the gold ring inscribed 'V & A' that his parents had given him at his confirmation, and swept her into his life. All of which meant social death for Lady Beresford whose husband penned a letter – which he did not send – to Bertie:

> you have systematically ranged yourself on the side of the other person against my wife . . . I consider that from the beginning by your unasked interference and subsequent action you have deliberately used your high position to insult a humbler by doing all you can to elevate the person with whom she had a quarrel . . .
>
> The days of duelling are past but there is a more just way of getting right done and that is publicity. The first opportunity that occurs to me I shall give my opinion publicly of YRH and state that you have behaved like a blackguard and a coward, and that I am prepared to prove my words.

YRH had reason to avoid such publicity. That year he was again in court giving evidence in what became known as The Baccarat Scandal. At a house called Tranby Croft in Yorkshire in September 1890 he and eight others played baccarat for high stakes. Sir William Gordon Cumming, ship-owner, lieutenant-colonel with the Scots Guards and worth £80,000 a year, was thought to cheat. In exchange for 'preserving silence', his accusers requested him to sign a document agreeing never to play cards again. All involved signed it including Bertie.

The story reached the papers. Daisy was thought to be the mole. Sir William brought action against his accusers. In court his counsel said it was anyway against regulations for Bertie, a Field Marshal in the army, to have signed the paper because all cases of alleged dishonourable conduct had to be put to the accused's superior officer.

The verdict went against Sir William but Bertie was hissed from the spectators' gallery and neither the Queen nor his nephew the Kaiser, nor *The Times* were amused. 'His signing the paper was wrong (and turns out to have been contrary to military regulations),' Victoria wrote to Vicky. More than that she deplored

the light which has been thrown on his habits . . . alarms and shocks people so much, for the example is so bad . . . The monarchy almost is in danger if he is lowered and despised.

The Kaiser wrote to her protesting at 'a Colonel of the Prussian Hussars embroiling himself in a gambling squabble'. *The New York Times* mooted that royalty had become an uneconomic proposition for the British taxpayer and *The Times* wrote:

We profoundly regret that the Prince should have been in any way mixed up, not only in the case, but in the social circumstances which prepared the way for it. We make no comment upon his conduct toward Sir William Gordon Cumming. He believed Sir William had cheated; he wished to save him; he wished to avoid scandal; and he asked him to sign the paper. This may have been, and probably was, a breach of military rule; but with that the public at large does not concern itself. What does concern and indeed distress the public is the discovery that the Prince should have been at the baccarat table; that the game was apparently played to please him; that it was played with his counters specially taken down for the purpose; that his 'set' are a gambling, a baccarat-playing set . . . Sir William Gordon Cumming was made to sign a declaration that 'he would never touch a card again'. We almost wish, for the sake of English society in general, that we could learn that the result of this most unhappy case had been that the Prince of Wales had signed a similar declaration.

Bertie took lessons in virtue from no one. He did, though, part from Daisy in 1898 when she espoused socialism. She took to talking and writing about nationalization as a solution to 'the great land problem', said the landed classes ought to earn an honest living, that public schools like Eton should be done away with. She called the rise of the Labour Party the triumph of effort over privilege and said socialism 'lies at the bottom of the salvation of our country'. She gave her money to the cause, started a magazine called *Outspoken Review*, turned her estate at Easton into a bird sanctuary and said the solution to life's problems lay in the Gospel of Love. She advocated the emancipation of women and expressed scorn 'at the hypocrisy that condemned a woman who made assaults on the Seventh Commandment and condoned any man who did so'.

Like fidelity, homosexuality and suffrage, socialism was not a concept of which Bertie approved. She asked questions about privilege, power, merit and excessive wealth and why it was that his set should have the upper hand. None of it appealed to him. This was dissent. 'Those who revealed unpleasant things were not liked the better for it,' she wrote of him. 'Only a sincere democrat desires to know the uncomfortable things of life . . .'. So it was timely when, in 1898, Mrs Keppel talked to the Prince the whole evening on the top landing of Lady Howe's house and an understanding arose overnight of how they might meet each other's needs and desires. For she knew a woman's place, was glittering, witty, curvaceous, discreet and had no socialist leanings or desire to discomfort herself or her lover with the uncomfortable things of life.

FIVE

In an unpublished autobiographical piece Violet wrote of her childhood confusion over Bertie's presence at the Keppel house at 30
Portman Square:

> Once upon a time there was a little girl who was usually exhibited
> when coffee was served. Her interest was centred mainly in the
> *canards*, those lumps of sugar grown-ups would dip into their
> coffee for her, a favour she used to ask of a fat, bald gentleman
> who smelt of cigars and eau-de-Portugal, whose fingers were
> covered in rings and to whom one curtsied endlessly. One day
> she took advantage of a lull in the conversation to inquire, 'Mama,
> why do we call Grandpapa "Majesty"?' A glacial silence ensued
> in which you could have heard a pin drop: 'No more *canards*
> darling, you don't look terribly well. Alfred, take Mademoiselle
> upstairs.' Aware that she had uttered an enormity, the little girl
> let the footman lead her off to the nursery. Not Grandpapa –
> but who? What?

Further questions were not encouraged nor the mystery explained.
The little girl was left to work it out. Grandpapa suggested family.
And this particular grandpapa was wooed, revered, served, far more
than Papa who inspired no curtsies or special ceremony. In time,
Mama's sexual flair set a standard to emulate: 'I adore the unparalleled
romance of her life,' was Violet's refrain. 'I wonder if I shall ever
squeeze as much romance into my life.'

The who and what of Papa was never clear either. He was not
perhaps Papa. His significance to Mama was less than Grandpapa's,
round whom her world revolved. And if His Majesty was not Grand-

papa and Papa was not Papa, then who and what of the little girl exhibited when coffee was served?

Mrs Keppel's photograph was frequently requested by magazine editors. Captions referred to her as the Prince of Wales's friend, commended her looks and clothes, noted her presence at regal functions. In September 1899 a portrait of her with Violet by Alice Hughes was printed on the cover of *Country Life*. Dressed by Worth in yards of lace with flowers at her bosom, her hair waved, pearls in her ears, she gazes with devotion at the little barefoot girl on her knee. The intimacy is contrived. Such clothes were never meant for cuddling a child. She is about to put her down and pack her off with nanny.*

Violet's quarters at Portman Square were on the top two floors; 'the fortress floors' she called them. She shared them with her sister Sonia, Nana, who wore a starched uniform and a false hairpiece and had gout, a maid and, until she was ten, a governess, Miss Ainslie, who lost her fiancé in the Boer War.

Sonia was born in 1900 when Violet was six, Queen Victoria ailing and Bertie soon to be King. Violet disliked the intrusion of her sister into her nursery world. She perceived her looks as plain, her teeth protruding and for ten years refused to talk to her. 'With one terrifying exception I cannot recall one spoken word during that decade of time,' Sonia wrote in *Edwardian Daughter*.

Sonia was almost certainly George's daughter for she had the Keppel nose. She adored her father, sided with him, and intimated her mother's treatment of him was less than kind. As mistress to the Prince of Wales Mrs Keppel perhaps did not intend to have a child with her husband. Perhaps she placated George for his displacement. But eight months after Sonia's birth Bertie was crowned and Alice elevated to the rank of Official Mistress to the King. It was not entirely appropriate for her to be mothering a baby.

Margaret Greville of Polesden Lacey, a Regency mansion at Great

---

* In 1995 this photograph was used by the Royal Mail on their 25p stamp – alongside the profile of Queen Elizabeth II.

Bookham, Surrey, was a close friend, had no children of her own, and offered to adopt Sonia. Mrs Keppel refused. 'When Mamma had refused to let me go always she remained near enough at hand to be a delightfully indulgent godmother,' Sonia wrote. Mrs Greville was the daughter of a millionaire Scottish brewer. Assertive and outspoken 'her standard of luxury was of the highest'. Sir Osbert Sitwell called her 'very ugly and spiteful but excellent company'. Sir Henry Channon wrote, 'there is no one on earth quite so skilfully malicious as old Maggie.' Gerald Berners liked to tell the story of when she gave Bacon, her drunk butler, a note one evening at dinner, 'You are drunk. Leave the room.' The butler put it on a silver salver and handed it to Sir Robert Horne, advocate, MP and third Lord of the Admiralty.

Grandpapa acceded to the throne of England on 22 January 1901. 'He desires me to say,' his Private Secretary wrote that evening to the Duke of Devonshire, 'that he would propose to call himself Edward 7th.' One critic said he should propose to call himself Edward the Caresser. Lord Randolph Churchill's son, Winston, wrote to his mother about the impending coronation:

> I am curious to know about the King. Will it entirely revolutionise his way of life? Will he sell his horses and scatter his Jews or will Reuben Sassoon be enshrined among the crown jewels and other regalia? Will he become desperately serious? Will he continue to be friendly to you? Will the Keppel be appointed 1st Lady of the Bedchamber? Write to tell me all about this . . .

The coronation on 9 August 1902 in Westminster Abbey was six weeks late. Originally planned for 26 June, a rehearsal was held on 27 May. Streets from Buckingham Palace to the Abbey were festooned with flowers and lights. The *London Gazette* gave details of routes, regulations, names of guests. Bertie prepared for the reception of foreign monarchs and heads of state. But the show was postponed. He developed acute appendicitis. Surgery was hazardous, there were fears for his life. The previous May he had written to Mrs Keppel and, in a circumspect but unequivocal way, declared his commitment to her:

May 1901
Marlborough House

My dear Mrs George
   Should I be taken very seriously ill, I hope you will come and cheer me up, but should there be no chance of my recovery you will I hope still come and see me so that I may say farewell & thank you for all your kindness and friendship since it has been my good fortune to know you.
   I feel convinced that all those who have any affection for me will carry out the wishes which I have expressed in these lines.
                    Believe me
                              Yours most sincerely
                              Edward R

Public comment on his sexual affairs and scrutiny by the law had made him chary. But the letter gave evidence of Mrs Keppel's elevated status. It was an implicit instruction. Nine years later when Bertie was dying she sent this letter to Queen Alexandra. It contained too, perhaps, a signal of obligation that his financial adviser, Ernest Cassel, would have understood.

On 23 June 1902 Bertie had his infected appendix removed. As he came round from a chloroform haze his first words were 'Where's George?' His surgeons supposed him to be asking for his son.

On 9 August at eleven in the morning a slimmer Prince of Wales left Buckingham Palace in a gilded coach. The ceremony lasted three hours, the congregation filled Westminster Abbey. There were sacramental vessels of gold and precious stones, magnificent robes, choirs singing hosannas. The Duke of Marlborough carried the crown on a velvet cushion, the Duchess, in velvet, ermine and a tiara, was canopy bearer to the Queen. At the altar Bertie took the Coronation Oath. He promised, with his hand on the Great Bible, to govern the peoples of Great Britain, Ireland, Canada, Australia, New Zealand, South Africa, India, Pakistan and Ceylon. He swore to defend the Church of England, to maintain the laws of God and uphold the Gospel. He accepted the Sword of State, the homage of bishops, dukes and peers. He left the Abbey with the crown of supreme office on his head, the orb symbolizing the domination of the world by Christ in his left hand and the sceptre, symbolizing supreme authority in his right.

Mrs Lionel Sackville-West was there with her daughter, Vita. She wore the Knole tiara made from Marie Antoinette's diamonds. Mrs Keppel, Sarah Bernhardt, and 'a number of other decorative ladies whose only claim to an invitation was His Majesty's esteem' watched the ceremony from a special box in the Abbey. Some wit called it the King's Loose Box.

As sole mistress to the crowned King, Alice needed money. She was unofficial Queen but not on a payroll or accorded public acknowledgement of the cost of her responsibilities. The King was a stickler for attention to details of dress, etiquette, ceremony and protocol. His standards, in consumer terms, were high. Wine on the royal yacht was drunk from golden cups. Such rituals required commensurate sartorial style. He was known to chide a man for not wearing a silk top hat at the races or for pinning on his medals upside down. To the Duchess of Marlborough, wearing a diamond crescent in her hair at a dinner in his honour, he said, 'The Queen has taken the trouble to wear a tiara. Why have you not done so?'

George could not meet Alice's needs. Once Sonia heard him say he was 'facing a financial crisis'. With Bertie's intervention he was found employment that paid a salary, got him out of the house at teatime and took him on business trips overseas. He was to work for Bertie's yachting friend Sir Thomas Lipton, 'the grocer millionaire', who owned vast tea plantations in Ceylon. He was given a job in Lipton's Buyers'

Association selling groceries, bedding, tobacco, cartridges, coal, motor cars. His office was at 70 Wigmore Street. On 8 April 1901 Lady Curzon wrote to her husband of

> the complete supremacy of Mrs George Keppel over 'Kinje' [Edward VII] & Sir Thomas Lipton just presented with a high class Victorian Order because he has made George Keppel his *American* messenger & sent him out to the States.

These were changing times. Trade, regarded as vulgar by aristocrats for whom riches were a birthright, had the virtue of yielding money. George's eldest brother Arnold, Lord Albemarle, accepted cash in exchange for letting his name appear on the letterhead of a company that promoted tyres, bicycles and cars. For George, serving the king required personal adjustments as a letter from him in 1902 to Bertie's friend the Marquis de Soveral shows:

> Dear Soveral
>   My wife tells me you contemplate buying a small motor car for use in London. May we offer our services in the matter . . . ?

The offer, a 'great bargain, only used for 4–5 months and in perfect condition', was a twelve-horse-power Sidley, £440 new, but to Soveral a snip at £300.

Mrs Keppel's wealth was acquired with the skilled intervention of Sir Ernest Cassel. Bertie called him 'the cleverest head in England'. Known as the 'King's Millionaire', he worked magic on Bertie's money. They looked alike. Both had beards, paunches, guttural voices, protuberant eyes, beringed hands and smoked cigars. 'Always curtsy to the King, dear,' the Keppel nanny adjured Violet and Sonia when she exhibited them in the drawing room as coffee was served. Sonia, as confused as Violet as to the significance of Majesty, curtsied to Cassel too. Both he and Bertie frequently gave the girls presents – a Fabergé egg, a jewelled bracelet. 'I came to rely on him as a living form of gilt-edged security,' Sonia said of Cassel, 'a likeness which was enhanced by his wearing shirts with parallel stripes on them, like the bars in front of a cashier's desk.' He was a frequent visitor at 30 Portman Square and Mrs Keppel relied on him in such a way too.

Bertie when he became King said he wanted enough to 'do it handsomely'. Parliament, with persuasion from his friend Sir Edward Hamilton, Joint Permanent Secretary to the Treasury, granted him an annual income of £470,000 — £85,000 more than to his mother and the equivalent of about £15 million now. But Bertie, a big spender, still had debts. His annual bills on his estates at Osborne on the Isle of Wight and Balmoral in the Highlands of Scotland alone were £40,000. Cassel helped. The poet and diarist Wilfrid Scawen Blunt recorded that at the time of the coronation the King's debts were paid off by his friends, 'one of whom is said to have lent £100,000 and satisfies himself with £25,000 in repayment plus a knighthood'.

On 7 March 1901, six weeks into his reign, Bertie gave Cassel all his spare capital to invest. At his office at 21 Old Broad Street, London, Cassel wrote in a ledger:

> I hereby acknowledge having received from His Majesty the King
> the sum of twenty thousand six hundred and eighty five pounds.
> This sum is deposited with me for the purpose of being invested.
> The records of this and any future investments I may make on
> behalf of His Majesty will be kept in an account opened on my
> books this day entitled Special AA Account.

The following year Bertie asked him for £10,000 as he was 'most anxious to pay off an acquisition of property' near Sandringham. A few weeks after this payment Cassel wrote to Bertie: 'Referring to our conversation about your Majesty's investments, I have the honour to report that there is upwards of £30,000 available.' Within a year, under Cassel's husbandry, £20,685 had multiplied into more than £40,000.

The relationship was symbiotic. Bertie grew rich on Cassel's 'sagacious advice', Cassel thrived on the King's endorsement, the flurry of honours received, the sanction of the aristocracy, the peerage, the elite, the landowning class that dominated parliament and the armed and civil services, made the laws and owned most of the nation's wealth. Bertie's head endorsed the £7 million Cassel accrued as his private fortune.

After his coronation, Bertie made him a Privy Councillor. Cassel swore to 'give his mind and opinion to the King', to give 'faith and allegiance', to 'keep secret all matters committed and revealed to him'. The King took him to the centre of his private life. Cassel dined and played bridge with him, absorbed his concerns about money, placed his bets, dealt with begging letters from ex-lovers, gave him and Mrs Keppel the use of his apartment in Paris and of his villas in Austria, Switzerland, Biarritz.

Giving faith and allegiance involved acceptance of the King's special relationship with Little Mrs George. 'My dear Cassel,' Bertie wrote in September 1901 to him at Grosvenor Square, a few doors down from where Mrs Keppel would in time reside:

> I have since heard that Mrs K will be back at the end of this month. So if you write to her at Hotel du Palais, Paris, I think she would probably be able to dine with you on Sunday week.

Cassel made Mrs Keppel and a number of influential aristocrats very rich – he invested for Lord Knollys and for Randolph and Winston Churchill. Lord Esher, responsible for the upkeep of the royal palaces, wrote of a visit to Churchill's Bolton Street house in April 1908:

> The drawing room is all in oak with books and one picture by Romney which is quite beautiful. The *whole* a gift from Cassel! These financiers always take up with the young rising politicians. It is very astute of them.

Cassel, though useful to the aristocracy, was not one of them. He was an *arriviste*, a Jew, without the genealogical credentials for acceptance into their closed world. He took no real pleasure in Edwardian patrician pursuits: country house weekends, shooting, bridge, gambling, adultery. He liked business, making money, acquiring status. His wealth secured him invitations, not friends. It kept at bay the anti-Semitism which writhed through patrician circles, detectable in the snide aside, private letter and dropped remark. Bourgeois, conservative and well-to-do, he wanted to assimilate. Proud to serve an English king, he avoided his fellow Jews and gave to gentile charities. Because of Bertie's endorsement he did not have to hear what aristocrats really thought of him: 'Israel in force,' Lord Carrington wrote of a dinner for Bertie given by Albert Sassoon in July 1900, 'Reuben Sassoon, Mr and Mrs Leo and Alfred Rothschild and that awful Sir Ernest Cassel who is in the highest favour, and of course Mr and Mrs George Keppel.'

Bertie's association with Jews was an embarrassment to many of high-born gentile blood. It was not as unmentionable as the sexual orientation of his eldest son and of his lover's eldest daughter, but it was a threat to their sense of society. Sir Edward Hamilton, Chief Secretary to the Treasury, wrote in his diary of a dinner for the King and Mrs Keppel given by Cassel:

> I quite made up my mind that when he came to the Throne, the King would have such a sense of his own dignity and be so determined to play the part of monarch that He would only dine at exceptional houses. But after dining with Cassel of course he can dine anywhere. I much regret it.

Bertie, if he knew of such sentiments, was above them. He appreciated racial diversity, entrepreneurial success and capitalist enterprise.

Born in 1852 in Cologne, Cassel came from an orthodox family, his father a banker with an unremarkable income. True to the legend of the self-made plutocrat Cassel left for England in 1869 when he was seventeen in the clothes he wore and with a violin. In London he worked for Bischoffsheim and Goldschmidt, merchant bankers who made loans to foreign markets then encouraged investment on the stock exchange. It was an area of finance prone to price rigging and crashes. If shaky governments defaulted on repayments bond-holders had no redress. Contentious loans were negotiated in central America and elsewhere.

Cassel steered a course, was promoted and, within ten years, had personal capital of £150,000, stakes in all manner of enterprises and worked only for himself. He did not entrench himself as a director or chairman of any of the companies in which he held substantial stakes. He was, said his biographer Anthony Allfrey, 'one of a new breed, an economic imperialist, a lone strategist'. Such partnerships as he formed were expedient and temporary.

He made a fortune on the new railroads which 'guzzled capital'. Thousands of miles of track were needed across the American prairies. In temporary partnership with Jacob Schiff, director of the New York bank Kuhn Loeb, he loaned capital to and bought shares in the big railroad companies: the Canadian Pacific, Chicago and Atlantic, Denver and Rio Grande, Texas and Pacific, Texas and St Louis, the New York Ontario.

He became a dollar multi-millionaire, a major stockholder worldwide. He drew dividend from investment in American beet sugar, South African gold and diamond mines, the Westinghouse Electric Company, the Central London Railway (now the Central Line), Vickers' armaments and shipbuilding factories. In Sweden he invested in the whole of the country's capital market and industrial infrastructure. He arranged government loans to China, Japan, Russia, Uruguay, Egypt.

With Cassel's sagacious advice and Bertie's indulgence, lucrative investments were made for Mrs Keppel, too. She had shares in the Argentine Great Western railway, the Cordoba Central, the Baltimore and Ohio, the Great Northern, the Illinois Central, the Chicago St Louis and New Orleans, the Royal Mail Steam Packet Company, the Transvaal Diamond Mining Company, the British South Africa Company. 'When she came into his life twelve years ago she was bankrupt,' Lord Esher said of her when Bertie died in 1910.

In her novel *The Edwardians*, Vita Sackville-West gave Mrs Keppel the pseudonym Romola Cheyne and mocked insider dealings and her acquisitive skills:

> investments bulked heavy in their talk, and other people's
> incomes, and the merits of various stocks and shares; also the

financial shrewdness of Mrs Cheyne . . . who cropped up constantly in the conversation; Romola Cheyne, it appeared, had
made a big scoop in rubber last week — but some veiled sneers
accompanied this subject, for how could Romola fail, it was asked,
with such sources of information at her disposal? Dear Romola:
what a clever woman. And never malicious, said someone. No,
said someone else; too clever to be malicious.

Kingship, politics, business, adultery and personal profit intertwined.
Wheels of enterprise need lubrication. In 1902 Cassel wrote to Bertie
from the Cairo Savoy about his new Egyptian Agricultural Bank: 'The
poorer classes have not been slow to take advantage of the borrowing
facilities placed at their disposal.' Within a few months the poorer
classes were paying interest on a million sterling. The Khedive — the
Egyptian viceroy — wanted to visit England and hoped King Edward
would visit Egypt. 'The Khedive is very susceptible of kind and consider-
ate treatment,' Cassel wrote. 'I think his Highness is very pleased to
have found in me a medium through which he can communicate
with your Majesty.'

Bertie encouraged Cassel's skills. Codes of practice were not scrutinized. 'You will have doubtless heard,' he wrote to him on 1 June
1902

that Peace is signed [the Treaty of Vereeniging ending the Boer
War] which is the greatest blessing that has been conferred on
this country for a long time! 'Consols' are sure to go up
tomorrow. Could you not make a large investment for me? It is
to be hoped that the Chancellor of the Exchequer may announce
on Wednesday not to put the extra pence on the Income Tax
. . . I send these lines by hand. Excuse great haste.

Beneath the trappings of great wealth Cassel remained a loner, his
private life bleak. After three years of marriage in 1881 his English
Catholic wife, Amalia Maud Maxwell, died of consumption. At her
dying wish he converted to her faith. She left him with a baby daughter

'Maudie' – Amalia Mary Maud. His divorced sister Wilhelmina Schön-brunn and her two children came from Germany to keep house for him. She reverted to the name of Cassel and some supposed her to be his wife.

Cassel emulated Bertie's style and extravagance but without his louche appetites. In 1905 he bought 28 and 29 Park Lane and, in three years, and with 800 tons of white Tuscan marble created Brook House, a mansion to match the King's Marlborough House. Twenty-foot-high pillars adorned the hall and glass-domed staircase. Visitors who climbed the crimson-carpeted stairs saw life-size portraits of Bertie and Ernest that showed how alike they looked. An oak-panelled dining room seated a hundred. There were thirty bedrooms, twelve bathrooms, six kitchens, a staff of thirty-one, hydraulic lifts, footmen in full livery with powdered hair, paintings by Frans Hals, Romney, Reynolds, Murillo and Van Dyck, Renaissance bronzes, Dresden china, Chinese jade, English silver and antique furniture, much of it chosen on the advice of Bond Street's Joseph Duveen.

Cassel went through the motions of aristocratic pleasures but was not to the manner born. From Crichel he wrote to his daughter Maudie:

> The party is like all these parties. Everything very well done . . .
> Weather delightful and the shoot excellent. I look on. The King
> is in good spirits and gracious as usual.

His games of bridge with Bertie and Little Mrs George were a service. 'The King,' he wrote to Maudie in April 1902 when he was a guest on the Royal Yacht, 'is rather pleased with me because I made one or two mistakes at bridge.' He hunted with the Quorn but looked, 'a stout Teutonic gentleman in a pink coat, uncomfortable in it and on his horse'. He bred horses and gave them to Bertie's friends. His colt, Handicapper, won the Two Thousand Guineas which earned Bertie's respect and congratulations. In 1895 he registered to join the Jockey Club. Even with Bertie's influence it took thirteen years before he was admitted.

In middle age, when he had massively accumulated all the trappings of success, he lamented, 'I have had everything in life that I did not want and nothing that I did.' Bertie had bestowed all honours: the Order of Merit, Knight Commander of the Royal Victorian Order, Knight Commander of the Order of St Michael and St George. 'Levee dress will be worn,' read Cassel's invitation to Buckingham Palace at noon on 18 December 1905,

> those attending the Investiture will leave their Cocked Hats, Helmet etc in the Lower Hall. They should wear one glove on the left hand. Swords are *not* to be hooked up.

In Frederick Ponsonby's view these decorations were cost-effective baubles. Bertie's

> greatest wish was to see men wearing as many as possible . . . A man who received a Grand Cross of some Order, value £25, was happier than a man who received a snuff-box worth £200, so monarchs saved their purses and pandered to the unwholesome craving of human beings to wear decorations which they had in no way earned.

Sir Edward Hamilton said Bertie 'liked to have a rich man at his beck and call and by this means is able to benefit the Favourite'. The benefit showed. At Portman Square Mrs Keppel's sham Louis XV chairs and imitation Meissen china were replaced by the real thing. Three bathrooms were installed and more staff acquired: the butler Mr Rolphe, the cook Mrs Wright, Miss Draper the housekeeper, maids called Katie and Peggie, George the 'boot boy', a nanny, a nurserymaid, a governess. Joseph Duveen of Bond Street advised on pictures and antiques for Mrs Keppel, too. She visited him in her electric brougham driven by Mr Freed.

Her social visits dovetailed with the King's. He hated being apart from her. Lord Esher, a close friend of Bertie's, who for two years worked as Cassel's partner, wrote to his son Maurice in July 1905 from Batsford Park, Lord Redesdale's Gloucestershire home:

The King is perfectly happy. His admiration of Mrs K. is almost
pathetic. He watches her all day and is never happy when she's
talking to someone else . . . she is never bored of him and always
good-humoured. So, her hold over him grows.

She, not the Queen, was with him for winter shoots at Chatsworth
as the guest of the Duke of Devonshire, or at Elvedon owned by Lord
Iveagh. For racing at Goodwood they stayed with Mrs Willie James at
West Dean Park in Sussex. For Cowes week they were guests on the
yachts of Arthur Morley or Sir Thomas Lipton. For the Doncaster
St Leger they stayed with the Saviles at Rufford Abbey. After Balmoral,
Bertie joined her at the Sassoons' Scottish house, Tulchan Lodge, or
at Duntreath. When separated from her on public holidays he sent
her notes: 'This woodcock wishes you a happy New Year' on a card
with a picture of a gamebird; 'Another Bonne Année. I think this girl
is like dear little Sonia' on a card with a sepia photograph of a child.
And he lavished presents on her: a brooch set with precious stones,
the initials spelling DEAREST, a silver cigarette case engraved with a
crowned E, a hatpin with stag's horns, a ruby tiara.

Mrs Keppel was compliant, available, flattering, firm, appeared to
submit, but dominated him with her charm. 'She sits next to him at
dinner irrespective of rank,' Esher observed. 'Mrs George Keppel very
smart and much toadied to,' Lord Carrington wrote of a dinner given
for the King by Lord Rosebery in February 1908. Like Cassel, politicians
knew that to win the King's approval they must first please her.
When Carrington wanted in 1906 to change Bertie's antipathy to the
prospective Liberal Prime Minister Sir Henry Campbell-Bannerman he
invited him, the King and Mrs Keppel to dinner:

HM was in capital spirits and remained till nearly one o'clock.
He played bridge and won £4. After dinner he had a long conversation with CB on foreign politics and the King told me as
he went away he was quite satisfied with CB's opinions and
declarations.

Mrs Keppel could amuse Bertie, use him and make him change his mind. Violet said her mother's investments by 1918 yielded at least £20,000 a year, which helped her stay luminous, resplendent and of the world of orchids, malmaisons, fine clothes, obeisance and romance.

In later life Violet in anger was to

wonder dully what relation I was to this woman to whom all beauty was non-existent, and who only judged people on their material worth . . . who hates music, never reads a line of poetry, or anything for that matter but the most trashy novels, who is not genuinely interested in art and cares nothing for even one of the things that mean such a lot to me.

When young such heresy was not overt. Mother, Violet said, was the star round which her own world revolved. She stored sensual memories of her: her geranium-scented bathwater, the flower smells of her bedroom, violet-scented cachous, chestnut hair, a lace dressing gown, a grey spring dress fastened from throat to knee with tiny braid buttons, a black velvet low-cut evening dress, a black feathered hat, a diamond and pearl collar.

As time went on to be Mrs Keppel's daughter was to have its problems as well as its vicarious glamour. For given a mother so endowed, luminous, desired and resplendent, it was difficult to feel as lovable, good-looking or successful. 'We do not equal still less surpass her.'

In some invincible way Mrs Keppel was resplendent and fêted because of His Majesty. And Majesty was Grandpapa or 'Kingy Gateau', a mix of Father Christmas and godfather, who must be curtsied to, attended and revered but never discussed. 'And if not Grandpapa – who? What?' Father perhaps? Or just a large mysterious stranger who smelled of cigars and *eau-de-Portugal*, wore rings set with rubies, came downstairs from Mama's bedroom in the late afternoon and around whom life revolved and to whom everyone deferred.

SIX

Each year Bertie, Alice and her girls took their Easter holiday in Biarritz. George went to the office, Alexandra visited relatives. For their spring wardrobe — straw hats with ribbons, light coats, dresses, stockings and black buttoned boots — Violet and Sonia were taken to the 'juvenile department' of Woollands in Knightsbridge. A dresser they knew as 'No. 10', whose mouth was always full of pins, decked them out.

Bertie travelled out separately, calling himself the Earl of Chester for decorum's sake. 'He seldom took more than thirty attendants apart from his suite.' Three motor cars with chauffeurs were sent on ahead for his personal use. He travelled through France in three private railway carriages — one furnished as a clubroom with Spanish leather armchairs, card tables, drinks, cigars. In Biarritz he and his retinue stayed at the Hôtel du Palais. Soveral 'the ladies' man', and guests for bridge and picnics were always in the royal party.

A palace courier accompanied Mrs Keppel, her daughters, Miss Draper and the nanny. They were all assigned cabins for the Channel crossing and a private railway carriage, divided into compartments. 'At Calais Mama was treated like royalty,' Sonia wrote. The *chef de gare* met her and escorted her through customs. On the French train a car attendant 'hovered over her like a love-sick troubadour'.

Their luggage filled a van. Violet and Sonia had a large trunk each, several baskets and a medicine chest. Nanny's trunk was small. Pride of place on the journey went to Mama's luggage:

> Studded wardrobe-trunks, standing up on end and high enough to stand in; hat-boxes; shoe boxes; rugs; travelling cushions; her travelling jewel-case. The 'big' luggage went in the van, but Miss Draper was in charge of the 'small' luggage.

By day they watched the scenery from large fawn-coloured armchairs. 'Mama disliked eating in the restaurant car,' so meals in baskets were brought into their compartments. At night double sleeping berths were unfolded, Violet and Miss Draper slept in one compartment, Mrs Keppel and Sonia in the other. Mother underwent a transformation that made her less than goddess-like in Sonia's eyes:

> Out of a square, silk case she brought a small pillow, a shapeless nightgown and a mob cap. Under the nightgown she subdued her beautifully curved body. And under the cap she piled her shining chestnut hair. Next she greased her face. Then she helped me up the ladder to my upper berth and kissed me goodnight. Lastly she took a strong sleeping pill, put on black night-spectacles and lay for dead till morning.
>
> I dared not move and any inclination to go to the lavatory had to be controlled until daylight filtered through the shuttered window. And even then I was terrified I would fall down the ladder and wake Mama. So I lay through the night rigid and wakeful . . . Sometimes I would peer over the edge of my berth at Mama and in the weird blue ceiling light her white face with its black-bandaged eyes looked ghastly.

Beauty was restored by the time they reached Biarritz. Ernest Cassel met them and took them to his Villa Eugénie built by Napoleon III. His sister 'Bobbie' kept house as she did in London. 'In fact,' wrote Sonia, 'Sir Ernest was fervently served by all his female relations and his approbation or disapproval governed their day.' The villa was like a vast conservatory with marble tiles and glass doors. Mrs Keppel had a floor to herself. Violet and Sonia stayed on the nursery floor with Cassel's granddaughters Edwina and Mary Ashley. Richer than the Keppel girls, Bertie was their godfather and their knickers were edged with lace.

At Biarritz Little Mrs George was Bertie's Queen:

> For her it must have seemed the nearest thing to a family life they could enjoy together . . . There was no question here as to

whether Count Mensdorff could or could not invite *La Favorita* to
a formal banquet at 14 Belgrave Square because of those awkward
problems of *placement* she might create around his Embassy dining-
table. There was even less question as to whether 'Mrs G.K.'
should be asked to stay for the weekend at Eaton because both
the King and Queen Alexandra were coming as well.

Every day at 12.15 like a staid married couple the King and Alice
walked arm in arm along the promenade with Caesar, the King's white
Norfolk terrier who was groomed by Wellard, the second footman.
They lunched in the royal suite at the Hôtel du Palais. One of the
menus cited hard-boiled plover eggs, salmon, chicken, asparagus,
strawberries, Chablis, champagne and Napoleon brandy. In the afternoons they went sightseeing or to the races. None of the entertain-
ments was with children in mind but Violet recorded a visit in 1906
to the Spanish village of Fuentarabbia where she saw posters for a
'*corrida*' and drank chocolate with cinammon 'which seemed like the
height of refinement'. The King and Alice dined at 8.15 and played
bridge until midnight. Bertie was an erratic bridge player and swore if
the cards did not suit him.

Cassel's daughter Maudie described the Biarritz visits as unbearably
tedious, the entire time focused round the King's dull routine. 'We
are his servants quite as much as the housemaid or the butler,' she
wrote. And Violet when older derided Biarritz as 'the most callous
and trivial of French watering places'.

On Easter Sunday they all wore new clothes and in the morning
gave presents. Sonia particularly liked the

> lovely little jewelled Easter eggs given by Kingy and Sir Ernest,
> particularly an exquisitely midget one in royal blue enamel,
> embossed with a diamond 'E' and topped by a tiny crown in gold
> and rubies.

In the afternoon in a convoy of cars they went for an elaborate
picnic. Caesar sat on Violet's knee. In *Triple Violette* she said she secretly

detested the dog, which smelled. Kingy chose the site — usually by the side of the road. Footmen set out lunch: a long table, linen cloths, chairs, china plates, silver cutlery, all sorts of cold food in silver bowls.

The King's cigars and cigarettes were not good for his health. Temper or laughter made him cough uncontrollably. In 1905 he had a swelling in his throat which his doctors feared 'might develop any time into cancer'. He sprayed it twice a day. One year on a day when Mrs Keppel visited Bayonne without him, Violet persuaded him to take her to a carnival at San Sebastiàn. There were crowds. He had a bronchial attack, went scarlet in the face, appeared to be suffocating, and was rushed back to Biarritz by his chauffeur:

> Mama was waiting for us on the villa steps and I was sent straight to my room. As for the poor King, it was decidedly the last time that he gave in to one of my childish whims.

The King and Mrs Keppel were at Biarritz in spring 1908 when Campbell-Bannerman resigned as Prime Minister because of illness and Asquith was elected. Bertie wrote to his Private Secretary, 'C-B was a great gentleman and poor Asquith is so deplorably common not to say vulgar!' Common or not, the Constitution required the King to swear in the new leader, preside over the Privy Council meeting, the delivering of Seals of Office, the 'kissing of hands'.

Bertie did not want to break his holiday with Mrs Keppel. He told his equerry to 'sound Asquith' and see if he would travel to Biarritz for the ritual kissing. There was criticism in the press and consternation in parliament. Mrs Keppel used her influence to defuse alarm. Bertie's equerry, Sir Arthur Davidson, told Knollys:

> Mrs George Keppel told me last night that when motoring with the King in the afternoon she said something casually with refer-ence to C-B and asked if his death would make any alterations to his plans. He said he could not say, but he meant to do whatever the future Prime Minister suggested.

Asquith caught the boat train from Victoria Station on 6 May 1908
and reached Biarritz next evening. Mrs Keppel briefed him on how to
behave. He saw the King on the morning of the 8th then wrote to his
wife Margot:

> I put on a frock coat and escorted by Fritz and old Stanley Clarke
> went to the King who was similarly attired. I presented him
> with a written resignation of the office of Chancellor of the
> Exchequeur; and he then said 'I appoint you Prime Minister and
> First Lord of the Treasury' whereupon I knelt down and kissed
> his hand. *Voilá tout*! He then asked me to come into the next
> room and breakfast with him. We were quite alone for an hour
> and I went over all the appointments with him. He made no
> objection to any of them and discussed the various men very
> freely and with a good deal of shrewdness.

Acknowledging the status of Mrs Keppel, the following day, on 9
May, Asquith wrote to her, too, on Hôtel du Palais stationery:

> Before leaving Biarritz I must send you a line of most sincere
> thanks for your kind words and wise counsels, which I shall
> treasure and (I hope) profit by.
>
> It was a real pleasure to see you at such a time, and to be
> made to feel that, whatever betides, I can count on your friend-
> ship.

The King and the Keppels returned from their Biarritz holidays via
Paris. Little Mrs George stayed a week or so in Cassel's apartment at
2 rue du Cirque to visit Worth for her dresses and the rue St Honoré
for gloves and shoes. Violet saw her mother received 'like a goddess':

> Monsieur Jean (Worth) supervising her fitting in person, the
> *vendeuses* quite shamelessly forsaking their other clients to vie with
> each other in flattering epithets ... My mother was everything
> that could appeal to them, lovely, vivacious, fêted, fashionable,
> with a kind word for each of the anonymous old crones who
> had been for years in the establishment ... Even I came in for a

little vicarious petting. *De Madame Keppel, je suis la fille, je suis la fille,*
I chanted.

It was an unusual chant for a child and from it problems flowed,
entrenching her view of herself as less lovely, less deserving of attention
or praise.

Violet preferred summers at Duntreath to Easters in Biarritz. Her
mother's ancestral castle seemed more apt, more romantic than the
Villa Eugénie or Portman Square. 'Every year I find it unchanged,'
Violet wrote with majestic imagery when she was sixteen,

> the same stone for stone as it was 500 years ago . . . the peacocks
> stalking round the house in the small hours of the morning
> uttering penetrating but unmusical cries . . . the gorgeous flaming
> sunsets that set the hills a-kindling for all the world like cabochon
> rubies . . . the haunted room and the Dumb Laird behind the
> dining room screen . . . the purposeless, incessant tick-tick of
> pigeon feet upon the roof and the jackdaws flying from turret
> to turret.

On 1 September every year she and Sonia travelled there by train:
Carlisle, Glasgow, Blanefield. In early childhood a wagon and roan
horses took them, by night, the last stretch of the journey. When
Bertie visited to shoot grouse in the heather all was displaced. For a
week's stay he would take with him forty suits and uniforms, twenty
pairs of boots and shoes, a valet, a sergeant footman, a brusher, two
equerries with their valets, two telephonists, two chauffeurs, two load-
ers for his guns and an Arab boy to make coffee the way he liked it.
There was no room for Violet and Sonia. They were sent to stay with
a neighbour. 'We used to come over for the day however,' Violet
wrote. 'The King was very kind to us children.' The more grouse he
shot, she said, the better his temper.

Quidenham, George Keppel's family home, defined Violet's childhood too. 'Places have played at least as important a part in my life as
people,' she wrote in her memoirs. In time her relationships with

places proved more rewarding than with people. Photographs show the King and his friends at Quidenham shoots, the King seated at the centre, George standing at the party's edge.

Quidenham was an eighteenth-century, red-brick mansion, in spring its gardens carpeted with daffodils, primroses and bluebells. Lord Albemarle – Uncle Arnold, George's eldest brother – adorned the house and grounds with sculptures of his own making: bronze drummer boys, model cannon and in the hall a lifesize marble nude which Violet doubted was of her aunt.

In Violet's room portraits by Sir Peter Lely testified to George's aristocratic past: William Anne, the second earl, 'fat and sallow' and named after his godmother, Queen Anne; Arnold Joost – William III's lover with curled periwig, robes, garters and red-heeled shoes; Louise de Kerouaille, Duchess of Portsmouth and lover of Charles II – 'her tapering Lely white fingers play luxuriously with a string of grossly inflated pearls.'

The Keppel Christmas was spent at Crichel. Augusta Alington decreed that ladies be given jewels or Fabergé ornaments as presents and the men be given gold. Violet and Sonia came 'in the category of extra Christmas luggage' and there was little for them to do. They lunched with the adults on Christmas day but for the most part stayed upstairs. Sonia described the drawing room as an 'amphitheatre of sardonic adult laughter'. Twice a day they were exhibited to the guests – after lunch when they shook hands with them all and after tea, wearing dresses with frills and sashes.

Mrs Keppel's world was glimpsed and admired by her daughters, her approbation courted, her disapproval feared. What she wanted she got and the world was as she ordained. 'When roused to anger, which was seldom, she cut with a remark.' 'You have no charm' was one of her withering judgements. 'Persuasion,' Violet wrote, 'was Mama's strong suit. She could have persuaded Florence Nightingale to become a ballet dancer.' When Sonia as a child said she did not like ham her mother countered 'but it doesn't taste like ham'.

Life on the nursery floors of Portman Square was regulated by

servants. They provided discipline and instruction, such cradling as
there was, and order to the days. There were lessons all morning,
walks in the park, visiting and sightseeing, bed at seven and when
older at nine. Violet was clever, liked reading, learned languages easily,
had a flair for drawing. She described herself as an unsociable child,
'suspicious, introspective and passionately possessive about the people
and things I cared for'. She wept for no reason and was more stormy
and temperamental than anyone could understand.

She said she always loathed London. 'I hated everything about it —
streets, climate, smell.' In her memoirs she derided Portman Square
for its lack of mystery or privacy and its occupants for their lack of
intellectual stretch. 'The most outstanding feature of Portman Square,'
she wrote, 'was a boiler, unaccountably situated in the schoolroom
cupboard.' It gurgled and was a topic for visitors — 'it could be counted
on to create a diversion'.

The household revolved around Mrs Keppel. In her boudoir on the
floor below no boilers gurgled. All was scents, velvets, pearls. She
breakfasted in bed. (In adult life Violet did too.) Miss Draper wound
her watches, ran her bath, scented it with rose geranium salts, put
out her underwear in a lace cover, helped her on with her stockings,
laced her stays, combed and waved her hair. Mrs Wright then brought
a black book inscribed with menus for lunch and dinner. 'This book
Mama would consider carefully, scratching out, writing in. And while
she did so Mrs Wright would stand motionless . . .'

Shopping was a crucial pursuit, a female equivalent to the hunting
fields. Miss Draper pinned Alice's veil, buttoned her gloves, put powder,
cigarettes, money into her bag. Violet's preferred visits were to Bumpus
the bookseller or to Joseph Duveen. Sonia favoured the trip across Hyde
Park to Albert Gate to Mr Montagu, manager of Westminster Bank. She
was given a sovereign and stayed in an anteroom while business was
done. Mama's attractiveness to bank managers was legendary and 'the
one at Albert Gate was as infatuated as the rest'. He met Mrs Keppel at
the door and ushered her to private rooms. When she put down her
umbrella or parasol and lifted her veil he 'seemed to catch his breath a

little as he beheld her beautiful face.' He talked, Sonia said, 'in a reverently low voice as though he was praying in church'.

In *Edwardian Daughter* Sonia chose a shopping story to show her mother's munificence. Together they visited Morrell's toy shop in Oxford Street. In the window was an 'exquisite' doll with eyelashes, frilled jacket, swansdown bonnet. Looking at it was a small girl 'raggedly dressed and dirty' who remarked on its beauty. Mrs Keppel left Sonia on the pavement, bought the doll, put it into the child's 'thin little arms' and said, 'Call her Alice.' Like a Queen to the derelict she offered a glimpse of grace and favour.

Trips to the bank manager and shopping were essential prerequisites to visiting. Mrs Keppel took her girls on the teatime rounds and country house awaydays: to Polesden Lacey, Clovelly Court, Appley Hall and Berkeley Square.

When Violet was ten her mother fired her English governess Miss Ainslie and hired Hélène Claissac. Moiselle, as Violet called her, came from Paris and suggested a life other than seduction, entertaining and bridge. A Republican, she was, Violet said,

> my first (and salutary) contact with French intellectual integrity,
> so remote from the breathy beatitudes Miss Ainslie would exhale
> over some cliché attributed to a member of the Royal Family.

She 'did not give a fig for riches, rank, renown'. Introduced to Bertie, she shook his hand. He responded with 'a Gallic kiss'.

In spring 1905 Portman Square was redecorated. Sonia went to the Alingtons at Crichel, which she hated. Violet, aged ten, went to Paris for three weeks with Moiselle, Aunt Jessie and Hornsby, a manservant.

She kept a diary which later she annotated and gave to Vita Sackville-West. She stayed in the Hotel Belmont, ate in its restaurant, met in the day with Moiselle's niece Germaine. She walked in the Champs-Elysées 'it was too lovely, all the horse-chestnut trees were out and smelt so nice', in the Bois de Boulogne, the Jardin d'Acclimatation, the Jardin des Plantes where Bertie as Prince of Wales had propositioned whores. She visited Nôtre-Dame, the Louvre, Napoleon's tomb, the Musée de Luxembourg, the Musée de Cluny, the Musée Carnavalet, the Panthéon. She climbed the Arc de Triomphe, bought hats and hairpins in the Bon Marché, ate chocolate eclairs, drank iced lemonade at Rumpelmayer's and was given a privileged view of the visit of the King of Spain. This Paris visit was a liberation, a relationship to a place where she felt she belonged. She determined to live there one day and to speak French without accent.

But the city was not entirely hers. Mother crossed the Channel to be with the King. Bertie was there to affirm England's allegiance to France and dissociate himself from his nephew the Kaiser's claims to 'world-wide domination by the Hohenzollerns'. Mrs Keppel stayed again at 2 rue du Cirque. She swept into Violet's life, bought dresses for her, took her to Fontainebleau and told her how the Empress Eugénie had asked to meet her and shown her the pen with which Napoleon I signed the Act of Abdication, which was not the pen shown to tourists. She wove a fabrication of personal anecdote and unmatchable charm round Violet's city then swept away to meet the King. 'The great lost the power to impress,' Violet wrote of her mother's anecdotes. Mother was of the inner sanctum where greatness lay. Where she went, history was made.

Missing from Violet's life was friendship with children her own age. Cleverer than her sister she kept to herself, shunned children's parties, snubbed her contemporaries. But then one afternoon in the winter of 1905 'of a sudden everything changed'.

She allowed herself 'to be dragged to a tea-party at Lady Kilmorey's' at Aldford Street, Park Lane. Lady Kilmorey's daughter had a broken leg. Violet went to talk to her. By the bedside was another equally unsociable girl, tall, gawky, 'most unsuitably dressed in what appeared to be her mother's old clothes'. They were drawn to each other. ('It seems to me so significant that I should remember with such distinctness my first sight of her,' Vita wrote fifteen years later.) Violet remarked on the flowers in the room. Vita ignored her. Violet was piqued but tried again.

Back home she asked her mother if she might have the girl to tea. Mrs Keppel agreed and wrote to Vita's mother. The invitation was accepted. Vita visited Portman Square.

They sat in the dark by the fire in George Keppel's sitting room ('he was never in at this hour'), dangled their legs over the leather fender, talked of their ancestors and books – stories of adventure and romance with passionate heroes and unequivocal feelings: *The Three Musketeers*, *The Count of Monte Cristo*, *Quentin Durward* and *Ivanhoe*. Violet alluded to the pleasures of Paris. Vita confided about her dogs, rabbits and the magnificence of Knole, her country home. In the hall when she left Violet kissed her goodbye. In her bath that night Vita sang to herself, 'I've got a friend.'

SEVEN

'One never loves more passionately than at the age of ten,' Violet wrote in her fifth novel, *Hunt the Slipper*. To her friendship with Vita she brought her childhood hopes and dreams. 'Everything changed.' 'Don't you see you are perfection to me as I am to you,' she wrote. She idolized Vita and bombarded her with letters 'which became more exacting as hers tended to become more and more of the "yesterday-my-pet-rabbit-had-six-babies" type'. All that winter they delved into each other's inner world. 'I', said Vita, 'who was the worst person in the world at making friends, closed instantaneously in friendship.'

The word friend resounded for them both. It meant intimacy, filled a need: for Violet, who scorned her sister, viewed her mother as queen, was bewildered by the King and served by hired staff; and for Vita, an only child with a capricious mother and the strange weight of her relationship to Knole, the Sackvilles' family home at Sevenoaks in Kent.

Violet was invited to stay. Even as a child she knew Knole was the key to understanding her friend:

> Vita belonged to Knole, to the courtyards, gables, galleries; to the prancing sculptured leopards, to the traditions, rites and splendours. It was a considerable burden for one so young. No wonder she wrote about rabbits.

Virginia Woolf sensed, when she fell in love with Vita twenty-four years later and wrote *Orlando* for and about her, that Vita inhabited Knole more crucially than her own body. Violet aged ten felt the resonance of Vita's past:

> It was necessary to see Vita at Knole to realise how inevitable she was. Knole was committed to produce a Vita. Generations of

74

Sackvilles, heavy lidded, splenetic, looked possessively down on their offspring . . . These selfsame features, painted by Van Dyck, Gainsborough, Lawrence, emerging from a ruff, a 'jabot', a 'choker', occurred in each generation . . .

Duntreath and Portman Square were lesser homes. Knole was the setting of true splendour. It epitomized the aristocrat's sense of having created the past and of owning the land. Mrs Keppel was the tinsel queen of a player king compared to Vita and Knole.

Based on the diurnal year, the house had 365 rooms, fifty-two staircases, seven courtyards. It covered six acres and had towers, battlements, twelfth-century buttresses, Tudor gables, long galleries, vast parks. Virginia Woolf called it 'a conglomeration of buildings half as big as Cambridge', capable of 'housing half the poor of Judd Street'. Bought by the Archbishop of Canterbury in 1456, it was added to, altered, given by Elizabeth I in 1556 to her cousin, Thomas Sackville, and stayed in the family from then on. 'It is above all an English house,' Vita wrote. 'It has the tone of England; it melts into the green of the garden turf, into the tawnier green of the park beyond, into the blue of the pale English sky.'

She called herself its soul. She and Violet thought old houses if understood lived and formed relationships. 'I really have antennae about places,' Violet wrote. 'I get their meaning, they tell me their secrets.' Vita said Knole was not 'haunted':

> But you require either an unimaginative nerve or else a complete certainty of the house's benevolence before you can wander through the state-rooms after nightfall with a candle as I used to do when I was little . . . But I was never frightened at Knole. I loved it; and took it for granted that Knole loved me.

She knew every detail: the leadwork on the pipes, the smells of woodwork, leather, tapestry. If scolded she 'took sanctuary' in the Chapel of the Archbishops. She saw the evening sunlight reflecting into the Cartoon Gallery on to the Renaissance fireplace and walls of

Genoese velvet. One winter in the banqueting hall she encountered a stag that had strayed in from the snow.

She showed Violet the ballroom hung with portraits of ten generations of Sackvilles, the chapel with Gothic tapestries, the Venetian Ambassador's Bedroom, the King's Bedroom where 'the great four-poster of silver and flamingo satin towered to the ceiling', coats of arms in the Leicester Gallery, the Poets' Parlour 'rich with memories of Pope and Dryden', the vaults with the stacked coffins of Sackvilles dating back to the fourteenth century. She showed her the high-walled gardens, orchards, hothouses, 'pineries' and beyond the gardens the park with hills, glades, deer and rabbits.

'Had you been a man,' Violet when adult wrote to Vita, 'I should most certainly have married you, as I think I am the only person who loves Knole as much as you do.'

Here was their palace. For Violet, Knole and Vita surpassed the outward glamour of her mother and the King. Vita was not a man but that did not stop her from falling in love with Violet. 'Violet is *mine*,' she was to write:

> I can't express it more emphatically or more accurately than that, nor do I want to dress up an elemental fact in any circumlocution of words.
>
> There *is* a bond which unites me to Violet, Violet to me . . . what that bond is God alone knows; sometimes I feel it as something legendary. Violet is *mine*, she always has been, it is inescapable.

She could not openly acknowledge or allow this elemental fact and legendary bond. Nor, because she was a woman, though her concept of self was rooted in Knole, though she loved the place and took it for granted that it loved her, would it ever be hers. Her father's brother Charles had a son, Edward, who would inherit the house and the Sackville title. From childhood on Vita was jealous. Her letters stressed his inappropriateness to the place, how he fussed about his stomach pains, wore make-up, bracelets and enormous rings, was 'as floppy as an unstaked delphinium after a gale' It was an irony that Eddy was gay, never married, had affairs with Duncan Grant and an American called Jimmy and painted swastikas and a large silver 69 on his bedroom walls:

> There he stands shivering between two suitcases in front of a door far too large for him – dwarfed by the grey architecture towering above him . . . a little mingy niminy-piminy man in a grey overcoat like a dressing gown.
>
> And then he knocks and the door is opened to him and I drive hastily away while he goes in.

She was dispossessed of Knole and Violet by inheritance law and matrimonial law. In their combined splendour they seemed like a paradise lost.

Visiting Knole Violet was 'almost oppressively conscious' of Vita's mother, Lady Sackville. As forceful a presence as Mrs Keppel at Portman Square or Queen Victoria at Buckingham Palace she was, Violet said, like the Cheshire Cat, 'intermittent, yet omnipresent':

> Her daughter, who admired and distrusted her, was, up to a point, the Cheshire Cat's plaything, but only up to a point. Knole, the Sackvilles, her charming if unobtrusive father watched over her.

When Violet came to code her life into fiction the portrait of a controlling matriarch recurred, a mother who invades the sexuality of her offspring. It was a creation with attributes of Queen Victoria and Mrs Keppel too, though she based it physically on Lady Sackville:

> In her too fleshy face classical features sought to escape from the encroaching fat. An admirable mouth of pure and cruel design held good. It was obvious that she had been beautiful. Her voluminous, ambiguous body was upholstered rather than dressed in what appeared to be an assortment of patterns, lace, brocades, velvets, taffetas. Shopping lists were pinned to her bosom. She kept up a flow of flattering, sprightly conversation, not unlike

the patter of a conjuror, intent on keeping your mind off the trick he is about to perform.

Fantastic and slightly barmy, Victoria Sackville had power, theatre and a conviction that what she wanted, she should have. Her volatility was an antidote to the usual Sackville lugubriousness. Her childhood did not prepare her for the mores of the English aristocracy. Her mother, 'Star of Andalusia', was Pepita the Spanish dancer, her father Lionel Sackville-West, an English diplomat. They made their home at Arcachon in south-west France, though Lionel travelled widely. They produced five children but did not marry. Pepita was Catholic and constrained from divorcing her husband and dancing teacher Juan Antonio de Oliva.

When Victoria was nine Pepita died. She and her two sisters were sent to a convent in Paris. The place was cold, the regime strict, at night in her prayers she asked the Virgin Mary to warm her bed. Chatter was punished. If she complained of feeling unwell she was sent to an extra church service, if she fainted she was given extra lessons. Holidays were trips with the nuns to Bercq near Boulogne. She was told not to mention that her mother had been a dancer called Pepita.

She was at the convent seven years and assumed her future would be as a governess. But in 1880 a Mrs Mulhall, sent by Lionel, arrived at the convent to take his daughters to England. On the boat she told Victoria and her sisters they were illegitimate.

In England, Lord Sackville of Knole and Lord de la Warr of Buckhurst were revealed as uncles and the Duchess of Bedford and Countess of Derby as aunts. The Duchess of Bedford refused to associate with this illegitimate brood. Lady Derby – Aunt Mary – was kind, but drew the line at inviting them to tea with visitors.

In 1881 Lionel was appointed British Minister in Washington. Victoria went with him as lady of the house. Unusual, exotic, French-speaking, unpredictable, she was a fascination and a success. In her diary she listed her offers of marriage from politicians and diplomats – the President of the United States, Sir Cecil Spring-Rice who himself became British Ambassador in America, Sir Charles Hardinge who became head of the Foreign Office and wrote Bertie's speeches, and half a dozen more.

She was in Washington seven years. In 1888 there was a presidential election. Lionel gave his views on who he would prefer as president, the indiscretion was publicized and he was asked to leave. Three weeks later his brother Mortimer, the 1st Baron Sackville, died and Lionel inherited Knole. Victoria, aged twenty-six, was to return with him to manage the estate.

On the way home they stopped at the French Riviera. Bertie was there. The company was dashing, smart and fast. 'All the fast women respect me because I never go anywhere without Papa,' Victoria wrote in her diary. Bertie wooed and teased her but she was not as yielding as Little Mrs George ten years later. 'I was horribly shy, *terriblement intimidée*, the first time I met him.' After dinner he sent for her to go to the smoking room. 'I refused to smoke but I was obliged to go there . . . He asked for my photograph which I shall delay sending him as long as possible.'

She did not understand his jokes but assumed they were funny because everyone laughed. He told her she brought him luck at baccarat:

> He made me sit at his right hand, and indeed he won. He gave me a big gold piece of 100 francs as a mascot with his name and the date engraved on it.

When she went to talk to someone else he looked for her 'all over the place'. 'He put me at his right hand at supper.' They went to his club and he danced the 'quadrille d'honneur' with her. 'He is amiability itself toward me.'

With convent primness she thought herself too popular and resolved to stop wearing her pink tulle frock trimmed with silver leaves. A French marquis whom Bertie said was a very good fellow wanted to marry her, but she worried he was not a Catholic. Life was dazzling. She reflected on the vanity of money, '*mais pourtant j'aimerais bien avoir un petit million à moi*'.

Then came Knole and her little million. She gave the servants orders, wore the family jewels, marvelled at the paintings, tapestries and treasures with which the place was stuffed and to herself repeated the refrain, '*Quel roman de ma vie*'. Her father, diffident and eccentric, took no notice of her or Knole. He whittled paper knives from the lids of cigar boxes, read Gibbon's *Decline and Fall*, walked in the garden followed by two pet cranes and refused to speak to visitors. Given the chance he went to London for the day to avoid them.

Her cousin — also called Lionel — visited. Heir to the Sackville title and to Knole, he was twenty-two, five years her junior, gentle and quiet. They played draughts in the library and he thought her exotic. 'I wonder whether I shall ever marry Lionel?' she wrote in her diary. 'How much people admire Knole! I should be very lacking in ambition were I to renounce it, but one's personal happiness should come before ambition.'

She prayed for guidance, worried about the French marquis and on 17 June 1890 married ambition, happiness and her cousin in the chapel at Knole. Bertie sent her a diamond and pearl brooch as a wedding present. The marriage caused jealousy and consternation among her brothers, sisters, uncles and aunts — the blood tie, the illegitimacy, her Catholicism, the huge inheritance.

At first she loved her husband, though she thought him unfathomable and took no notice of his work. In her diary she recorded how, when and where they had sex: in the library, on the sofa, in the bath, in the park. She called him Tio and his penis Baby. 'Baby very naughty this morning while I was pretending to sleep . . . Tio is getting more passionate every day . . . Tio was perfectly mad tonight . . . He really is a stallion — 4 times . . . Delirium. Afterwards Tio said, "Was it nice Vicky?" '

For a while sex and organizing Knole concealed their incompatibility. She enjoyed installing electric lights, bathrooms and modern conveniences. 'Everybody says that I made Knole the most comfortable large house in England, uniting the beauties of Windsor Castle and the Ritz.'

Lionel, like his uncle, took no interest in running the estate. He was commander of the West Kent Yeomanry and on various civic committees in Kent. Virginia Woolf called him 'the figure of an English nobleman, decayed, dignified, smoothed, effete'. Conversation between him and his wife stalled when Baby tired: 'L says that I talk a lot and I do,' Victoria wrote in her diary on 9 April 1891, 'as I am always trying to keep the conversation going at meals, which I dread. I think there is so little small talk in England.'

On 9 March 1892 Vita was born. Giving birth was an experience Victoria resolved not to repeat. She begged for chloroform and longed to die, said it was a hundred times worse than she had expected and that she would drown herself sooner than have another child.

By 1904, the year Vita and Violet met, sex with Lionel had lost its appeal. She told him her nervous system was out of order and she must be left in peace. Lionel said little but found himself other women. Victoria found consolation with Seery – Sir John Murray Scott. He was six feet four, weighed twenty-five stone, had a red face and white mutton-chop whiskers. In summer he sweated and flies buzzed near. Vita once measured the region of his waist and said it was five feet round.

He was as rich as he was large. From the collector Sir Richard Wallace, to whom he was secretary, he inherited Hertford House, its paintings and treasures (now known as the Wallace Collection), money, land, a huge Paris apartment 'packed with the most wonderful furniture and bibelots', Bagatelle (a pavilion in sixty acres in the Bois de Boulogne), a shooting lodge at Sluie in the Scottish Highlands where Vita as a child, like Violet at Duntreath, felt at her most free,

> those lovely, lovely hills, those blazing sunsets, those runnels of icy water where I used to make water wheels, those lovely summer evenings fishing on the loch, those long days when I often walked fifteen miles or more with the guns and the gillies.

Seery worshipped Victoria, called her a little Spanish beggar and let her have whatever she wanted. 'At times she wanted a good deal,' Vita wrote. 'Mother became absolutely the light and air of his life.' She bullied, charmed, teased and fought with him. The first evening he met her he added a codicil to his will leaving her £50,000. He gave her large sums of money for the upkeep of Knole. She told Vita he was in love with her and that he pleaded outside her bedroom door at night. She said if he were to have a fit she would come and wake Vita and together they must bump him downstairs back to his room to avoid scandal.

Seery came into Lady Sackville's life when Vita was six, as Kingy came into Mrs Keppel's life when Violet was four. Both girls were used to the presence of immensely rich, genial, fat men who adored their mothers and turned their fathers into shadowy figures. 'Went to tea with Violet and stayed to dinner. The King was there' was an offhand diary entry of Vita's in 1905. Years later she wrote of her childhood visits to Portman Square:

> Often when I went to their house I used to see a discreet little one-horse brougham waiting outside and the butler would slip me into a dark corner of the hall with a murmured 'One minute, miss, a gentleman is coming downstairs' so that I might take my choice whether it was the King or the doctor.

Often, too, Violet would be sent for to go to the drawing room to be exhibited to Kingy, and the girls would say, O bother, much as they did when Vita was sent for to see Seery. They were left to make whatever sense they could of these men who visited mother's boudoir in the afternoon, or pleaded outside mother's door at night. And though infidelity and acquisitiveness lurked beneath the glittering surface of charm and manners both girls, too, were aware of the sexual power of their mothers, a power that had no moral dimension, made men seem slavish and weak and was rewarded with riches and flattery. 'How my mother puzzled me and how I loved her!' Vita wrote. 'She wounded and dazzled and fascinated and charmed me by turns.'

At times the wounds surpassed the charm. 'She loved me as a baby, but I don't think she cared much for me as a child,' Vita wrote. Herself

'MY MOTHER, ALL DYNAMISM, INITIATIVE,
AND YES, VIRILITY'

Mrs Keppel in 1900

'WE ARE NOT AS LOVABLE,
OR AS GOOD-LOOKING, OR AS
SUCCESSFUL AS OUR MOTHERS'

Above: Mrs Keppel in 1890

'I WONDER IF I SHALL EVER
SQUEEZE AS MUCH ROMANCE INTO
MY LIFE AS SHE HAS HAD IN HERS'

Left: Violet Keppel in 1918

'MAMA, WHY DO WE CALL GRANDPAPA "MAJESTY"?'

King Edward VII in 1901

emotionally neglected as a child, Lady Sackville was an erratic parent. In adult life she could not talk without tears of her own mother's death. Sometimes she said Vita was beautiful; at others that she could not look at her because she was so ugly. Once she unjustly accused her of lying and made her kneel at her feet and ask God for forgiveness. Capricious with discipline, she bewildered with changes of heart and mood,

> one moment she would be in tears saying that my father wanted to kill her with worry because the electric lighting at Knole had broken down and next moment she would be mopping her eyes with laughter because a gardener had stumbled over a flower pot.

Her moral guidance confused too: 'One must always tell the truth darling if one can' she told her, 'but not *all* the truth; *toute vérité n'est pas bonne à dire*.' 'Never refuse a good offer my child' was another piece of advice. 'I have refused a good many offers in my life and always regretted it.'

Lady Sackville pried into Vita's inner world then lamented when she refused to speak of what she felt,

> it has been rather hard to live all my life with Papa and Lionel who are both so cold on the surface and now I find the same disposition in my child. I like my old Seery because he is so *sympathetique* and I want that so much with my Spanish nature.

But it did not lead her to treat him very well.

Mrs Keppel in contrast was sharp, straightforward and unambiguous. She took no interest in the complexity of her daughters' states of mind. 'Too clever to be malicious', she appeared charming to both Kingy and her husband. Vita, though, witnessed her mother shouting at her father and goading Seery:

> I thought they would quarrel for good ... It was all very unpleasant and they called each other names and I hated it ... I am awfully sorry for Seery ... he cried this afternoon.

Such scenes made Vita create her own world of stories, choose the company of her pony, dogs and rabbits and observe her mother's eccentricities from a haven of her own control.

Capricious with money, her mother veered from indulgence to parsimony. She casually purchased antiques and pearls but picked the stamps off unfranked letters. She bought the most expensive writing paper then wrote her letters on stationery she had taken from railway hotels, or on the backs of letters received or catalogues. 'I think she touched the peak' Vita said 'when she wrote to me on the toilet paper she had found in the ladies cloakroom at Harrods.'

At Knole she had one room entirely papered with postage stamps. In her gardens she liked a display of flowers, so into gaps in the herbaceous border she stuck delphiniums made from painted tin on metal stalks, 'annual, biennial, perennial meant nothing to her; it merely irritated her that plants shouldn't flower the whole time and in exactly the right colours'.

Her oddness matured with the years. She obsessed about the benefits of fresh air, refused to have fires in the biting cold, and kept every door at Knole open – not with mundane door stoppers, but statues of Nelson, Cupid and the Duke of Wellington. Vita was given a wooden Shakespeare: 'You like poetry darling so you will like to have Shakespeare holding the door for you. *N'est-ce pas que c'est bien trouvé?*'

She took to eating meals in the garden even when it snowed. Her husband found it worse than idiosyncratic, went round shutting all doors and withdrew into his own thoughts. Vita disliked having to eat dinner in a fur coat and with hot-water bottle, foot muffs and mittens, but 'never lost the sense that no ordinary mother could introduce such fairy tales into life'.

Her mother's extravagant relationship to material things contrasted with Mrs Keppel's orderly acquisitiveness. With bizarre facility Lady Sackville acquired and abandoned stately homes, fortunes, admirers, jewels. In the back drawing room of her London house at Hill Street, Berkeley Square, she created a Persian Room with murals of exotic

flowers, latticed windows and 'improbably spiky cities'. It delighted
her,

> she possessed, more than anybody I have ever known, the faculty
> of delusion. When once she went into her Persian Room she
> ceased to see the fog or to hear the taxis. She entered the only
> world she knew, the world of unreality which she made real to
> herself, and into which she persuaded other people by the sheer
> strength of her own personality and conviction to enter.

Violet, too, was a fantasist with the faculty of delusion. In her letters
she wooed Vita with images as seductive as her mother's Persian Room.
Like Lady Sackville she created her own world. 'Do you know', she
was to write to Vita in 1920,

> that my only really solid and unseverable lien with the world is
> *you*, my love for you? I believe if there weren't you I should live
> more and more in my own world until finally I withdrew myself
> inwardly altogether. I'm sure it would happen.

As a child her romantic heart went out to a friend whose English
heritage spanned the centuries, whose home was the size of Hampton
Court and whose mother trailed the romance of Pepita the Spanish
dancer, the austerity of a French convent and the needs of a deprived
child.

Together Violet and Vita attended Helen Wolff's School for Girls
in South Audley Street. They were both clever, though Vita was better
at exams. 'Brilliant performance' she wrote of her results in April
1908. Their education was formal and academic, free thinking was
discouraged, sex was not discussed, views on social superiority went
undisturbed. Vita knew which girls were Jewish or 'bedint' — the
dismissive Sackville term for the middle class. 'Genealogies and family
connexions, tables of precedence and a familiarity with country seats
formed almost part of a moral code,' she wrote.

She and Violet took piano lessons, learned Italian with Signorina
Castelli and dancing with Mrs Wordsworth, lunched sometimes at

George Keppel's office, went to matinées with him and out to tea. 'Mr Keppel is really a dear and so kind, he gave me a huge box of chocolates,' Vita wrote in her diary.

In spring 1906 Violet again stayed in Paris with Moiselle in an apartment in the Quai Debilly belonging to a friend of her mother's. She visited Vita in Seery's apartment in the rue Lafitte. Vistas of rooms opened into each other and there were 'old and magnificent' servants and footmen. There were paintings by Boucher, Fragonard panels, chandeliers in every room. They staged, in costume, *Le Masque de Fer*, a play in French by Vita. It rhymed and was in five acts. Their audience comprised their governesses, the concierge and his wife, the chef and the butler. 'It speaks highly for their good manners that they sat it out,' Violet wrote.

Spurred by Vita's fluent grammatical French, Violet went to classes in the Faubourg St Honoré, was 'forever poring over a French grammar and a French dictionary' and planned one day to write novels in French. They talked in French and *tutoyered* to show what friends they were. 'Without the stimulus of Vita it is doubtful whether I should have taken so much trouble with my lessons,' Violet wrote:

> If I'd read all the Elizabethans by the time I was twelve and quoted Marvell, Herrick and Pope . . . it was because she liked them. If I learned Rostand's plays by heart and agreed to get myself up in Cyrano's beard and Flambeau's moustache, it was only in the hope of making her like me.

Mrs Keppel visited her daughter: 'my mother paid me the supreme compliment of coming to stay in "my" flat.' She feared Violet was becoming too bookish, clever, avant-garde. She taught her to order the dinner menu, rebuked her for choosing mayonnaise with three courses and took her, as ever, to the dressmaker.

In spring 1908, when she was thirteen, Violet told Vita that she loved her. In reply Vita 'stumbled out an unfamiliar "darling". Oh God, to remember that first avowal, that first endearment!' she wrote twelve years later. That summer both went to Florence to improve their Italian. Violet and Moiselle stayed at a pension in the Via Venezia, Vita and her French governess in the Villa Pestellini. They went to the Uffizi and saw Botticelli's *Primavera*, to Fiesole – 'It was very hot, but the view one gets to the top' – to the church of the convent of San Sacramento 'where the nuns sing too beautifully'. The nights, in recollection, 'were lit by fireflies and serenaded by frogs'.

They had a farewell tea together when Vita left. Violet cried and gave her the doge's lava ring she had cajoled from Joseph Duveen when she was six. Vita kept it on a piece of lapis lazuli. 'I don't think I was ever more sorry to leave any place,' she told her mother. 'Violet Keppel seemed very sorry to say goodbye to me; at least she cried very much.'

Violet cried again that autumn when she feared Vita might break her plan to stay with her at Duntreath. Vita's grandfather, Lord Sackville, died in September and she was, ostensibly, in mourning. But she arrived and Violet 'in a carefully thought out Scottish get-up' met her at the station. 'I am afraid I forgot to sorrow much while I was there,' Vita wrote. Mrs Keppel was at the castle with Colonel Forbes, Mrs Alec Farquharson, Sir Archibald and Lady Edmonstone and their sons. Violet filled Vita's room with tuberoses, they walked together in the rain, dressed up and acted in Vita's play *The Viper of Milan*.

On Vita's first night there, when she had gone to bed, Violet went to her room. They talked all night while owls hooted outside. It was the first time in either of their lives that they had shared the night with anyone. 'I can't hear owls now without recalling her soft, troubling presence in my room in the dark,' Vita was later to write.

Their childish passion for each other was, she said, too fierce even then to be sentimental. For Violet it was from the start obsessive and unswerving. Duntreath became haunted by Vita. 'How I loved you then! I was always afraid of your guessing how much I loved you . . . The place is inviolably yours, the lanky, awkward, adorable you that wrote historical novels and had no sense of humour . . .'

Violet's love was not for a king but for a girl with whom she shared a sense of legendary allegiance, the capricious splendour of mothers, the expectation of a palatial home. This girl held sexual power for her while men and their desires were 'no more than amourettes'. To this girl she took a romantic sensibility, an uncertainty of the worth of kings and princes and a fierce determination that what she wanted she might one day have:

Darling, how dreadfully happy we were before we grew up, you and I! I am terribly against being grown up. It does nobody any good.

EIGHT

King Edward VII died in 1910. He set off for Biarritz on 6 March. The night before leaving Buckingham Palace he did 'full justice' to a menu of turtle soup, salmon steak, grilled chicken, saddle of mutton, several snipe stuffed with foie gras, asparagus, a fruit dish, 'an enormous iced concoction' and a savoury. He also had words with his Queen about 'Mrs Keppel and the affront of his going openly with her'.

Alexandra took a Mediterranean cruise in the new yacht named after her. Bertie stopped over in Paris and went to the Théâtre de la Porte St Martin to see *Chantecler*, a play by Edmond Rostand. He thought it stupid, childish and like a pantomime; the theatre was damp and cold, he caught a chill and arrived at the Hôtel du Palais in Biarritz with a chest infection. Mrs Keppel, flustered, wrote to Soveral:

> The King's cold is so bad that he can't dine out but he wants us all to dine with him at 8.15 at the Palais. *SO BE THERE.* I am quite worried *entre nous* and have sent for the nurse.

Alexandra when told blamed 'that horrid Biarritz'. She suggested Bertie join her in April when her yacht docked at Genoa and that together they sail to Corfu to visit her brother, the King of Greece. Bertie said that was 'quite out of the question'.

Cassel was not at the Villa Eugénie that spring. His daughter Maud was chronically ill with tuberculosis. In a vain attempt to cure her he took her, his sister and niece, on a cruise up the Nile to Aswan. To ensure her peace he booked three floors of all hotels. He and the King wrote regularly to each other about money and Maudie's health. Bertie's annual accounts were due. On 28 March he told Cassel 'the matter you generally report to me at this time of the year is as satisfactory as the preceding ones.'

He said his bronchitis was no more than a cold. With Little Mrs George he followed his routine of sightseeing, picnics and promenades. They saw Blériot fly at the local aviation ground, watched pelota in the Basque mountain village of Sare, spent afternoons at the Biarritz golf club and the racecourse at Anglet. On 20 April they took a trip to Pau, stayed in the Hôtel de France there, lunched in the mountains at Cauterets and went on to Lourdes to seek a cure for what was left of his lungs.

On 25 April, after seven weeks, Biarritz bade the King farewell. Soldiers of the 49th Infantry Regiment who went out each year with him, local French soldiers and the fire brigade held a military tattoo under his hotel balcony. There was a fireworks' display, parades. 'I shall be sorry to leave Biarritz,' Bertie said. 'Perhaps it will be for ever.'

He arrived home on 27 April. He wrote to Cassel saying he looked forward to meeting him on 7 May at Buckingham Palace and to 'talking over many matters' with him. He went to Sandringham for the weekend, supervised some gardening, 'stood about in the cold wind' and on 2 May returned to London. He played bridge with Mrs Keppel but she sent him off home at 10.30 to go to bed early. Over the next few days he was ill and she visited him each day at the Palace.

Alexandra arrived home on the evening of 5 May. She had heard of the seriousness of this illness when she got to Calais. Bertie had chest pains, fainting fits, was a terrible colour and choked when he smoked his cigars. Cassel, too, returned to Brook House that day from his cruise. Mrs Keppel called to see him right away. He wrote to Maudie:

> Poor Alice met me on arrival in despair. There is grave ground for anxiety . . . but there is no reason to despair. I shall go to the Palace tomorrow where my appointment for tomorrow still holds good.

Next morning his butler, Davidson, had a phone call saying the King was too ill to receive Cassel. Half an hour later Lord Knollys left a message instructing him to go to the Palace at once. Cassel took with him for the King an envelope with £10,000 in banknotes.

He first saw the Queen. She asked after his daughter Maudie. She and the physician Sir Francis Laking advised him not to let the King speak much. Bertie, dressed and in his sitting room, tried to rise from his chair to shake hands but 'looked as if he had suffered great pain and spoke indistinctly'. He too asked after Maudie and was glad the cruise had done her good. He said, 'I am very seedy, but I wanted to see you . . . He then talked about other matters, and I had to ask his leave to go as I felt it was not good for him to go on speaking.'

Late in the afternoon the Prince of Wales brought news that Bertie's horse, Witch of the Air, had won the 4.15 at Kempton Park. 'Yes, I have heard it,' said the King. 'I am very glad.'

In his last hours Mrs Keppel went to see him. She had sent the Queen the letter Bertie wrote her in 1901, when he had appendicitis. It stated that if he were to die he wanted to 'say farewell' to her and that he was 'convinced that all those who have any affection for me will carry out the wishes which I have expressed in these lines'. The Queen shook hands with her, said, 'I am sure you have always had a good influence over him', then turned away and walked to the window.

Bertie had had a series of heart attacks and was incoherent. He kept falling forward in his chair and did not recognize his Little Mrs George. Cassel's envelope of money was by his bed.

In a rare display Mrs Keppel lost control and kept repeating, 'I never did any harm, there was nothing wrong between us, what is to become of me.' Princess Victoria tried, but failed, to calm her. Mrs Keppel was carried to Frederick Ponsonby's room in a 'wild fit of hysterics'. It was hours before she quietened down. Lord Esher wrote in his journal, 'Altogether it was a painful and rather theatrical exhibition and ought never to have happened.'

Bertie died at a quarter to midnight. Alexandra said Biarritz had killed him. She wanted to hide herself away in the country but 'there was this terrible State funeral and all the dreadful arrangements that had to be made'. Francis Knollys sent the envelope of banknotes back to Cassel: 'I presume they belong to you and are not the result of any speculation you went into for him.' Cassel returned the money, saying it represented 'interest I gave to the King in financial matters I am undertaking'.

It was a large sum to have in notes – about half a million pounds in today's money – and an odd offering to bring to the bedside of a dying King. 'It was the fruit of a quite exceptionally lucrative investment' said Cassel's biographer, Anthony Allfrey, who surmised that the money was intended for Mrs Keppel. It was, perhaps, an indication of the casual way her fortune was accrued.

The atmosphere was grim on 5 May at 16 Portman Square. Strangers gathered outside the house. 'I was afraid to approach my stern, unsmiling mother,' Sonia said. George was abstracted and serious, Nannie evasive, Moiselle silent.

Next morning Violet and Sonia woke to learn the King was dead. Their mother and George had left the house in the night to stay with Arthur and Venetia James in Grafton Street. He was a racing friend of Bertie's. To Venetia, Mrs Keppel said the Queen had sent for her to go to the dying King's bedside, had kissed her and given her the promise that the royal family 'would look after her'. Mrs James spread this story round the Ritz, 'telling everyone about Mrs Keppel's visit to B. Palace'. 'Mrs Keppel has lied about the whole affair . . . and describes, quite falsely, her reception by the King' Lord Esher wrote.

Violet and Sonia, too, were taken to Mrs James's house by Nannie and Moiselle. The Keppel family never returned to Portman Square. Mrs James was rich and childless and her house severe. The hall was of yellow marble with nude classical figures in niches. Manservants of 'untouchable dignity' opened and closed the doors to 'frigid reception rooms'. Blinds were drawn, lights dimmed, everyone wore black. The girls were shown to darkened rooms, given black clothes – even their underwear was threaded with black ribbon – and told their mother was in bed. They tried to go and see her but Mrs James prevented them. Late in the day she escorted them to her bedside:

We went up to her bed and she turned and looked at us blankly and without recognition, and rather resentfully, as though we were unwelcome intruders.

It was all too much for Sonia, who was only nine. She sought out her father, wept 'on his ever-comforting shirt-front,' and confided her anxieties of the preceding day, her distress at leaving Portman Square, her dislike of Mrs James's house, her 'terror of Mama's non-recognition.' 'Why,' she asked with resentment, 'does it matter so much, Kingy dying?'

'Because,' her father replied, 'Kingy was such a wonderful man.'

The newspapers, bordered in black, wrote of nothing but the King's death. His body lay on a catafalque at Westminster Abbey from 17 to 19 May, until the funeral there on the 20th. Attending the service were the German Emperor and the Kings of Spain, Portugal, Denmark, Belgium, Norway and Bulgaria. Vita went with her father. 'Everyone cried when they saw the King's little dog following the coffin,' she wrote in her diary.

Sir Frederick Ponsonby arranged the funeral. 'With memories of Queen Victoria's funeral only nine years earlier I found no difficulty in organization,' he said. The Order of Service was bound in purple velvet, the Archbishop of Canterbury in his benediction spoke of eternal life, the Bishop of Winchester thanked God for delivering Bertie from the miseries of this sinful world, the Archbishop of York asked God to resurrect him.

The nation mourned. Church services were held in every village, town and city. Eulogies abounded to the King's greatness, wisdom and glory. Voices of dissent were few and private. Wilfrid Scawen Blunt wrote in his diary on the day of the funeral:

Today the King was buried and I hope the country will return to comparative sanity for at present it is in delirium. The absurdities written in every newspaper about him pass belief. He might have been a Solon and a Francis of Assisi combined if characters drawn of him were true. In no print has there been the slightest allusion to Mrs Keppel or to any of the 101 ladies he has loved, or to his gambling or to any of the little vices which made up his domestic life. It is not for me or perhaps any of us to censure him for these pleasant wickednesses, but his was not even in make-believe the life of a saint or of an at all virtuous or respectable man, and according to strict theology he is most certainly at the present moment in hell. Yet all the bishops and priests, Catholic, Protestant and Non-conformist, join in giving him a glorious place in heaven and there were eight miles of his loyal and adoring subjects marching on foot to see him lying in state at Westminster Hall.

For myself I think he performed his duties well. He had a passion for pageantry and ceremonial and dresssing up, and he was never tired of putting on uniforms and taking them off, and receiving princes and ambassadors and opening museums and hospitals and attending cattle shows and military shows and shows of every kind, while every night of his life he was to be seen at theatres and operas and music halls. Thus he was always before the public and had come to have the popularity of an actor who plays his part in a variety of costumes and always well. Abroad too there is no doubt he had a great reputation. His little Bohemian tastes made him much beloved at Paris . . . He did not affect to be virtuous and all sorts of publicans and sinners found their place at his table. The journalists loved him. He did not mind being snap-shotted and was stand off to nobody. If not witty he could understand a joke, and if not wise he was sensible . . . He liked to be well received wherever he went and to be on good terms with the world. He was essentially a cosmopolitan and without racial prejudice and he cared as much for popularity abroad as at home . . . He wanted an easy life and that everybody should be friends with everybody. He sank his English nationality on the Continent, talked French and German in preference to English, and English with a foreign accent. He knew Europe well and exactly what foreigners thought of England.

... he never succeeded in making friends with his nephew Wilhelm and I fancy they hated each other to the end ... he may rightly share with Solomon the title of the 'Wise'. They each had several hundred concubines and as we know, 'The knowledge of women is the beginning of wisdom.' At least it teaches tolerance of the unwisdom of others.

Of all this the newspaper writers say no word, being virtuous men and fools.

The nation was denied full revelation of the King's little vices and pleasant wickednesses. In his will he directed that letters and private papers should be burned after his death. This was done by Sir Francis Knollys and Lord Esher. After Alexandra's death hers were burned by Knollys's wife Charlotte.

~

Life at Court changed with Bertie's death. 'Are we as welcome as ever?' was the caption to a cartoon by Max Beerbohm showing Ernest Cassel, Arthur Sassoon and Leopold Rothschild creeping along a Palace corridor. Scawen Blunt predicted a 'regular sweep' of

the Jews and the second-rate women that the King preferred to his aristocracy because they amused him ... [George V] hates all these and would have nothing to do with them.

Cassel subscribed to a bust of Bertie by Sir Thomas Brock and continued for a while to oversee the royal portfolio and to donate large sums to charity. But for him and Mrs Keppel royal intimacy was over, the special relationship gone. He retired in December 1910. *The Times* gave him a respectful appraisal and, in private, he continued his flair for making money.

For Mrs Keppel life changed overnight. The King's death left her wealthy but uncrowned. Without a role she could not publicly parade her grief or continue as part of Palace life. She was cold-shouldered by Bertie's son and rebuffed when she went to sign her name in the visitors' book at Marlborough House.

Soon after Bertie's death she moved into a huge house at 16 Grosvenor Street. Originally an eighteenth-century mansion, converted in the late nineteenth century into piano showrooms with flats above, she set about having it restored to its former glory. Violet described it as 'a great improvement' on Portman Square. Osbert Sitwell called it 'surely one of the most remarkable houses in London':

> Its high façade, dignified and unpretentious as only that of a Georgian mansion can be, very effectively hid its immense size. Within existed an unusual air of spaciousness and light, an atmosphere of luxury, for Mrs Keppel possessed an instinct for splendour.

Hostessing came later. She sought to scotch rumours from critics like Lord Knollys that her appetite for partying was as keen as ever. To his wife she wrote from Grosvenor Street, after Bertie's death, on paper framed in black:

> My dear Lady Knollys
> I feel sure *you* cannot think I should give a dinner party, feeling as I do. Tomorrow, Soveral, Louise Sassoon and Captain Fortescue come. Soveral because he does not dine out, & I told Ld Knollys of Louise, who is coming up simply to see me. How people can do anything I do not know, as life with all its joys, have come to a full stop, at least for me.
> Sincerely
> Alice Keppel

Three guests, she let it be known, did not constitute a dinner party. She withdrew temporarily from the social scene and while builders worked on improvements to 16 Grosvenor Street, arranged a year's trip to Ceylon, China and round the world.

She went to Duntreath for the summer months and in August

announced to her daughters that they would sail with her to Ceylon on 3 November. 'No young lady's education is complete without a smattering of Tamil,' she told Violet. The journey out would take three weeks. For three months they were to be guests of Bertie's friend and George's employer Sir Thomas Lipton. Their destination was his bungalow and tea plantations at Dambatenne.

Mrs Keppel's brother, 'beloved Archie', was in the party along with his wife Ida, their son Ronnie and his wife Eva, Nannie, Moiselle and a male escort for the girls, Watty Montgomery, who already had a smattering of Tamil and whom Sonia liked because he reminded her of Papa – who stayed at home.

In October Violet wrote to Vita telling her how she did nothing but try on dresses all day. 'I want you to come to Ceylon if only to see them. O Vanity Thy Name is Violet.' She did not want to part from Vita. She again told her that she loved her and Vita asked her why. Violet who was sixteen replied,

> you ask me pointblank why I love you . . . I love you because
> you never capitulate. I love you for your wonderful intelligence,
> for your literary aspirations, for your unconscious (?) coquetry.
> I love you because you have the air of doubting nothing! I love
> in you what is also in me: imagination, the gift for languages,
> taste, intuition and a host of other things . . . I love you Vita
> because I've seen your soul.

But Vita, two years older, was busy. She had 'come out' into society. A Florentine Marquis, Orazio Pucci, wanted to marry her and pursued her to Rome and Paris. She called him poor Pucci and did not in the least want to marry him. Her friend Rosamund Grosvenor, whom she called 'the Rubens lady' because she was pink and white and curvy was besotted with her. Vita desired, kissed and shared a bed with her, but thought her stupid. ('O my dears do consider your illustrious names,' her governess said as she saw their amorous displays.) And at a dinner party she had met Harold Nicolson, liked his curls and boyish ways and thought him witty, amenable and not in the least boring.

Violet warned she would become the 'wife of a gentleman . . . I pray
that my prediction will not be realized.' But Vita was easy about men.
'I didn't think of them in what is called "that way".'

On 31 October Violet met her to say goodbye. They went to a play
and drove round Hyde Park. 'The end of that motor-drive was one of
the very rare but extremely disturbing occasions when she kissed me,'
Vita recalled ten years later. She warned Violet to stay true while she
was away and threatened to kill her if she did not. From Grosvenor
Street Violet wrote:

> Your speech impressed me profoundly . . . if only your imagina-
> tion could take it in, you were holding, so to speak, my soul in
> your hands. You could mould it any way you liked . . .
>
> My curiosity on the other hand is so great that I would let
> myself go to the extreme just to see how you would arrange to
> kill me. Would it be a stiletto thrust between the shoulder blades
> by a traitor at midnight or a poisoned cup by daylight? Do tell
> me so that I know where I stand . . .

Dambatenne, 6000 feet above sea level, had panoramic views of
mountains, lagoons, camphor trees and mile after mile of plantations
of tea. Ceylonese women in bright clothes picked the leaves for a
pittance. The Keppel party travelled out via Naples and Tangier, across
the Red Sea and Indian Ocean. For the journey by road from Colombo
to Dambatenne three cars carried them all, their luggage and guns,
spears and nets for hunting in the jungle. As they drove through
mountain villages local people gathered to look. Alice said they
thought the cars were gods.

In one village a woman, a basket of fruit on her head, seemed
mesmerized by the cars and stood in their path. In Sonia's account:

> The chauffeur sounded his horn. The next thing I remember was
> a bump, and then fruit from the basket flew all over the road
> . . . Then the crowd began to scream . . . Dimly, I sensed that we
> had killed the poor old woman . . . A native policeman appeared,

and Watty towered over him, quietly answering his excited questions. Mama and Uncle Archie stood beside him while the villagers crowded round vociferously. Eventually the legal points appeared to be settled. And evidently Mama's generosity placated the old woman's relations. Like an old rag-doll I saw her carried limply away.

Though life with all its joys had come to a full stop, charm and money had its way.

〜'

Two days after Violet left for the East and five days after warning her to be faithful while she was away, Vita wrote a letter, on 5 November 1910, from Knole to Harold Nicolson:

> My dear Harold
>   I have been asked to 'ask a man' to dine on Thursday with Mrs Harold Pearson and go to a dance, so would you like to come? I promise you shan't be made to dance! I think it might be rather amusing.

She told him to let her know as soon as possible or 'better still' to come to tea with her and the Rubens lady.

In the winter she had a persistent chest infection and her mother sent her to the south of France to recuperate in the sun. She stayed in the Château Malet outside Monte Carlo. Rosamund and Harold stayed too. Violet wrote exotic letters evoking the Orient and the *Thousand and One Nights*. She wrote of pawpaws for breakfast, lagoons girded by nutmeg trees, swaying bamboo, purple orchids, camphor trees, white peacocks, the jungle, mountains, starry skies and weary oxen with bloodshot eyes, 'a vermilion land, enamoured of light, drunk by sunshine . . .'

But behind the endeavoured seduction she was disquieted as she scanned Vita's letters – less frequent than her own and half the length

— for proof of fidelity or signs of betrayal: 'Do try not to get married before I return,' she asked her on 4 December 1910.

And though Vita spared the details, clues were there. They gave some inkling of Harold 'so fresh, so intellectual, so unphysical' whom Vita liked better than anyone as a companion and playfellow, and for his brain and 'delicious disposition'. It was enough for Violet to write on 12 December without embellishment, some ten days after she arrived at Dambatenne that as she read, again and again, Vita's latest letter, 'a sort of heavy anguish', an 'apprehension' made her heart beat fast and her hand tremble. In French, her language of the heart, she voiced fear:

> For the first time your two extra years seem to me so real, arrogant, sinister. Don't think I haven't anticipated it. I've often thought of it. Oh God, tell me I'm wrong — carried away by my fiendish imagination.
>
> After all, I'm hardly a woman. I ought to have known that at your age you'd have a liaison with a man. I'd be wise to accept this. I feel I'm about to say inappropriate things. Don't laugh. Promise you won't laugh. For so long I've asked nothing of you, so grant me that. *It would hurt so.*

Violet did not enjoy the trip to Ceylon. In her memoirs she described it as 'a completely irrelevant interlude'. She was there not to learn a smattering of Tamil, but because it suited her mother. It was discreet for the previous King's mistress to absent herself from London society while changes took place at the Palace. For Mrs Keppel travel was a compensatory way of putting Biarritz, Portman Square and her now uncertain social position behind her. She intended to be away for more than a year and so her daughters must be away too.

Violet suffered the heat and spicy food and felt herself 'essentially an occidental'. She liked, she said, hints of the Orient — as in Bucharest, Sicily and southern Spain — but 'the unmitigated East disturbs'. She spent the time in 'a mood of settled melancholy', bought a ruby for Vita but sensed she was losing her. 'What a bitch you are!' she wrote on 2 January 1911. 'Do you know that you have ceased to be a reality for me?'

Mrs Keppel's days at Dambatenne were spent lazing on divans. The heat was intense. Archie got migraines. Ida embroidered. Nannie, fractious, quarrelled with Moiselle and was shocked by the bare breasts of the women who picked tea. A house snake kept to catch mice terrified Sonia. One lunchtime a servant walked through the dining room with chamber pots stacked on his head. It was not Grosvenor Street, the Villa Eugénie or Portman Square.

They had picnics in the hills and admired the unfamiliar sight of monkeys, parrots and hummingbirds in the wild. They visited the buried city at Anuradhapura. The day after Violet wrote her premonitory letter to Vita they went into the jungle at Nuwara Eliya with rifles, huge nets, wading boots and cameras for big game hunting. It was the kind of trip Kingy passionately loved. 'I hope terribly they won't force me to participate,' Violet wrote to Vita. 'Those enormous beasts all bleeding – pouah! It makes one shudder!'

In February Mrs Keppel, her beloved Archie and his family sailed for China. Violet and Sonia, accompanied by Moiselle and the nanny, were despatched to Munich. Violet was nearly seventeen, Sonia ten. At Colombo they said goodbye to their mother whom they would not see for many months. 'The parting with Mama was terrible,' Sonia wrote.

At San Remo they were reunited with George Keppel for a few days. Violet met up with Vita who was still at the Monte Carlo villa. 'I remember admiring to myself the thick plait of her really beautiful hair,' Vita wrote. Violet gave her the ruby she had bought her. She did not waver from her love of Europe, its languages and culture, her desire to live in Paris and to write, her derision of marriage and social conformity, her serious love of Vita. If she saw her unawares the colour drained from her face. Lord Sackville, as a joke, when Vita mentioned seeing Violet, would say: Did she turn pale? 'O Vita,' Violet wrote that year:

I get so sad when I think how like we are to two gamblers, both greedy to win, neither of whom will risk throwing a card unless the other throws his at the same time! You won't tell me you love me, because you fear (wrongly most of the time) that I will not make the same declaration to you at the same moment!

Vita took conquest and possession — of people and place — lightly. She liked Harold but he seemed too diffident to make any physical move. She 'tyrannized' Rosamund and desired her. Violet she regarded as hers. 'I knew it then, albeit only through my obscurely but quite obstinantly proprietary attitude.' Most of all she liked Knole, Kent, her dogs and writing stories, plays and poems.

After a week in San Remo the Keppel girls went on to Munich. Moiselle and Nannie, usually discordant, united in criticism of Mrs Keppel for dumping her daughters 'like the Babes in the Wood' in a country where they knew no one. They all booked in at a pension at 5 Maximilianstrasse owned by Frau Glocker, once an opera singer now a landlady who tippled brandy. Mrs Keppel had not vetted the place and would not have approved of it. The bedrooms had lino on the floors and inadequate stoves. Of the six other boarders one, Frau Leeb, had a wooden leg which she unscrewed at mealtimes and left propped by the fire. Violet and Sonia ate breakfast and lunch with the other guests and had tea in their own sitting room.

It was snowing when they arrived. The cold, the upholstered furniture, feather bedding and anxiety at being separated from her mother in unfamiliar surroundings exacerbated Sonia's asthma. Nannie wrapped her in a cotton-wool pack which made her wheeze the more. She became chronically ill.

She and Violet went to an international school. Violet, more at home in Europe than England, learned German easily, proved witty and moved in a cosmopolitan set. Sonia was confused by the language, wore a brace on her protruding teeth, was homesick and sought out English girlfriends:

I liked the two Molesworth girls because their grandmother had written *The Cuckoo Clock*. And because most of our lives we appeared to have gone to bed at the same time and to have had milk and biscuits for supper.

Neither she nor Violet truly knew what mother was doing in China or why they were in Munich and she was there. For unexplained reasons the death of Kingy meant they lost her, too. The glittering goddess had disappeared to an unknown corner of the world as bewildering as Dambatenne.

George Keppel visited Munich once a month. While there, he saw much of the singer Nellie Melba who called him a 'charmeur'. In the afternoons he took Sonia shopping, out to tea and to museums. In the evenings he often took Violet to the opera. She liked Wagner best. Mother, Duntreath and Grosvenor Street all seemed part of another life. Violet wrote to Vita and asked her to visit. 'But I never did,' Vita, absorbed in her own life, said.

In summer 1911 Mrs Keppel offered Violet a holiday in the country of her choice and told her she was welcome to bring a friend. Violet asked Vita to join them in the Austrian Tyrol. Vita declined and Violet's disappointment was keen. 'No I am not angry,' she wrote on 31 July from the Grand Hotel Reichtenhall:

Why should I be? It is merely a pity. That is all I can say.

... No, I am afraid you will not see me again till goodness knows when! I don't think I shall return to England before i'm married. To say the least of it I have forgotten everybody in England except you, which is not a compliment – only the truth which somehow or other never manages to be complimentary.

O Vita come! If not for your sake for mine. Don't you *understand*. Can't you see it can never be the same again. If I have ever wanted you I want you *now*. Come, I implore you. My pride forbids me to say more. I could kill myself for having said so much.

Their letters became infrequent. At Christmas Violet sent her a card of two cherubs floating in the sky.

Mrs Keppel visited Munich. At the station Sonia did not recognize her:

> A lady caught my arm and said: 'Here I am, darling!' I gave her a brief look and tried to brush her aside. But the lady persisted. 'Here I am!' again she said.
>
> I looked up at her and, rudely, I stared. The turquoise-coloured eyes were the same, smiling down at me ... But what had happened to the hair?
>
> The last time I had seen it, under the ship's lights at Colombo, it had shone like gold. Now it was snow white.

Like a fairy Mrs Keppel transformed her daughters' lives. Dismayed by the Pension Glocker she moved them to a spacious sunny apartment furnished with rented antiques. Disturbed by Violet's weight gain and clothes she said 'My poor child! You can never leave Germany!' decked her out and told her to diet. Disapproving of her college friends, she contacted Sir Vincent Corbett, British Ambassador in Munich, and through him introduced Violet to young people she deemed more suitable. 'They were a jolly, extrovert lot, given up to shooting and skiing,' Violet said. For Sonia she found a new doctor, who threw out the feather bedding and cotton-wool padding and advocated opening the windows.

She then returned to Grosvenor Street, rose from the ashes of bereavement, tinted her white hair blue and re-established herself in society life. She took with her treasures from the East to adorn her Georgian mansion: porcelain and Coromandel screens, Chippendale chinoiserie furniture, eighteenth-century painted silk panels to line the walls of her boudoir. She turned 16 Grosvenor Steet into a spectacular townhouse. 'In these spacious rooms Mama had all the scope she needed to demonstrate her matured taste and knowledge,' Sonia said. 'Not only were the rooms beautiful,' Osbert Sitwell wrote, with their grey walls, red lacquer cabinets, English eighteenth-century people in their red coats, huge porcelain pagodas [a gift from Bertie] and thick, magnificent carpets, but the hostess conducted the running of her house as a work of art in itself . . .

From Bond Street she bought Old Masters, china, cut-glass candelabra, chandeliers. The dining room seated seventy. Her Angora cats matched the carpets. Twice as many servants as in Portman Square lived in the basement area.

Mrs Keppel's suite was on the first floor, George's on the floor above. All the old Portman Street furniture went into his rooms: screens, *chaiseslongues*, leather chairs, his photos of 'masses of beautiful ladies with well-developed bosoms and tiny waists'. Sonia's and Nannie's rooms and the schoolroom were on the second floor, too. Violet and Moiselle had the floor above. Violet's sitting room was converted out of an attic.

Mrs Keppel, her social confidence unimpaired, resumed her life of bridge, visiting and choosing the menus. In March 1912 she retrieved her daughters from Germany. Sonia was to be despatched to London, Violet to Paris. From the Grand Hotel Heidelberg Violet wrote to Vita that she 'would suffocate with rage' if she did not see her in Paris. She was eighteen and it was time for her to 'come out' into society. Mrs Keppel bought her brassieres, corsets, chic clothes, got her hair curled, her nails manicured. On this metamorphosis much money was spent. Vita wrote to Harold Nicolson, who was in Constantinople and to whom she was unofficially engaged: 'My erratic friend Violet Keppel is coming home in April so you will know her; I am so glad. She will amuse you more than anybody.'

'After a month in Paris, who would have recognized the Bavarian Backfisch?' Violet said:

Patiently, tirelessly, my mother dealt with my appearance, item after item; complexion, hair, figure, clothes, adding here, subtracting there. A whole *quartier* concentrated on my uninviting person.

Mrs Keppel's coming back and her daughter's coming out were to dazzle Grosvenor Street and Berkeley Square.

NINE

Mrs Keppel 'determined to give Violet a wonderful season' whether she wanted one or not. Life at 16 Grosvenor Street focused on entertaining, parties and who was getting married to whom. Ostensibly it was all for her daughter's sake. Each day she would say 'So and So's engagement was in *The Times* this morning'. Her table, Sonia wrote, was graced by

> exquisite beauties like Zia Torby and Diana Manners and Bridget Colebrooke and Vi de Trafford. And romantic young men like John Granby and Charles Lister, and Julian and Billy Grenfell.

Violet did not enjoy herself. She seemed 'much less gay than she had done in Munich'. On her own admission she cared for no one in England but Vita. Men thought her too acerbic, too clever. She sprinkled her conversation with phrases in French and German, alluded to her painting classes and love of Wagner and scared the 'pink and white' young men introduced as putative husbands.

All agreed she could be very amusing, a good mimic, and that she sparkled when she chose. She liked dancing — particularly the foxtrot and tango. But at heart she found her mother's social world intolerable. It brought with it constraints, hypocrisies and obligations of a sort she hated but was not strategic enough to defy. These were the people who by virtue of their wealth and class *were* society — royalty, politicians, beauties — but she was not attracted to their lives. Vita, too, rejected them as role models and satirized them in her novel *The Edwardians*:

> their conversation seemed to consist in asking one another what they had thought of such and such an entertainment and

whether they were going to such and such another . . . investments bulked heavy in their talk, and other people's incomes,
and the merits of stocks and shares; . . . These are the people
who ordain the London season, glorify Ascot, make or unmake
the fortunes of small Continental watering places, inspire envy,
emulation and snobbishness . . . they spend money, and that is
the best that can be said of them.

Mrs Keppel invited three hundred people to Violet's coming-out
ball in April 1912. George and Mr Rolfe the butler planned it all like
a military manoeuvre. 'The house was full of men moving furniture
and of florists arranging flowers.' Guests dined at little tables, the
Italianate garden was 'spanned by a tent', Casano's band played soft
music throughout dinner. Sonia panicked and elected to stay with
Lady Elizabeth Williamson who was eighty and lived in Curzon Street.
    The old Edwardians regrouped at Mrs Keppel's command in their
brilliant jewels and grand dresses, with their now grown-up children,
still confident of power and privilege despite King Edward's death.
Violet scorned them. She extolled art and freedom. She shared the
pre-war craze for Diaghilev's productions of the Russian ballet, saw
Nijinsky and Karsavina dancing in *Scheherezade* and, influenced by the
set designs of Bakst, decorated her rooms at the top of the house with
gold lamé curtains, subdued lighting, the painted head of a sphinx
over the fireplace. She festooned the divans with cushions, burned
incense, filled the place with ikons, missals, Persian jackets and feathered turbans. It was a setting for less orthodox seduction than Mrs
Keppel's bedroom two floors down.
    Vita was abroad and did not attend this 'coming out'. But a month
later Violet and her mother went to Knole for a Saturday to Monday
party. ('Weekend' was considered vulgar, resonant of trade and the
necessity for paid occupation.) Violet was discomfited to see Vita's
popularity and social success: 'she had all the prestige that two years'
precedence *dans le monde* can confer. I felt resentful, at a disadvantage.'
She thought Vita beautiful, not a Bavarian Backfisch like herself:

She was tall and graceful. The profound hereditary Sackville eyes were as pools from which the morning mist had lifted. A peach might have envied her complexion. Round her revolved several enamoured young men.

Violet, marginalized, flirted with one of the guests, went with him to the park and did not return until everyone was in bed. She made her way to Vita's bedroom 'down miles of passages', past the state rooms, through the long gallery. She went in without knocking and did not turn on the light. 'Moonlight poured through the uncurtained windows on to the carved historical-looking bed.'

Vita was not asleep. She was caustic about Violet's flirtatiousness with men. They kissed. Violet felt betrayed, thought her condescending, feared rumours about her impending engagement to Harold Nicolson were true and that their own intimacy was at an end. She asked if Vita was in love and Vita said she was not.

To her mother Violet confided her disappointment that Vita gave more time to Rosamund Grosvenor than to herself. Mrs Keppel mentioned this to Lady Sackville, which irritated Vita. 'This jealousy between R and V will end badly,' she wrote in her diary. But such feelings were of no social significance, no more than girlish moods. And now Violet was 'out' they all met at country house parties, at Knole, Coker, Crichel, Crewe, Sutton Courtney.

On 8 June Violet wrote to Vita from Buckhurst, Withyam, Sussex:

This is a rather nice place with a divine garden. Of course it is not Knole . . . Knole is quite unique & I love it far better than you have any idea of . . . I would not at all object to being housemaid at Knole.

From Crichel at Christmas she thanked Vita for a jade claw, sent love to Rosamund, hoped to meet 'sometime next year etc., etc.' They met at Knole at New Year in 1913 and at Vita's birthday party in March. On 10 March they walked together in Hyde Park. 'She is mad,' Vita wrote in her diary, 'she kissed me as she usually does not, and told me she loves me. Rose does not know that I went out with V. this evening.'

None of them considered the implications of these kisses and declarations of love. In May, Violet and her mother stayed in Ravello at the villa of Lord Grimthorpe – the banker reputed to be Violet's father. Vita stayed, too, to vex Rosamund who was having a romance with a sailor.

On 29 May Mrs Keppel gave a dinner party for seventy at Grosvenor Street. Vita was there. Violet, responding to social expectations and knowing jealousy unleashed possessiveness in Vita, got engaged to Gerald Wellesley, heir to the title of Duke of Wellington, a diplomat and colleague of Harold Nicolson. He bought her a ring but the engagement was one of her 'parlour tricks' and she broke it. Vita, disturbed, wrote to Harold:

> He lays down the law so he is positively rude, and I never knew anyone so critical . . . He is excited about Violet Keppel but she doesn't like him. How you will hate her, or perhaps you will be completely bowled over, so on the whole I think you had better not meet.

The following year Gerald Wellesley found a new, very rich fiancée, Dorothy Ashton, stepdaughter of the Earl of Scarborough. The marriage lasted until she started an affair with Vita in 1922.

Marriage and its prospects prompted the parties, dinners and dances given by mothers. If the sexuality of the daughters in ballgowns and the family pearls appeared equivocal or complicated, marriage would sort that out. Marriage was the main tide, other liaisons squalls and eddies of the heart. But Violet would not or could not go with the tide. She had her mother's bold love for a king to match. She put a regal premium on her own feelings. She found Vita's engagement to Harold Nicolson intolerable, a betrayal, and would not observe the social niceties surrounding it. Her jealousy was acute. On 28 July he wrote to Vita from his parents' home at 53 Cadogan Gardens:

Isn't it funny — Violet is so jealous of Gwen [his sister] getting nearer to you (legally) than she is — and has not answered any of her letters. G is terrified that she will be catty to you about her. She (Violet) is a vulgar little girl.

A week later on 5 August 1913 Vita's engagement was formally announced in the papers. Violet wrote a scornful letter:

Accepté mes félicitations les plus sincère *à la nouvelle de tes fiançailles!* I never could write letters on this subject in any language but somehow it sounds less sickening in French. I wish you *every possible happiness* (et cetera) from the bottom of my heart (et cetera). Will you and Mr Nicholson come and have tea with me? Also Mama *me charge de te demander* if you would both care to spend the week at Clingendaal beginning Sunday 10th of August.

. . . I see in the evening papers that the rumour is contradicted, in which case the effusion would be (officially at least) in vain. *Ma non importa.* You can keep it till the day when it ought publicly to be forthcoming. It will suit the same purpose at any age, with no matter whom.

Behind Violet's love for Vita was contempt for the hypocrisy of marriage as she had seen it practised by her mother and the King. For herself she knew marriage would be a meretricious show. She wanted proof that Vita was dissembling too.

The night before her wedding Vita cried for an hour at the thought of leaving Knole. She was married in the chapel there on 1 October 1913. She wore a gold gown, a veil of Irish lace; Rosamund Grosvenor and Harold's sister Gwen were bridesmaids. Six hundred wedding presents were displayed in the Great Hall: emeralds and diamonds from Lady Sackville, an amethyst and diamond ring from Mrs Keppel on Violet's behalf. Violet stayed away — a measure of how betrayed she felt. Lady Sackville stayed in bed. She disliked not being the centre of attention and parting with her daughter made her ill.

She had had a difficult year. Seery died in January 1912. She was waiting for him at Spealls, the interior design shop in South Audley Street which she managed, erratically, for a few years. He was going to take her to lunch. She had told him to bring a bottle of port wine for one of the staff who was ill. Instead he had a massive heart attack. He left her £150,000 in cash, the contents of 2 rue Lafitte estimated at £350,000, and valuable antiques, jewels and artworks. His relatives went to court alleging she had mesmerized him and exerted 'undue influence'. She was defended by Sir Edward Carson, famous for his prosecution of Oscar Wilde. Mr F.E. Smith — later Lord Birkenhead defended the Scott family. Lady Sackville knew him socially and with her inimitable capacity for intervention wrote to him before the case:

19 June 1913

Dear Mr Smith

I hear that Mr Malcolm Scott has approached you on the subject of attacking me and my husband and my daughter in his iniquitous suit, coming next week.

I can't believe that you would let yourself be mixed up in this painful affair when you and I meet among our friends in society and I meet your wife often too.

The whole Defence put forward by Mr Scott is a tissue of falsehoods against a woman who has behaved well all her life and tried to help saving one of the finest places in England.

I do hope you will think over the undeserved pain you will give so unnecessarily . . .

    Yours sincerely

      V. Sackville

I swear on my honour that I have *never* influenced Sir J. over his will, except to leave us much less than he intended and that I have never seen or destroyed any signed Codicil.

She won and made a friend of the judge, Sir Samuel Evans. Summing up he called her a lady of high mettle, 'very high mettle indeed'. She sold the contents of 2 rue Lafitte (though Seery had hoped these works of art would enrich Knole) and in the year of Vita's marriage spent money wildly. 'How she flung money about that year . . . It was almost terrifying to go out shopping with her,' Vita wrote. She invested £60,000 in the goldmine of a Canadian whom she met on a train. Walking down Bond Street she saw in a jeweller's window a chain of emeralds and diamonds and bought it for Vita. Her victory made Lady Sackville very rich, but it was a public humiliation for her husband, who turned to his lover, Olive Rubens.

For Vita marriage to Harold was supportive, companionable, calm. His background was not exotic like hers and he had no money other than what he earned. Born in Teheran in 1886, the third son of a Scottish diplomat, Sir Arthur Nicolson, and Catherine Rowan Hamilton, he spent his childhood in embassies and legations in Constantinople, Tangier, Madrid, St Petersburg. He went to Wellington College and Balliol, Oxford, and in 1909 joined the Foreign Office.

He was, Vita said, 'a merry angel', enthusiastic, intelligent, jokey, avoiding of confrontation. Mild disdain for Americans, Jews and the middle class and a dislike of women, left him easy and charming in the company of aristocratic men. He admired and adored Vita but preferred to write of emotion not show it.

They honeymooned in Italy and Egypt, then sailed to Constantinople where he was third secretary at the British Embassy. She was homesick for Knole and Rosamund, but life was new and happy. By December she was pregnant. The following June war loomed and Harold was recalled to England:

> I remember a divine voyage by sea from Constantinople to Marseilles, through the Aegean, a second honeymoon. We met Mother in Paris and both thought that she was going off her head, as she was obviously in an extraordinarily unbalanced state of mind. Then we went to Knole. War was declared on the 4th of August and Ben was born on the 6th. Scenes immediately began with mother over his name.

Lady Sackville was having a difficult menopause. Excluded by Vita's harmonious family life, she marginalized Harold, was disparaging about his parents and tried to claim the new child by insisting he be called Lionel. She filled Harold with dread. Four years later, he felt equal loathing for Violet whom he thought resembled her. Emotionally manipulative women who claimed Vita made him venomous:

> Everything in me cries out in loathing of BM [Bonne Maman], of her vain empty insincere nature — and I get hot with shame to think that I have allowed myself to pander to her vanity, to adulate her emptiness and to abet her insincerity.

Vita and he moved out of Knole. BM's money bought them 182 Ebury Place in Pimlico, rebuilt by Edwin Lutyens. Her money too bought them, a year later, Long Barn, a Tudor house two miles from Knole, a Rolls-Royce to get them between the two places, and then the adjacent property, Brook Farm and the surrounding fields.

In the summer of 1914 Mrs Keppel and Violet went again to Clingendaal near The Hague. It belonged to Daisy, Baroness de Brienen, who inherited it from her father. He had no sons and willed it to whichever of his daughters did not marry. Daisy de Brienen wore nautical suits, shirts, collars, ties and round her neck a pearl chain with a whistle to call her dogs.

Clingendaal spanned a canal, had rose-garlanded bridges, stables, carnation houses, a Japanese garden and an observatory. Mrs Keppel and Daisy de Brienen shared the expense of elaborate summer holidays there. Guests travelled out by night ferry from Harwich to the Hook of Holland. Cars were sent to meet them and bring them back in time for breakfast. They ate at a long table laid with embroidered linen and oriental china. There was bacon, eggs, grilled kidneys, devilled chicken, cold ham and galantine, freshly made rolls, pyramids of fruit. Footmen in tail coats, liveries and white cotton gloves served them from a sideboard with tiers of silver-plated breakfast dishes and coffee pots of antique Dutch and English silver.

Among the guests, that last summer before the lamps went out over Europe, were Violet, Duchess of Rutland, who lived in Belvoir Castle and arrived off the boat wearing a silver turban and opera cloak (the Duke owned large parts of the Midlands); her daughter Lady Diana Manners, acclaimed for her beauty; Lady de Trafford in a tailored suit and tiny plumed toque; her daughter Vi; Sir Fritz and Lady Ponsonby with their children Loelia and Gaspard; the Ilchesters who lived at Melbury House near Dorchester and at Holland House, Kensington; Sir 'Lulu' and Lady Harcourt; Sonia's godmother Maggie Greville; her brother-in-law Sydney; Henry Stonor; Harry Cust, poet, politician, editor of *Pall Mall Gazette* and the father of the Duchess of Rutland's daughter Diana. Included among the guests were 'a suitor or two' for Violet, young men soon to be annihilated by the war.

Mrs Keppel's former authority was restored. She carried on the tradition of hospitality, hedonism, entertainment on an extraordinary scale. Daisy de Brienen provided the palace but deferred to her queenly status. Alice was ensconced in the best rooms. At dinner the young liked to sit near to hear her humorous gossip and observe her social skills. What she disliked did not intrude. Sonia that summer, aged thirteen, wrote a novel about a loveless marriage, her mother called it extraordinary, 'not very attractive for someone of your age', and burned it.

George organized them all. His invitation book was divided and subdivided into columns headed Invited and Accepted, Old Men, Young Men, Ladies, Girls. He assigned rooms, recorded proposed lengths of stay and activities and amusements for each day. 'Mama disliked such details,' Sonia said. He arranged swimming sessions, barge expeditions, visits to cheese factories and picture galleries, cycling trips, games of golf, afternoons at the races, picnics on the lawn. He drew up lists of which guests were to travel in which car and provided them with maps, stopwatches and mileometers. Harry Cust called his efforts 'George's summer manoeuvres'.

Summer manoeuvres ended when news came that Germany had invaded Belgium. The journey home, usually a matter of state cabins and leisurely farewells, was chaotic. The privileged class became 'mere units of a struggling crowd, pushing and shoving to board the last boat back to England'. Mrs Keppel, still La Favorita, was allocated two cabins by the purser. In London the banks were shut and 16 Grosvenor Street closed with no food ready. George went to his club, the Marlborough, and Mrs Keppel and her daughters walked across Berkeley Square for boiled eggs, coffee and toast at the Ritz.

War interrupted their lives. It put a stop to foreign travel, the casino in Monte Carlo, essential trips to Worth in Paris. It brought an unwelcome dimension of rationing, shortages, restrictions. It curtailed Violet's flirtations with men. It was difficult to get engaged, however insincerely, between 1914 and 1918. For young men conscription was hard to avoid. Harold Nicolson was exempted on the grounds that his work as a civil servant was 'indispensable' but he was an exception. Conscripts died at a rate of 5600 a day. 'It required' Violet said, 'superhuman courage to open a newsaper. George Vernon, Volley Heath, Patrick Shaw Stewart, Raymond Asquith, Bim Tennant, one after the other were struck down.' First to go was Julian Grenfell, who only briefly wrote poems about the joys of battle. He had wooed Violet, Sonia said, with 'poetry and pugilism':

> He would arrive at Grosvenor Street dressed in an old sweater and crumpled grey flannel trousers with frequently a black eye, and, more than once, a split lip (having been boxing the night before).

At a ball patronized by the royal family he locked himself in the ladies' cloakroom with Violet. Once Sonia heard her calling for help from her sitting room at the top of the house. 'His courtship was too spectacular,' Violet wrote. 'Father was infuriated by his dress, his recurrent black eye ... Julian was banned ... The war was imminent; he was one of the first to go. The war saw to it that we never met again.'

George Keppel rejoined the army and was made a captain, then a major and sent to France. His weekly letters to Violet and Sonia detailed route marches, outdoor sports, kit inspections and parades. He did not mention the horrors of battle. He spent his fiftieth birthday in the trenches. Alice sent out a hamper from Fortnum and Mason. When it arrived rats had eaten the cake and delicacies packed in cardboard. He asked that in future she send tinned food.

Mrs Keppel displayed support for the war effort but kept allegiance to her notions of civilized life. For about a month she did secretarial work at a hospital in Étaples run by Lady Sarah Wilson. Violet served in a canteen in Grosvenor Gardens – until fired for confusing cleaning powder and cocoa. Sonia served soup in Lady Limerick's Canteen for Soldiers at London Bridge.

Back in England Mrs Keppel rented a house at Watlington Park, Oxford, for weekends. It was a nice house, Osbert Sitwell said, with beautiful grounds and views of the Chilterns. And at Grosvenor Street she gave mid-week lunch parties for women friends, politicians and service chiefs. Winston Churchill, Henry Asquith 'or some leading soldier like Sir John Cowans' were among those attending these. 'It was tacitly understood that the conversation should remain on a light level with the darker shades of war excluded from it.'

But the dark shades of war were not entirely excluded. The bright colours of Bakst were eclipsed by the stark canvases of Paul Nash; the jingoism of Julian Grenfell was followed by the epitaphs of Wilfred Owen. When there were zeppelin attacks on London Violet and Sonia slept on camp beds in the drawing room among the Louis XV consoles and tapestry chairs, Persian carpets and Chippendale mirrors.

George Keppel came home at Christmas 1915, his appearance altered, his shoulders rounded from crouching in the trenches. 'Mamma did her best to entertain him,' Sonia said. She invited pretty women to dinner, arranged theatre outings and games of bridge. But George seemed abstracted and found Grosvenor Street and armchair politics hard to bear. Men like him did not tell women how terrible this war was. 'Even Mama stung him sometimes,' Sonia wrote. He was irritated when she contradicted him then said, 'Well after all Georgie darling,

Winston told me so.' He was most at ease with Sonia with whom he liked to sit in his living room in silence by the fire. 'Is it awful at the Front, Papa?' she asked him. 'Not too good, Doey,' he replied.

They spent Christmas at Crichel but without the ritual exchange of Fabergé. Gerard Sturt, Lord and Lady Alington's son, paralysed from the waist down from wounds inflicted in France, was a reminder that the halcyon days had passed. Never happy at Crichel he had wanted to leave but was now dependent on his family. On Christmas Day tension between him and his father was high. There were difficulties as to where his nurse should have her meals and because he had asked for his own sitting room. Lord Alington complained his wheelchair pulled tacks from the carpet and took up room at the dinner table.

He stumbled over Gerard's dog and in temper said,

'You and your dog are nothing but a nuisance in this house.'

'Then obviously the solution is for me and my dog to move elsewhere,' Gerard replied.

'Which I hope will be to us in Grosvenor Street,' Alice said. 'You can have your own sitting room and we can put up your nurse. As for you Humphrey you ought to go down on your knees and beg Gerard's pardon. And then pick the rest of the tintacks out of your beastly carpet with your teeth.'

Gerard moved to London to the house of a friend, Mrs Julie Thompson, not to Grosvenor Street. He died at Crichel from his wounds on Armistice Day, 11 November 1918.

In spring 1916 Mrs Keppel managed to get to Paris to buy clothes. For Sonia's sixteenth birthday party she bought her a dress by Jean Lanvin of royal blue tulle edged in mink. She sent out invitations: 'Mrs Keppel At Home 31 May 1916 Dancing 9.30'. The naval Battle of Jutland began that night. In a display of patriotism, she told the band to play the national anthem and the guests to go home.

In August George was posted to Ireland to train soldiers. He found a house for the summer at Connemara for Alice, her brother Archie, Ida, Violet, Sonia. The morning bugle calls disturbed Alice's sleep and she asked George to cut Reveille or have it an hour later. 'There's a war on, Freddie darling,' he said (her middle name was Frederica), 'and I'm not here to train the men to lie in bed.'

A month later a telegram brought news of the death of the nineteen-year-old son of Ida and Archie. Archie went to bed. Mrs Keppel sent for George. Sonia sat with Ida who was embroidering something in greens, yellows and blues. In the hall they heard Alice say to George, 'Poor Archie, poor darling Archie, luckily dear Ida doesn't feel things like Archie.' When Alice came into the sitting room Ida did not look up from her embroidery.

To Quidenham, where the Keppel family motto was 'Do not yield to misfortunes', came news that Violet's cousin Edward had been killed at Ypres. Another cousin, Rupert, was for three years a prisoner of war.

Violet saw little of Vita during the war, though sometimes they had tea together or went to a matinée. 'At her own sarcastic request,' she was godmother to Vita's son Benedict. In late August 1916 Vita and Harold stayed at Watlington Park. In the party were Osbert Sitwell, Lady Lily Wemyss, Daisy de Brienen, the Hwfa Williamses, Lord Ilchester. They all played poker and games when it rained.

Violet took drawing lessons at the Slade but seemed without direction. She was expected to marry but could not take the idea seriously. She found another unlikely fiancé — Osbert Sitwell. He had, she said, 'a schoolboy adulation' for her mother, who teased him because he adored her so:

> The idea of matrimony crept insidiously into our conversation. Everything to do with Osbert filled me with awe: his magnificent ancestral home, Renishaw, his dim and mysterious mother, his unknown ogre of a father ... his fascinating but intimidating sister Edith who made me feel uncouth and ungraceful, his more accessible brother 'Sachie'.

Edith Sitwell, according to Violet, was sure the marriage would work.

At Christmas Osbert Sitwell was among the house guests at Polesden Lacey. Maggie Greville had turned the north and west side into a convalescent home for King Edward VII's Hospital for Officers. She kept the rest for herself. From there Violet wrote to Vita of tangles with another man, too. She said she hated being at Polesden but her mother would not let her remain at Grosvenor Street when she herself was away. Osbert complained to Vita's mother that he was 'very unhappy' about the way Violet treated him.

Lady Sackville for her part was perturbed when all the male staff from Knole were called up. She asked Lord Kitchener to help:

I think perhaps you do not realise, my dear Lord K, that we employ five carpenters and four painters and two blacksmiths and two footmen and you are taking them all from us! I do not complain about the footmen, although I must say that I had never thought I would see parlourmaids at Knole! I am putting up with them, because I know I must, but it really does offend me to see these women hovering round me in their starched aprons, which are not at all what Knole is used to, instead of liveries and even powdered hair! Dear Lord K., I am sure you will sympathise with me when I say that parlourmaids are so middle class, not at all what you and me are used to. But as I said that is not what I complain about. What I do mind is your taking all our carpenters from us. I quite see that you must send my dear Lionel to Gallipoli; and he would be very cross with me if he knew I had written to you. Of course all the gentlemen must go. There is *noblesse oblige* isn't there? And you and I know that – we must give an example. You are at the War Office and have got to neglect your dear Boome which you love so much. I think you love it as much as I love Knole? And of course you must love it even more because the world says you have never loved any woman – is that true? I shall ask you next time I come to luncheon with you. But talking about luncheon reminds me of parlourmaids and I said I would not complain about them

(because I am patriotic after all), but I do complain about the
way you take our workmen from us. Do you not realise, my
dear Lord K, that you are ruining houses like ours? After all there
is Hatfield where Queen Elizabeth spent her time as a young
princess, and that is historic too, just like Knole, and I am sure
Lord Salisbury would tell you he was having frightful difficulties
in keeping Hatfield going, just as we are having in keeping Knole.
What can you do about it? It seems to me a national duty, just
as important for us as keeping up the army and our splendid
troop. I do admire them so much. Do help me all you can.

She briefly offered Knole as a hospital ward but when five Belgians
were assigned to her decided they were spies in German pay and that
Knole would be bombed. She contacted the local police and had them
taken away.

Violet visited Long Barn and mocked the cosiness of the Tudor
architecture — low ceilings, small leaded window panes, oak beams,
sloping floors. Excluded and betrayed by Vita's family life she denigrated
it if she could. Here, married and committed to a man, was the girl
to whom she had sworn to stay true, declared her love and given the
doge's ring. In June 1917, when Harold phoned her to say Vita could
not go to a party, Violet 'was *so* disappointed'. But she jumped at his
suggestion that he should not go either. 'Damn that little too too,'
he wrote to Vita, 'it hates me and misses no opportunity of letting
me down.'

That summer Violet formed a new friendship. Pat Dansey lived with
her elderly uncle Lord Fitzhardinge 'a crochety ogre' in Berkeley Castle,
Gloucestershire, a medieval castle dating back to 1153. She weighed
seven stone, had dark hair, a brittle manner and a stutter. Violet
intrigued her by confiding her love of Vita. She invited Violet to the
castle, allocated her the Blue Room, showed her the dungeon where
Edward II was murdered, told her of how when young she would sit
like a mouse in the Great Hall listening to her uncle and his cronies
in their evening hunt clothes talking about vintage wines and playing

whist. Violet liked the grandeur of Berkeley and its haunting sense of the past. Pat had formed a relationship with the Duke of Argyll's granddaughter, Joan Campbell. This relationship was to last a lifetime and took on the closeness of marriage. But it did not preclude Pat's interest in other women. She told Violet that she loved her and gave her photographs of herself. 'I used to invent the most erotic pastimes to appeal to her taste,' she said to Vita in later years.

PART TWO

Portrait of a Lesbian Affair

TEN

Mrs Keppel and her daughters moved as guests from stately home to country house as the war went its way. In April 1916 they were at Cassel's seaside home at Branksome Dene, Bournemouth – 'all chintz and white paint', sea breezes and games of piquet. He was there with his sister and granddaughter Edwina – who in 1922 married Queen Victoria's grandson, Louis Mountbatten. His only daughter Maudie had died in 1911.

Despite the 'old undercurrent' Violet's meetings with Vita were of the social sort appropriate to good friends. In March 1917 they went to a matinée at the Garrick theatre, in May they saw the Russian exhibition at the Grafton Galleries, in September Violet stayed at Long Barn and they went for walks together.

In October Violet and her mother were at Coker Court near Yeovil, Somerset, a Tudor house owned by Dorothy Heneage who was rich, hypochondriacal and sympathetic to Violet. From her Violet heard that Vita intended renting out her Ebury Street house for the winter. She feared if that was so they would meet infrequently:

> I simply can't get on without a periodical glimpse of radiant domesticity and you will become smug to an intolerable degree if the vagabond – what Dorothy calls 'rackety' – element as supplied by me, is indefinitely withheld from you. We mustn't let it happen. We are absolutely essential to one another, at least in *my* eyes!

She had she said 'a sudden craving' for Vita's company. Her letter was at Lady Sackville's Hill Street house when Vita returned with Harold from a weekend at Knebworth, Hertfordshire, the country estate of Lord Lytton, Parliamentary Secretary to the Admiralty. Guests included the portrait painter Sir John Lavery, Sir Edward Marsh MP, Sir Horace Rumbold, Ambassador to Switzerland, Sir Louis Mallet, Ambassador to Turkey, and Osbert Sitwell.

The following week Harold sought treatment for a venereal infection caught from a male guest. From the Foreign Office he wrote to Vita in anxiety and distress. He warned if he had passed it to her she would need treatment. He feared they might have 'a bloody time ahead'. The implication was that they had had sex together after he became infected. Afraid of her rejection he wrote of 'untidy or crawly tadpoles', the end of his bright sunlit world 'like a searchlight going out'. 'And I shall be left all alone and dim'. He asked her not to leave his anxious letters lying around and said nothing in the whole world mattered to him but her, 'my whole soul, my darling'.

Vita was in the clear. Harold's doctor forbade him to have sex with her, even protected sex, for six months. He was disappointed. There was a holiday coming up and 'it is a part of holiday isn't it?' By 20 April 1918 there would be no risk and the doctor was 'frightfully opty about it not happening again'.

Vita had pause for thought. Married four years, she had two children — Nigel was born in 1917 (a second son had been born dead in 1915) — Harold was 'a sunny harbour', their relationship 'open, frank, certain'. She was pleased to be a mother, he was even more pleased to be a father. 'We were in fact,' she wrote in 1920, 'a nice young couple to ask out to dinner.'

Her desire for women was muted by marriage, she had no lovers, her life focused on writing, her house, garden, husband, family. Harold for his part had not told her about his sexual encounters with good-looking intelligent young men of his own class. They were *boffes de gaîté*, 'a jolly vice' and held no promise of commitment or obligation. But he must have felt some compulsion of desire for they were against the law. He was ambitious, a diplomat and not a man lightly to put at risk his career, civil liberty, marriage and social position. The ruin of Oscar Wilde in 1895 showed the destructive power of the law. Harold told Vita she was the only one he loved. He cherished his domestic life and hoped for a daughter to complete the unit. Neither he nor Vita wanted an airless marriage, they were independent of each other by circumstance and choice. But on the Knebworth weekend when he caught the clap, whatever the tactful disposition of bedrooms and brass-framed names on the doors, Vita was in a room in the same house.

At the beginning of April 1918 Violet wrote again to Vita. She asked if she might come and stay at Long Barn. She hoped to travel by train to the Slade some mornings but was afraid of air raids in London after nightfall. Vita wanted to work but felt she could not refuse. Violet arrived on 13 April with an architect friend, 'Bear' Warre. Harold returned to town.

Five days later on 18 April, two days before the six-month curfew on marital sex was through, Vita put on trousers of the sort issued to Land Army women for the war effort. She had bought them for gardening. Their effect prompted a symbolic liberation on a par with long hair for poets, earrings for gay waiters, cockatoo hairdos for punks,

> in the unaccustomed freedom of breeches and gaiters I went into wild spirits . . . in the midst of my exuberance I knew that all the old undercurrent had come back stronger than ever and that my old domination over her had never been diminished.

Breeches, gaiters, undercurrents and domination had their way. Violet and she dined alone, talked until two in the morning, then kissed in the dark. Violet wore a red velvet dress 'exactly the olour of a red rose'. Her skin was white, her hair tawny, she was, Vita wrote, 'the most seductive being'. Vita confessed her 'duality', her gentle 'feminine' feelings for Harold, her rougher passionate feelings toward women. Violet talked of how she had loved Vita since childhood. She lay on the sofa, took Vita's hands, parted her fingers and counted the points of why she loved her. 'I hadn't dreamt of such an art of love . . .' Vita wrote. 'I was infinitely troubled by the softness of her touch and the murmur of her lovely voice.'

In her account of their affair, written in 1920, Vita portrayed Violet, that spring day in 1918, as the experienced seducer, the wily courtesan, as knowing as Mrs Keppel or Louise de Kéroualle — Charles II's mistress — 'infinitely clever', 'adept at concealment', determined to conquer. 'I might have been a boy of eighteen and she a woman of thirty-five'. In fact Violet was twenty-four, two years younger than Vita, watched over by her mother and with no particular experience of sex or life. 'I am young, headstrong, exceptionally passionate. I am in love for the first time in my life,' she wrote to Vita that year. It was Vita who had loved Rosamund Grosvenor, married Harold, published poems, given birth to three children.

Violet's love for Vita was the unequivocal focus of her life. Her perception of it had not changed from when she declared it in October 1910 before leaving for Ceylon. But she had no pragmatic plan for life, or idea of how to channel this love. When Vita married, she was hurt, made scathing comments, but did nothing to intrude. To please her mother she 'came out' into society but scorned its hypocrisies and double standards. The war frightened her but beyond a surface display of patriotism she took no interest in it. She flirted with its heroes to show her mother that she could, if she chose, have a man, but backed off if marriage loomed.

Mrs Keppel was not a role model for candid relationship. She put a premium on seduction, elided duplicity and discretion and did not seem to value her own marriage in an intrinsic way. Her daughters when small were neglected guests at her Court. Violet fantasized that the King was her father. Kingy was a wonderful man not least because mother was his heartfelt queen. A mother so gilded could not be courtesan to a rich, fat, bronchial philanderer overly fond of food and horses.

For Vita sex with Violet was a revelation. 'How eventful a day!' she wrote in her diary and marked it with a cross. In retrospect she wrote, 'I felt like a person translated or reborn; it was like beginning one's life again in a different capacity.' Violet stayed all week at Long Barn. Then in high spirits they went on holiday to Cornwall. They had lunch at Claridges, took the train to Plymouth, lost their luggage and stayed overnight in a fisherman's cottage, 'very primitive, nice pudding, no drains'. Harold arranged for them to have Hugh Walpole's cottage at Polperro. He said if it rained Vita would miss him, if the sun shone she would want him and that Violet would fall into the sea.

Called The Cobbles, perched on the cliffs above the sea, reached only by a footpath, the cottage was a perfect lovers' retreat. They read books, walked along the headland, went to Fowey in the local butcher's pony cart, drank cider in a little restaurant. Violet picked white lilac for Vita from a deserted garden. They saw themselves as gypsies, free and made for love, talked in a secret Romany language, called themselves Mitya and Lushka. 'How triumphant we were,' Violet wrote,

> that little room . . . the sea almost dashing against its walls, the
> tireless cry of the seagulls, the friendly books . . . the complete
> liberty of it all . . . And sometimes we loved each other so much
> we became inarticulate, content only to probe each other's eyes
> for the secret that was secret no longer.

For Violet this was it. Commitment was now total. 'She no longer flirted and got rid of the last person she had been engaged to, when we went to Cornwall,' Vita wrote. But Vita had a husband who hated what was happening. Harold travelled a great deal, but this was the first time Vita had chosen to go away without him and he was angry at how gratuitous it seemed 'just for a whim'. He was at the Foreign Office struggling with memoranda on the prospects of Germany invading Holland and of America fighting with Turkey. He sent her five letters a day. Couched in brittle humour, with drawings of Violet in towny clothes pretending a spartan life, their reality was alarm, anger, jealousy. 'I wish I was more violent and less affectionate . . . I suppose that you will now want to go to California with Violet and grow peach-fed hams.'

Vita wanted neither to lose nor hurt him. She returned to Long Barn on 11 May and wrote him a letter, though she was to see him that evening. She could talk with Violet until two in the morning but

not with him. Her letter belittled Violet yet let him know they would
go away together again. She was, she said, extraordinarily lucky to
have Harold's love, her boys, cottage, 'money, flowers, a farm and
three cows'. She loved him, he was an angel, but she had wanderlust
badly — for new places, excitement 'where no one will want me to
order lunch or pay housebooks . . . yes it is silly little things like that
which have got on my nerves. Being interrupted, being available.' She
wanted to travel with him but that was impossible because of his work.
In the meantime Violet, whose life at heart she told him she loathed,
saved her from 'intellectual stagnation and bovine complacency'. He
should not be jealous because 'Darling one day we will go off with
two little toothbrushes and the bloody war will be over.'

But it was Violet and she who were to go off with two little toothbrushes when the bloody war was over. And it was not only intellectual
stimulus which Violet provided or respite from the *ennui* of ordering
lunch and paying the servants. It was passion, love, desire, of an
overwhelming sort. Harold knew it and blamed and hated Violet for
it. His other dangerous option would have been to blame and hate his
wife.

Violet 'discovered' the letter. It focused on facts she wanted not to
see. 'God Mitya do you wonder I mistrust you? If you were capable of
that, what *aren't* you capable of?' It showed the whole scenario, beginning, middle and end: the choices to be made, the division of allegiance,
the prospect of corrosive jealousy, obsession, manipulation, insecurity,
pain. Someone was going to lose and get hurt, that much was clear.
Had she been the skilled operator, the thirty-five-year-old seductress
who knows life's sexual laws, she would have run from the scene.
What was not clear was the extent to which events would proceed to
spoil her life.

On 16 May Harold lunched at Grosvenor Street with Mrs Keppel,
Violet and Sonia. Mrs Keppel 'raved' about Vita whom she had seen
the day before. She said how she had changed, that her yellow dress
was 'too lovely', that she had never seen her so '*en beauté*' before. 'She
really is one of the most beautiful young women I have ever seen.'

'NONE OF YOU CAN *EVER* BE PROUD ENOUGH OF
BEING THE *CHILD* OF SUCH A FATHER WHO HAS
NOT HIS *EQUAL* IN THIS WORLD'

The Prince of Wales, his mother and bride, 1863

'A LIVING FORM OF GILT-
EDGED SECURITY'

*The 'King's Millionaire',
Sir Ernest Cassel*

'A FAT, BALD GENTLEMAN WHO
SMELT OF CIGARS AND EAU-DE-
PORTUGAL, WHOSE FINGERS WERE
COVERED IN RINGS AND TO
WHOM ONE CURTSIED ENDLESSLY'

Right: King Edward VII

'ONE COULD PICTURE
HIM WALTZING SUPERBLY
TO THE STRAINS OF *THE
MERRY WIDOW*'

Colonel George Keppel

'FOR MAMA, LACK OF SELF-
CONFIDENCE WAS UNTHINKABL

Lithograph of Mrs Keppel, circa 190

Harold said Violet looked very pretty too, basked in the compliment
and relayed it to Vita: 'Hadji put on his little face like this'

Violet too basked, and relayed:

I am drunk with the beauty of my Mitya! . . . Even my mother
who is not easily impressed shared my opinion. You have changed
it appears . . . They said you were like a dazzling Gypsy. My
sister's words not mine . . . they noticed a new exuberance in
you, something akin to sheer animal spirits that was never there
before. You may love me Mitya, but anyone would be *proud* to be
loved by you.

She went down to Long Barn next day, Vita wore her Land Girl
clothes and they walked to Knole. Lady Sackville raved too. She said
Vita should have her portrait painted wearing them, 'she looks so
charming in her corduroy trousers. She ought to have been a boy.'
Next day in London for tea with Violet and Bear Warre Vita wore a
red dress and hat. They decided she should be painted by William
Strang 'who does Spanish women so well'.

Violet spent nights with Vita at Grosvenor Street, Ebury Street,
Long Barn, and bombarded her with letters. In envelopes franked with
'Buy National War Bonds Now', or 'Feed the Guns with War Bonds',
and with Bertie's son's head on the three-halfpenny stamp, she wrote
of how she belonged to Vita, revered her superior beauty and wisdom,
cared not a damn for anyone else, was nothing but an empty husk
away from her, how 'you alone have bent me to your will, shattered
my self-possession, robbed me of my mystery, made me yours, yours.'
She spoke of drawing 'curtains' to conceal her real self from

everyone but Vita 'for you there are no curtains not even gossamer ones'. She listened to Brahms and Debussy and daydreamed of her, read Swinburne and imagined making love with her, took lessons at the Slade and fantasized that in their shared gipsy life only Love, Art and Beauty would signify:

> God knows it is aesthetically incorrect that the artist should be hampered by domesticity. Pegasus harnessed to a governess-cart ... an artist must necessarily belong to both sexes ... the artist striding the mountain tops, silent, inspired and alone.

For them both hamperings of domesticity were no worse than approving the lunch menu, telling the maid, or scolding the boot boy. But gipsies epitomized romance and artists dwelt in the realm of inspiration, exempt from moral behaviour of an ordinary sort:

> O Mitya come away let's fly – if ever there were two entirely primitive people they are surely us: let's go away and forget the world and all its squalor – let's forget such things as trains and trams and servants and streets and shops and money.

At the beginning of July they went again to Polperro. 'How happy we were. And the second time still happier. Mitya do you remember Plymouth the second time?' They sat on the rocks, looked at the sunset, talked of freedom and of love. Mrs Keppel, perhaps curious as to what was going on, invited Harold and Lady Sackville to dinner on 4 July, but cancelled when two of the housemaids got flu. Harold did not go to Long Barn while Vita was away. It depressed him to be there without her.

Vita asked for patience from him. She did not want to lose him, or her two little boys, aged four and one, her cottage, farm, flowers and three cows. But she was cold and unavailable, turned aside when he tried to kiss her, disliked social occasions with him if Violet was not there. Her previous diary entries had been about her boys – their words, weight gain, temper, songs. Now it was Violet who filled her life. She told her she loved her, that they were made for one another, colluded with plans to go away with her, said she would not have sex with Harold and took off her wedding ring.

But between Violet's dream and the real world a wide gap loomed. When they got back from Cornwall Vita went to Esher Place in Surrey with Harold. The Foreign Secretary, Arthur Balfour, the Duchess of Marlborough, Lord Stanmore, Lady Lancaster were guests. They all played tennis. 'Beastly party,' Vita wrote. 'I hate it.' Violet was 'utterly lost, miserably incomplete, sleepless and depressed.' Two nights running she had 'appallingly jealous dreams' about Vita. 'I adore you as I shall never adore anyone in my life again,' she wrote to her. 'It breaks my heart to be without you.'

Gossip wormed its way into smart drawing rooms. That month Violet discussed Vita 'at great length' with Oswald Dickinson, brother of Virginia Woolf's friend, Violet Dickinson. 'Ozzie' as described by Harold's friend and biographer James Lees-Milne was 'a cosy, gossipy, "queer" bachelor'. Violet and he talked of the 'dormant depths of passion and abandon' in Vita, her temperament and dazzling beauty and of how domestic, condescending, cocksure and 'not in the least thrilling' Harold was.

From Ozzie Lady Sackville heard of how Harold snapped at Vita in public. She hoped with all her heart, she wrote in her diary, that she would never see their love on the wane. She had her own problems with waning love. Her husband, unable to be civil to her, was ousting her from Knole. He removed portraits of her from his library and spent more and more time with Olive Rubens, who was charming and warm and sang songs after dinner. He turned the laundry into an apartment for her.

'Married life under these circumstances even in a magnificent house is miserable work,' Lady Sackville wrote. 'I feel absolutely miserably unhappy and I want to go away miles and miles from Knole.'

Miserable work or not, married life in a magnificent house was ordained by society and alternatives not countenanced. Mrs Keppel did not like gossip about her daughter's sexual ways. She impressed on Violet that when the war ended, marry she must. Violet was twenty-four. The disruption of world war and the killing of most eligible men were the only acceptable excuses for her spinsterhood. She had no history of disobeying her mother. Mrs Keppel encouraged her correspondence with Denys Robert Trefusis, a major with the Royal Horse Guards, serving in Belgium. She required a husband for her daughter and thought that he would do. Violet, always flirtatious, met him when he came to London on leave and wrote to him when he returned to the Front. He was an aristocrat, twenty-eight, the fourth child of the Honourable John Schomberg Trefusis, who was the fourth son of the nineteenth Lord Clinton. His family had served as courtiers to successive sovereigns, could be traced back to the thirteenth century, had a family seat in Devon, a coat of arms, the family mottos 'Neither rashly nor timidly' and 'All things come from God'. He had no money but Mrs Keppel was an astute businesswoman and would see to that.

Violet encouraged him enough. On 23 July she received a letter from him but at a party that night felt so 'possessed' by Vita she could not dance twice with the same partner or talk of other things. She put it to Vita that the truthful path was for them to be open about their love and to go away together:

> What sort of life can we lead now? Yours an infamous and degrading lie to the world, officially bound to someone you don't care for ... I, not caring a damn for anyone but you ... condemned to leading a futile purposeless existence which no longer holds the smallest attraction for me ...

Together they began writing a romantic novel about their love and the conflict between passion and marriage. They called it *Rebellion* though it was eventually published as *Challenge*. Its central evasion was that the lovers were of different sex. Vita was Julian, 'a tall, loose-limbed boy, untidy, graceful', at heart responsible and sensible, but 'flushed with the spirit of adventure, the prerogative of youth'. Violet was Eve, older, wilier and burdened with the 'female' temperament: jealous, untrustworthy, vain, coquettish, wickedly irresistible, 'all things seductive and insinuating',

> the provocative aloofness of her self-possession, the warm round-
> ness of her throat and arms, the little moue at the corner of her
> mouth, her little graceful hands and white skin . . . the pervading
> sensuousness that glowed from her . . . the marvellous organ of
> her voice . . . a dusky voice.

Eve is a cross between Alice Keppel and Carmen. Julian cannot help himself . . .

> his fingers moulded themselves lingeringly round her throat; she
> slipped still lower within the circle of his arm and his hand almost
> involuntarily trembled over the softness of her breast.

It was all Mills and Boon except of course that they were Vita's fingers and arm and Violet's throat and breast.

Rebellion was principally Vita's book though Violet contributed. They added to it each day throughout the summer of 1918 from letters and notes. In it, Vita showed admiration for Violet and sympathy for the bravado of her social manner. Only Julian knows the real Eve . . . knows her 'like his sister'. Witch though she is, he prefers her company to any in the world:

> Her humour, her audacity, the width of her range, the pic-
> turesqueness of her phraseology, her endless inventiveness, her
> subtle undercurrent of the personal . . . He knew that his life
> had been enriched and coloured by her presence in it; that it
> would, at any moment, have become a poorer, a grayer, a less
> magical thing through the loss of her.
>   . . . Her frivolity is a mask. Her instincts alone are deep; how
> deep it frightens me to think. She is an artist, although she may
> never produce art. She lives in a world of her own with its own
> code of morals and values. The Eve that we all know is a sham,
> the product of her own pride and humour. She is laughing at

us all. The Eve we know is entertaining, cynical, selfish, unscrupulous. The real Eve is . . . a rebel and an idealist.

Her idealism takes the shape of unswerving love and adulation of Julian/Vita:

> I have believed in you since I was a child; believed in you as something Olympian . . . I have crushed down the vision of life with you, but always it has remained at the back of my mind, so wide, so open, a life so free and so full of music and beauty.

It was difficult for Eve's prototype to live in the real world. On 14 August she lunched with Pat Dansey, 'broke down and sobbed her heart out'. Pat reacted vicariously to her story, absorbed its details, offered to help. Next day Violet went with her mother to Clovelly Court, Devonshire. As ever she was not permitted to remain at Grosvenor Street alone. Mrs Keppel, star guest at Clovelly, was 'so marvellously witful that I could forgive her anything,' Violet wrote: 'She is a clever woman. I do admire her.'

Romance for Mrs Keppel, 'Chinday' as Violet and Vita called her in their Romany language, was strategic work. She meant to squeeze the lesbian version of it out of her daughter's life. Gossip was rife and Violet unrepentant. Pained when she did not receive letters from Vita, obsessed with the when and where of their next meeting, she stayed aloof from other social exchange. There were rows when Chinday found her writing to Vita. Violet spoke of her mother's 'brutal and heartless treatment'. At Clovelly guests asked why she put up with it. 'God knows I feel too despondent to take any steps.'

'I hate lies,' she wrote to Vita. 'I am so fed up with lies' She referred to promises Vita had made and hoped she was summoning courage to tell Harold his marriage was over and to go away with her for good:

> How right you were when you said we were made for one another . . . What a perfect life we could have together & have had together (for a fortnight).

She was herself uncompromising:

And the supreme truth is this. *I can never be happy without you* . . .
You are the *grande passion* of my life. How gladly would I sacrifice
everything to you — family, friends, fortune, EVERYTHING.

Which was not what her mother would have her do. Violet wanted
equivalent sacrifice in return. On 25 August she wrote to Vita of how
she wanted her 'hungrily, frenziedly, passionately' — and exclusively:

I want you for my own . . . I want to go away with you. I must
and will and damn the world and damn the consequences and
anyone had better look out for themselves who dares to become
an obstacle in my path.

There were to be plenty of obstacles in her path. Next day Violet
received a letter from Denys. He said his company had won a boxing
competition and he a silver cup for horse jumping. He addressed
her as his 'fairest Fialka' — Russian for Violet — said she brought him
luck and was his mascot. Violet showed Vita the letter to make her
jealous:

I have greatly dared and now I am terrified. If you knew how
poignantly true is all I wrote you last night you would realize
the futility of making plans for 'after the war' . . . I don't care a fig
for the remote future and what happens after the war. Whatever
happens is going to happen now.

She was, she said, 'sick to death of all this camouflage'. None the less
camouflage plans were made for after the war, an unworkable prospect
of lies and the desire for truth.

Somewhere in Violet's perception of social behaviour was the idea
that marriage was a socially acceptable cover for socially unacceptable
sex. It was the fulcrum of those Edwardian house parties, the cover used
by her mother, the King, Harold, Vita. Denys Trefusis was oblivious to
the emotional intricacy of his postwar fate. He did not know how he
was to be used. He had had an awful war, fought in the battle of the
Somme, endured years of slaughter, threat and fear. He was emotionally precarious, not strong or well. Mrs Keppel wanted him to make

her daughter respectable. Violet wanted him not for himself but to appease her mother and provoke Vita into breaking with Harold so her love would be for her alone. Vita hoped Violet, like herself, 'would gain more liberty by marrying'. But the marriage must not preclude fidelity to her. 'Violet is *mine*,' she wrote in 1920 in her Confession. But so, if not in the same way, was Harold hers, and Long Barn, the boys, the farm, the garden, the cows. And so should Knole have been, she felt, by rights.

Denys admired Violet's intelligence, humour, originality and status. He wrote again to her on 1 September. He said he loved her as much as one person could love another, that he was 'waiting for her reply' and that he hoped for lucrative employment at the war's end. Thus Violet sailed into the wind, her feelings in turmoil. Five months into her affair with Vita she was acting out a charade of courtship to oblige her mother, distract society and provoke the woman she loved into claiming her.

From Clovelly Court Mrs Keppel took her daughter to Appley Hall at Ryde on the Isle of Wight. She forbade her to return to London until the end of September, when Denys Trefusis would be home on leave. In her mother's social milieu Violet had the status of a rebellious child. 'O Vita get away we must,' she wrote from Appley Hall:

> It has become an obsession with me. To see the much vaunted cliffs of Dover retreating in the mist, the intoxicating swish s' ish of the waves becoming more emancipated every moment . . . Let's go to Paris, the Riviera, anywhere.

Harold, diplomatic and conciliatory, looked for a solution that would concede to Vita and save their marriage. He suggested on 2 September that she buy a little seduction cottage 'in Cornwall or elsewhere' where she could go whenever and with whomsoever she liked. It would be a rule that he never visited it or asked who she was with. The arrangement would, he thought, 'make a real escape from the YOKE'. And when he was rich he would have one too, 'just the same and on the same condition'.

This was the kind of set up Violet at heart resented and abhorred. It was the pattern of adultery acceptable to her mother and the King. As she saw it Vita belonged to her and should never have married. She wanted monogomy founded on passion. Now she was compromised by Vita's marriage and was compromising Denys and herself:

What *is* the good Mitya? I get far more unhappiness out of love than happiness. Jealousy, immediately omnipotent, is at the root of all my misery . . . You see it is never without something to feed on. The only time when I forget it temporarily is when I'm with *you* – when I'm away it rules supreme. You see there is always the insurmountable Nicolson to deal with; if only he would disappear some day, but he won't. I have almost ceased in a sense to be jealous of what he is to *you*, I am jealous of what he is to you in the eyes of the world . . .

It would be absurd for you to be jealous of me because you know at the bottom of your heart that it is impossible for me to care for more than one person at a time – when I say care, I mean it is *impossible* for me to be even *fond* of anyone but you or merely superficially interested, whereas you admittedly have affections, very deep ones . . . for people who, God knows, are no concern of mine. The bargain is a one-sided one: you are all in all to me – and I am the dominating interest of several interests for you. I know you love me but not at all in the same way as I love you. How can you help it? You have inevitably other affections, other resources – if I fail you, you have plenty of other people to fall back upon. If you fail *me* what have I got?

It was all true but not useful for being so.

Introduced at Mrs Keppel's dinner parties, Denys Trefusis was praised, Violet said, for his appearance, 'manliness' and sense of humour. He was tall, slim, with reddish hair, blue eyes, looked smart in uniform. Vita met him, compared him to 'an ascetic in search of the Holy Grail' and liked him. 'I could afford to like him because I was accustomed to Violet's amusements.' But she was sexually possessive. She could not countenance him – or anyone – touching Violet with desire. She was jealous when Violet visited Pat Dansey. She took Violet's photographs of Pat and went to see her when Violet was away:

> Mitya, even you in your blindness were fully aware that your visit to Pat would not exactly fill me with rapture. You do these inevitably mischievous things, and then profess surprise at the result.

Harold called Violet evil, tortuous, erotic, irresponsible, a 'fierce orchid glimmering and stinking in the recesses of life'. He wished she was dead, said she had 'poisoned one of the most sunny things that ever happened'. As for Vita he supposed it was 'a sort of George Sand stunt', or a 'scarlet adventure', or perhaps she was a bit deranged like the rest of her family.

On 1 October Vita wrote him a love letter before he left for Italy. She told him she loved him 'unalterably', with a love that would survive passing passion. Their love, she said, after five years had 'long strong roots'. With him and no one else she had a sense of belonging, 'a sense of "He is MINE" – I don't think that often happens.'

Violet received similar avowals and the claim "She is MINE". The following week they went to *Scheherazade* – twice. 'Marvellous.' At Ebury Street Vita changed into men's clothes, browned her face, put a khaki bandage round her head, walked down Piccadilly smoking a cigarette, bought a newspaper from a boy who called her sir, went with Violet to Charing Cross station, then by train to Orpington.

She was Julian, Violet was Eve. 'This is the *best* adventure,' Vita wrote, 'The extraordinary thing was how natural it all was for me . . . I had wondered about my voice, but found I could sink it sufficiently.' They booked in at a lodging house as husband and wife. The following day they 'went to Knole which I think was brave. Here I slipped into the stables and emerged as myself.' 'Leave Julian at Knole,' she wrote in her diary and that night dreamed a wish-fulfilment dream of the escapade.

Gossip swelled. Ozzie Dickinson told Lady Sackville that Violet wanted to separate Vita and Harold. Violet told her she intended to marry Denys who had not got a penny, that Harold was stifling Vita's writing career, that Vita was not in love with him. Vita told her Harold was too sleepy and quick to be a good lover. Harold told her Violet was trying to destroy his home life by constantly ridiculing it. Lady Sackville told Harold that Violet was pernicious and amoral. Vita made Violet promise not to have any sexual exchange with Denys. And Violet told Vita how she loved her overwhelmingly, devastatingly, possessively, exorbitantly, submissively, incoherently and insatiably.

The war moved to an end. Mrs Keppel was concerned as to how George would fill his time. Vita suggested talking to her uncle Charles (who became the 4th Lord Sackville) to see if there was room at Knole on the staff. Mrs Keppel said George was too senior. She went into battle with Violet, whose behaviour made fissures in the structure of her world more damaging than war. There were 'hideous rows' when Violet tried to meet alone with Vita. She would not let her go to Long Barn unless Denys went with her. In London Violet felt incarcerated at Grosvenor Street:

> It does seem unfair that you aren't limited and supervised like
> me – that you can be in the country in a lovely place and day
> in day out I am made to stay in the place I hate most of any
> place on earth.

When separated from Vita, Violet was so miserable Denys suggested they both go and talk to Vita about it. Violet said she wanted to marry Denys in a registry office to get away from home. She asked Vita to be a witness.

In October Mrs Keppel took her daughter to Bideford to a house party of statesmen and their wives. On the train down she berated her

for the embarrassment she caused. Violet felt the tough side of
'Chinday' her beloved mother, whose life was unparalleled romance:

> Chinday was at her worst, at her snobbiest, at her unholiest
> coming down here – the things she said hurt so much, that after
> a time I ceased to feel them . . . Then an awful thought struck
> me: perhaps she didn't love me after all, how was it possible to
> love someone and yet say such things to them? How was it
> possible to be so nearly related yet so utterly apart? . . . God, how
> I longed for you, Mitya . . . I was so completely unhappy . . . It's
> impossible, it's intolerable, and always the note of slight conde-
> scension that obtrudes itself on everything she says to me, as
> though I were her social, moral and intellectual inferior. I may
> be the first two but I swear I'm not the last.

In London on Saturday 26 October, Denys returned to his regiment.
He proposed to Violet at Grosvenor Street before he left but she was
equivocal in her reply. Mrs Keppel was away for the weekend. Vita
stayed the night then bolted round in a taxi to Harold's parents at
Cadogan Gardens before she got back. On 31 October Mrs Keppel
took Violet to be photographed professionally so Denys might have a
permanent image of his mascot. The appointment foiled Violet's plan
to see Vita who had the flu. She sent gardenias and an apology. She
told Vita that going abroad with her was 'the *only* thing that can save
me from an otherwise CERTAIN FATE'.

She applied that same day to a Mr Sidney Russell Cooke for ; :rmits
and visas for her and Vita to go to Paris. He told her she must first
obtain passports from the Foreign Office and Harold was the logical
person to arrange this:

> As Mrs Nicolson could no doubt get a medical certificate advising
> her to go to the South of France after her flu & as she would no
> doubt require a 'companion' I think it would be possible to
> arrange the matter of the permits, but I doubt it could be done

under a fortnight from the time you get the passport as there is
rather a congestion of traffic.

Violet asked Harold and he helped. It was not his nature to obstruct
their plans. To Vita he said he was so busy with the prospective Paris
Peace Conference he would not 'mind much' if she went. Mrs Keppel
was agreeable as Denys would be in Paris and the ostensible point of
the trip was for Violet to meet him there. She viewed with relief the
prospect of her daughter out of the country and away from gossip. It
was not what Violet felt or did but how her behaviour was perceived
that vexed her most. 'She says we may go abroad whenever we like,
the sooner the better and for as long as we like,' Violet wrote.

Lady Sackville, suspicious, loathed the idea of her 'lily of a Vita to
go with such a dreadful immoral girl'. But she was busy renovating
and furnishing a big house in Brighton. She wrote in her diary that
Violet would shoot herself if Vita did not go. 'It is a real case of
blackmail.' Violet, she said, could copy handwriting and would leave
forged incriminating letters for the inquest.

On 5 November Sonia had a severe asthma attack and Mrs Keppel
nursed her. 'Mama is marvellous when anyone is really ill,' Violet told
Vita. 'So cool and calm and competent. She has not been to bed all
night.' On 7 November in London Denys was cheered as a hero by his
regiment. Three days later he again asked Violet to marry him. 'I said
"no" with more emphasis than I usually do. *Je t'aime, je t'aime*', she
wrote to Vita.

On 11 November Winston Churchill phoned Mrs Keppel at >.15 in
the morning with news that the Armistice was about to be signed. In
Brighton Lady Sackville rang an enormous dinner bell out of an
upstairs window which impressed her grandson Ben. Violet 'went mad'
with the rest of London. She dashed to Selfridges, bought flags and
with George Keppel festooned the balconies of Grosvenor Street. Then
she cheered her way with the crowds down Bond Street to Trafalgar
Square.

On 13 November she accused Vita of ruining her whole life and said if they did not go away together she would marry Denys 'in order to forget you'. On 18 November a new nanny arrived in Brighton for Vita's sons. On 24 November Harold wrote in his diary 'a tiresome day explaining to BM why Viti is going to France'. Two days later Violet and Vita spent the night in a hotel in Folkestone, then sailed the Channel the following day. Vita had packed her 'Julian clothes'.

ELEVEN

'I shall never forget my joy on arriving in Paris' Violet wrote in her autobiography. It was she said the culmination of her dreams, the happiest day of her life. France was her country, Paris her city. She liked hearing Vita talk 'beautiful rhythmical French'. This, away from the hypocrisy of Grosvenor Street and Kent was a new life of freedom, dedicated to love, art and truth.

She had saved from her allowance 'in order not to arrive impecunious in Paris'. All her money came from her mother. In January 1918 Mrs Keppel had invested an additional £50,000 in war stocks for her and these yielded extra dividends. Violet and Vita stayed at 30 rue Montpensier in the Palais-Royal. The apartment belonged to Edward Knoblock, author of *Kismet* and himself gay, like Hugh Walpole who owned the Polperro cottage. Denys visited on Wednesday 27 November. 'He lunched and dined with us, our guest, a casual friend, an outsider.' His presence, Violet said, 'was intended as a camouflage, to give Chinday, to her mind, excellent reason for my going there'.

'I had never felt so free in my life' Vita said, as she lived the role of Julian. Violet dressed as herself. They went to the opera, to a musical, *The Season of Love*, ate in the cafés. 'I was madly insatiably in love with you,' Violet wrote. At a play by Pierre Louys, *The Woman and the Puppet*, she 'lay back in an abandonment of happiness and gave myself up to your scandalously indiscreet caresses in full view of the theatre'.

'I shall never forget the evenings,' Vita wrote in her 1920 Confession, 'when we walked back slowly to our flat through the streets of Paris. When we got back to the flat the windows all used to be open on to the courtyard of the Palais-Royal and the fountains splashed below. It was all incredible — like a fairy-tale.'

Denys returned to Belgium after a week. They moved south without telling anyone where they were. Their uncertain plan was to live the life of their novel *Rebellion*, to go to Monte Carlo, Ajaccio, Greece. They booked in at the Hôtel Beau Rivage, St Raphael, 'riviera weather, palms, moonlight and the sea', then moved on to the Hotel Bristol, Monte Carlo. 'The weather was perfect, Monte Carlo was perfect, Violet was perfect,' Vita wrote. It was a place of pleasure – sunshine, flowers, ornate villas, domed hotels, cliffs studded with brightly painted houses, quays filled with yachts. Over the town loomed the casino with marble steps and perfect gardens, the Temple of Chance, where they gambled their money away. They were Eve and Julian, lovers and artists, in the backstreet bars and cafés. Sometimes they stayed in bed all day.

On Monday 16 December they caused a stir by dancing together at a *thé dansant* at the hotel. They left in a flurry with Vita pawning jewels to settle the bill. She wired for cash to Gerald Wellesley, Violet's erstwhile fiancé. They moved to the Windsor Hotel, to rooms on the third floor and with a lift that was worked by ropes. One evening Violet stood at the open window with Vita. They looked down over Monaco in the setting sun, there was the sound of waves and of singing from the other side of the harbour. She thought,

> Mitya will never leave me. O Beloved and that night we slept in each other's arms . . . I feel it is so dreadfully wrong of us to attempt to conceal . . . There would never be a particle of happiness in my life away from you . . . .

Violet extolled romantic feelings. She wanted to emulate her mother and have an equivalent love. She only obliquely realized her mother used her head far more than her heart. Letters from home pursued them and at 16 Grosvenor Street trouble brewed. On 29 November Mrs Keppel went to a dinner given by General Sir Archibald Hunter and his wife Mary. Among the guests were Lady Lowther, wife of Sir Gerard Lowther, Harold's ambassador when he was in Constantinople, Lady Muriel Paget, Maud Cunard the society hostess, Sir Ian Hamilton,

Lord Farquhar who had been lord-in-waiting to Bertie, and Harold. They had oysters, snipe, champagne, dessert, coffee and cigars. Mrs Keppel talked of her vexation with the faulty self-starter on her new car. She did not speak of her vexation at the 'inquisitiveness' Harold said all the guests showed as to the whereabouts of Vita and Violet.

Two days later she phoned Harold in a fuss because she had not heard from Violet. He said he was expecting a telegram from Vita and would let her know. No telegram arrived so he did not phone. Next day George, 'Pawpaw' as Harold called him, phoned before breakfast to say Mrs Keppel had not slept all night worrying.

On 5 December Harold sent an aggrieved letter for Vita to Edward Knoblock's flat. He did not know where to get hold of her. He put the whole mess down to 'that swine Violet who seems to addle your brain' and accused his wife of mooning on from day to day 'with the future in a sort of sloppy fog'. Two days later he sent another letter instructing Vita to tell Violet she was 'not the *only* second string to our bow'. He had in anger started an affair with Victor Cunard, nephew of the baronet of ocean liner fame. Victor Cunard was twenty, sharp and explicitly gay. Harold stayed with him in his family's house in Leicester then invited him to Knole. But Vita was not jealous of Harold's affairs, only Violet's.

The story of their dancing together reached London. 'I can't forgive you if you have really done something as vulgar and dangerous as that,' Harold wrote. He found it hard to believe because Vita could not dance. Nor did he like Vita 'telegraphing to Gerry behind my back. Whenever you have been long with that clammy fiend you get crooked.'

Violet was a bad smell, an illness, he said. 'She flatters you – that is it – every silly ass woman is bowled over by flattery. *How* I hate women.' He dined with Mrs Keppel on 10 December and described her as 'magnificent as ever'. Socially she expressed no grievance toward Violet or Vita. She said they were having a holiday on the Riviera after the privations of the war. Lady Sackville for her part told friends Violet had 'demoralized' Vita and was a sexual pervert, pernicious, amoral and on a par with 'that snake in the grass' Olive Rubens who had taken her own husband from her.

At Christmas Violet gave Vita corals. They went to church, then to the casino and lost 350 francs. Harold spent Christmas at Knole with his sons and invited the composer Lord Berners to stay. Gerald Berners had a spinet in his Rolls-Royce and dyed the doves at his home, Faringdon Hall, bright pink. Lady Sackville, no stranger to theatrical display, made friends with both him and Victor Cunard. Gay men were entertaining provided they were discreet and did not disrupt the social show. 'It is nobody's business to know our private lives . . . The less said about it the better . . . Silence is wiser,' she wrote in her *Book of Reminiscences*. Lord Sackville liked neither of them. Nor did he want to speak to his wife or hear of the marital troubles of his daughter. Lady Sackville felt unwanted and ousted from Knole. She dined in the garden on 30 December.

Harold went to Paris on the last day of 1918 as a Foreign Office official at the Peace Conference. Alone at the Majestic Hotel he felt himself to be 'terribly overworked' and 'unnaturally upset' by the sorrow and confusion of his private life. Edward Knoblock sent round bits and pieces left by Violet and Vita. Reminders of Violet, her cosmetics and shoes, made Harold feel sick. On 11 January he wrote he would spit in her face he hated her so. 'All Paris,' he said, was talking of his separation from Vita. He hired servants and waited for Vita to join him at the end of January. She did not come.

Moreover she told him it was 'indecent' to write to him when she was with Violet, 'oh, do, do try to see it!'. He told her she was irresponsible and 'lured into corruption' by Violet. Vita did not want him to blame Violet. She urged him to see that she was acting because of a 'great force' within herself. This he did not want to believe:

> You say Violet has no influence over you. Then what is it has made you so hard and selfish and unkind — not only to me but to Ben, Nigel and even Dada [Lord Sackville].

The only explanation was that Violet — the witch, Eve, the snake, the seductress — had done her primeval worst. It could not be that Vita 'like a person translated or reborn' was following her own desires.

Lady Sackville made it clear Vita would lose her if she did not give Violet up. She had had enough of organizing the lives of her grandchildren who were shunted from Knole to friends in Hampstead, to Harold's mother, Lady Carnock. 'Vita ought to come back and look after them,' she wrote to Harold. Violet, she let it be known, was a viper with a putrid mind. Lord Sackville wrote to Vita of how he hated the 'loathsome' things people were saying. He thought the sun and 'hand to mouth existence' of Monte Carlo had turned her head. Olive Rubens wrote 'you must, you simply *must* come home.' And from Mrs Keppel came letters for Violet letting her know that when she returned to London, as she must, she would marry and that would be that.

It was all too problematic, the pressures too great. Violet wrote to Harold. She told of the depth of her love for Vita, her despair at the anguish this love was causing, the tragedy she could see unfolding, her inability to sort things out. 'I have destroyed her letter,' Harold wrote to Vita:

> How sad it was! I like her to love you like that darling — it is the best thing Violet has done — and I really don't feel that anything so deep and compelling can be called unnatural or debasing.

He felt concern for Denys Trefusis with all the rumours of marriage and hoped if she was going to marry him she would announce the engagement soon and end the gossip. He thought Vita would advise Violet for the best.

Violet returned in the middle of March, after the four happiest months of her life, she said. Vita joined Harold in Paris and wrote to her on British Delegation paper saying her anguish at separation was exquisite. 'I'm glad,' Violet replied. 'I wish I could say as much for my own.' She was back at Grosvenor Street facing the wrath of her mother.

On 19 March Vita returned to England and was delighted to be reunited with her boys. Lady Sackville had moved to Brighton, the children and their nanny were there too. She refused to accept the presents Vita offered. 'She talks in a voice trembling with passion,' Vita wrote to Harold on 20 March. 'I HATE her tonight . . . I want you so dreadfully badly. I know I have brought it all on myself.' Harold, always forgiving, resolved to do everything he could to protect her and bring her back to 'calm and security' away from the scarlet adventurer.

Mrs Keppel, determined and practical, moved into action. The errant desires of the King of England were one thing, those of her daughter another. Violet would marry, discretion and society dictated this must be. She was ashamed of Violet, scornful and unkind, concerned for the family reputation, unprepared to attempt to understand. It was not a negotiable situation. She had spent a long time gambling at the King's side for high stakes. She was not going to lose her elevated position because of her wayward daughter. The accepted form was marriage into the aristocracy, the preservation of status, the semblance of propriety. Sex was a private matter, adultery an art, but this sort of scandal was beyond the pale.

A week after Violet's return she took her to a society ball where there were seven hundred guests. Mrs Keppel had announced that Violet was engaged to be married to Denys Trefusis. Violet was congratulated by everyone. She wrote to Vita when she got home at two in the morning 'at the conclusion of the most cruelly ironical day I have spent in my life'. She could she said, have 'screamed aloud':

Mitya I can't face this existence . . . I am losing every atom of self respect I ever possessed . . . I want you every second and every hour of the day, yet I am being slowly and inexorably tied to somebody else . . .

Nothing and no one in the world could kill the love I have for you . . . I have given you my body time after time to treat as you pleased . . . All the hoardings of my imagination I have laid bare to you. There isn't a recess in my brain into which you haven't penetrated. I have clung to you and caressed you and slept with you and I would like to tell the whole world I clamour

for you ... You **are** my lover and I am your mistress, and
kingdoms and empires and governments have tottered and suc-
cumbed before now to that mighty combination – the most
powerful in the world.

But the only kingdom which was to totter was Violet's own. The
Crown, government, Grosvenor Street, Kent and the Foreign Office
stayed intact.

Her kind of love was beyond mention even in the gossip columns
of the London papers. Lesbianism was not a subject for discussion, the
word was not used. Such feelings were aberrant and manifestations of
them an embarrassment. 'You know how I loathe and abominate
deceit and hypocrisy,' she wrote to Vita:

> To my mind it is the worst thing on earth and here I am putting
> it all into practice – all the things I have most loathed and
> denounced to you ... I belong to you body and soul. I ache for
> you all day and all night. You are my whole existence – O Mitya
> it is so *horrible*, so *monstrous*, so *criminal* to be with someone one
> doesn't care for when your whole being cries out for the person
> you *do* love and *do* belong to. In all my life I have never done
> anything as wrong as this.
>
> How can I get out of it? What am I to say? What is this hideous
> farce I'm playing?

Her 'great love affair' with Vita was shaping into a quagmire of
confusion, lies, deception and sham. She did not know what to do.
She wrote of the 'hell of having to endure the caresses of someone
you don't love'. Hell or not, Mrs Keppel when determined was a
formidable opponent. Violet did not have the courage to resist her.
She depended on her and craved her love.

She let Vita know that she alone could save the situation. 'What's
going to happen?' she wrote to her:

> Are you going to stand by and watch me marry this man? It's
> unheard of, inconceivable ...

If we could go away, you and I, even for a few months I would get out of it — but if I got out of it, and remained here alone and without you my life would be unendurable.

Chinday would make everything hell for me. If I had to go off and live alone at this juncture I should put an end to myself.

O my love and this time last week we were still free and happy and — together, and all life seemed full of youth and spring and Romance . . .

Mitya you must know how repugnant it is to me to tolerate this relationship. It is *absolutely contrary* to all my ideas of morals. I mayn't have many, but this absolutely does them in. I hover between indescribable self-loathing and plans of suicide.

Five days later, on 26 March 1919, Mrs Keppel gave the details of her daughter's engagement to the press. The wedding was set for 2 June. Vita bought all the papers at Brighton station and felt faint when she read the facts in print. Harold was sympathetic. He rightly feared the strain and unreality of this engagement would be too much for Violet. 'I feel really that it would be better if she broke it off — but you will know best,' he wrote to Vita. The next day he wondered if marriage would 'prove her salvation' and if she would become fond of Denys. Vita said she was almost sure Violet would break the engagement. 'Poor Denys but it is a little bit his own fault.' Harold did not know what she meant by that.

Poor Denys did not know what was going on. He had come from a war where it was useless to articulate feelings. He believed /iolet wanted him. She had said 'yes' to his marriage proposal, had declared herself 'thrilled' when he came home on leave the previous October, had told people she was in love. 'I certainly told people that' she wrote to Vita, 'and why? to camouflage our going away . . . You yourself told Pat I was on the verge of falling in love, you admitted, for the same reason.'

But the prime player was Mrs Keppel, manoeuvring and arranging, promising him a world after the hell of the trenches and the battlegrounds of France. He was malleable in her hands. She offered him an income if he married her daughter, an undemanding office occupation, a house, the prospect of travel. Violet was witty, attractive, strong-willed, artistic, his prize, his mascot, the living emblem of the luck and fortune that had brought him if not his compatriots home from the war.

Four days after the official announcement of their engagement he gave Violet 'his word of honour as a *gentleman*' never to do anything to displease her, 'you know in what sense I mean' she wrote to Vita. It meant, in code, no sex together. He put his assurance in writing to her. He wanted to behave honourably, to impress her with his trustworthiness. He viewed women as pure and less corruptible than men. He refrained from kissing her hair or taking her arm because that seemed to be her wish. He became despondent when she said she could not marry him, accepted she was fonder of Vita than of himself and tried to respect what he could not begin to understand. If he was jealous he did not or could not say. The closest he got to criticism was silence. One evening, when Violet returned from Vita, he said as she entered the room, 'You look as though you have been very demonstrative,' then took up a book and started to read: 'I began to read too, but I was really wondering all the time what he was thinking about. He is a sphinx that man.'

Denys was like those 999 out of every thousand women who, in Lord Birkenhead's view, had 'never heard a whisper of these practices' of lesbianism. He was straight from the killing fields and not acquainted or tainted with 'horrible and noxious suspicions'. He might have understood had Vita been a man. He was correct, musical, physically fearless, reserved, aloof. He had been through what he called a 'disastrous war' in which he killed men and saw men killed in swathes. He had symptoms of trauma: sleeplessness, bad dreams, an inability to talk of what he had seen. He wanted to build a civilian life, get married, work, write books, travel and be free.

He spoke fluent Russian. At the outbreak of war he was working in St Petersburg as tutor to the sons of a Monsieur Balaschoff. In a letter to an uncle in 1910, he declared his intention to 'specialise in Russian subjects — language, economics, trade, etc. Russia is the future field of investment,' he said. 'I am looking forward immensely to going into business.'

War and revolution foiled such plans. He volunteered for active service in France and Flanders. In 1915 he was poisoned by gas and invalided to England for two months. He was left with respiratory problems and recurring chest infections.

He felt 'caged up' at home and 'longed to breathe the open air'. His parents, respectable, 'very county and stuffy', viewed Violet as an 'absolute outsider'. She arrived to see them in Devon smelling of French perfume and in unsuitable clothes for the country. Colonel Trefusis was deaf, had little money and was dominated by Mitty, his wife, who was large and did charitable work for prisoners and unfortunates. Denys's two sisters were professional musicians. His elder brother Kerr had converted to Catholicism and was about to marry a rich divorcee older than his mother.

Violet recoiled from them all. She called them adamantine:

I *hate* them, Mitya ... I hate their overbred appearances, their academic mind, their musical aloofness and superiority, their inflexible point of view, their incredible *pride*, their extreme reserve and insurmountable indifference, their lack of humour, and — let it be faced! — total absence of any outward manifestation of humanity! ...

I hate them. I would like to tweak their aristocratic noses. I would like to tear their immaculate clothes from off their backs. I would like to give them penny dreadfuls to read, and make them listen to *Helen of Troy* for 4 hours a day on the gramophone!

I'm trying to find the dominating adjective for them, because they're not exactly *bien*, or prigs — no certainly not prigs — or old-fashioned — no! It's *aloofness*, that's what it is, sheer arctic aloofness ... They were unutterably disgusted because I cried at Ivan*.

* Glinka's opera, *A Life for the Tsar*.

Oh my sweet, how I miss you . . . I hate *them* Mitya, and
sometimes I hate *him*. I should be *miserable* with him. I feel trapped
and desperate.

It was not a propitious start to married life. The Trefusis family had
reason to ponder Violet joining their ranks.

Vita wished Denys 'was just a stray friend and not engaged to V'.
Violet hoped the engagement would sting Vita into 'claiming' her.
'Living permanently with me had become an obsession in her mind'
Vita wrote. She was extravagantly jealous at the thought of Denys
touching Violet, but when it came to commitment her own reality
was England, family, Kent, gardens, servants and a place to work. She
played a double game of colluding with the plan to run away with
Violet and of reassuring Harold that love with him was the real
thing.

Harold hoped for a diplomatic solution. He believed in the essential
goodness of his wife. His tactics were patience and forgiveness. He
preferred to negotiate terms, not talk of feelings. He told Vita he did
not expect her to break with Violet but he would not allow them
again to go away together for a long period. 'You simply can't go on
sacrificing your reputation and your duty to a tragic passion.'

Such terms suited Vita, provided Violet used Denys as a decoy and
had no sexual exchange with him. But for Violet it was all unworkable.
Her lover was insisting on fidelity without commitment, her mother
on marriage without love, her fiancé had expectations of relationship
however inchoate these were. On 17 April she spent three days with
Vita at Knole. Vita said it was 'an oasis'. For Violet it opened old habits,
old wounds. On 23 April Vita joined Harold in Paris and left Violet in
an entirely unstable state of mind, her wedding six weeks away. 'You
don't know, you'll never know the loneliness that I feel,' Violet wrote
to her. 'You'll never know how unhappy I am. You'll never know
how intolerably I miss you.'

It would have been difficult for Vita not to know. She was in Paris
a fortnight and deluged with the knowledge. It riled Violet to get

155

letters written on Délégation Britannique paper. She was desperate at
Vita being with Harold again: 'he will say "My little Mar" [his nickname
for her] and *kiss* the back of your neck. *Tu me fais horreur Mitya, parfois tu
me fais horreur.* The depths of duplicity in you make my hair stand yon
end.' As Violet saw it she had given an assurance and a promise that
no physical intimacy had or would take place between her and Denys
and yet Vita was intimate with Harold. 'Hadji this and Hadji that and
you are strolling almost arm in arm . . . And I, who love you fifty
times more than life, am temporarily forgotten – set aside.'

Hadji could not feel victorious. Vita was 'terribly unhappy' in Paris
with him. He felt overworked, stale, depressed about the peace negoti-
ations and despairing about his private life: 'O darling I have suffered
so this long dark year: have I to go through another?' He said he was
resigned to not seeing much of her in his life. He accepted that for
three months in the year she should go off alone somewhere and not
leave him her address. But he had seen her for only fourteen days in
six months and the children had seen her less. 'You can't say that
marriage is a bore to you or motherhood a responsibility.' What sad-
dened him was that she wanted to be away for even longer. He thought
Violet had 'thrown the evil eye' on them all.

The concept of Violet the evil manipulator absolved Vita and
explained everything. But in spring 1919 Vita worked in the gardens
at Long Barn, was encouraged by the publication of her first novel,
Heritage, which was well reviewed and knew that in the wings Harold
waited: 'All I can do,' he wrote to her on 22 May, 'is to love you
absolutely, and understand you absolutely, and let you do whatever
you like. That is easy . . .'

But Violet was heading for the rocks. She was filled with panic at
the prospect of marriage and with self-loathing for the mess she was
in and the distress she caused. She appealed to Pat Dansey to go away
with her. Pat refused and said it would not make Violet love *her*, if she
did. 'She says I would only go on loving you,' Violet wrote to Vita,
'and that I would throw her over at the first opportunity, all of which
is undeniably true.'

Vita told Violet she would elope with her before the wedding and that they would live together. 'I don't absolutely remember the process in detail,' she wrote two years later,

> but I know that I ended by consenting. After that we were both less unhappy; I could afford to see her ostensibly engaged to Denys when I knew that instead of marrying him she was coming away with me. I really intended to take her; we had every plan made. We were to go the day before the wedding – not sooner, because we thought we should be overtaken and brought back. It was of course only this looking forward which enabled me to endure the period of her engagement.

She gave consent but not commitment. At the beginning of May she wrote to Denys, insisted he not mention to Violet that she had done so, asked if he was happy and if all was well with his marriage plans and sent him a copy of her novel, *Heritage*. He replied from the Marlborough Club, Pall Mall:

> My dear Vita
>   Yes, I am *very* happy and everything goes well – though I must admit LMG [Little Mrs George] is somewhat worrying at times to both of us – quite charming at others!
>   This you will readily understand! The wedding has been put off till June 16th now.
>   I am more than delighted to hear that one of V's poems is to appear in print. Also she is doing what I think to be an *extremely* good portrait of me. Not that these two comparatively small achievements probably mean much in themselves, but what I greatly hope is that she will eventually find what she wants to do & then pursue it to the uttermost. I should like to see *one* really absorbing interest develop itself for her – I should be equally sorry to see whatever talent she has dissipated over a wide variety of subjects without any real devotion to one. If you agree about

this please try & influence her in that direction, though perhaps there is no need to hurry her to any conclusion yet.

Meanwhile I am just reading your book. I would not presume to criticise even after finishing it, much less now — I will only say that it will be quickly read — and carefully.

Yours

Denys

I will not mention your letter to V, so you must not mention this!

Whatever he felt, he was not going to show it. Even before the war, in a letter to his sister in 1909, he described himself as 'rigidly suppressed'. He said this was because of the 'sausage machine' public school system. A true Englishman, he said, after school was strong, healthy, honourable 'but he has had all his personality squashed out of him'.

Denys avoided analysis of motive or mood, took his fiancée to the Ballets Russes, to the opera, escorted her at dinner parties, planned trips to Venice and Spain, behaved as a gentleman, however capricious her affections. But he floundered when she flailed at the institution of marriage and said it 'ought to be confined to temperamental old maids, weary prostitutes and royalties!' He told her to make up her mind whether she wanted to be an artist or to marry and bring up a family, 'But whatever you do, *don't attempt to run both!*'

Mrs Keppel was more emphatic. There were frequent rows and Violet felt trapped and stifled in her mother's house. When she told her of the poem to which Denys referred, published in *Country Life*, Mrs Keppel said:

'Really, how nice. How much are they paying you for it?' And later in the day she remarked: 'Of course it's no use writing poetry unless you get paid for it.' . . . The point of view! . . . I nearly said: 'It's not possible that you should be my mother. I won't, I can't believe that we are any relations!

Violet said she wanted to burn to the ground St George's Church in Hanover Square where her wedding was to be held. It was delayed for a fortnight – from 2 to 16 June – ostensibly because so many people would be at the races. 'I don't think any objection was made by Mrs K at the change of date,' Pat Dansey wrote to Vita. 'It was changed for purely convenience sake.' (She would, she added, be 'truly thankful' when Vita came and sorted matters out.) Violet worked at the escape plan with Vita, whose equivocation took her to her wits' end.

At the end of May she told Denys Vita meant more to her than anyone and that she would die if she ceased to love her. He said he felt sorry for her. When she threatened to back out of the wedding he feared the wrath of Mrs Keppel and the 'appalling scandal' that would follow. He promised when they were married she could come and go as she pleased, he would be content if she spent three months of the year with him and would try to be her 'safe and loyal friend'. Pat Dansey, at Violet's request, talked to him. He told her, too, that he would keep to the pact of protective friend, with no sex.

Like Harold he sought to shield his temperamental wayward woman. Perhaps he thought time and patience would change her. But Harold and Vita had built a life and had much to preserve. Denys had nothing with Violet but bright hopes and fragile promises. As these began to tarnish and break, he brought into play qualities that made him a good soldier and a good Englishman: courage, trustworthiness, self-sacrifice. 'O Mitya,' Violet wrote to Vita:

> We are making a sort of brawling tavern out of what was once a Greek temple. Soon it will be ruined . . . There are no words strong enough for what has happened. I have ruined everything in my life . . . The only really effective thing would be for us to transplant our temple stone by stone and set it down in some new site . . . We can't, Oh we can't go on as at present. It makes me sick with disgust and self-loathing.

She needed a kind of help that was not on offer: disinterested advice and the chance to get away. She was learning hard lessons about her sort of love: society would not condone it, there was no context for it, it led to social ostracism, which led to self-dislike. Had her temperament allowed, she might have copied her mother, Vita, the King and Harold, and had sex with her lover while her spouse was out. But she had spoken the truth when she said that it was impossible for her to care for more than one person at a time. 'When I say care, I mean it is impossible for me to be even *fond* of anyone but you or merely superficially interested.' She was in too deep a mess to dissemble well.

On 6 May she had the worst of rows with her mother:

> I nearly struck her she was so terribly unkind. But all the time
> I thought in three days I shall have Mitya and it didn't seem to
> matter so much.

On 9 May she went with Pat Dansey to look at a house in the country for herself and Denys to live in when married. 'I can't, *can't* have one with anyone but you,' she wrote to Vita. In the train she felt faint with desire as she thought of her. 'I am terribly and unashamedly passionate. All the force of that passion is centred on you. I want you, I desire you . . . as I have never desired anyone in my life.'

Time passed, no divine intervention put matters right. The muddle swirled. Pat Dansey, attracted to them both, tried to signify in the drama. Vita's jealousy, she told her, was making Violet's marriage impossible. She wrote to her, demanded the return of photographs of herself she had given Violet which Vita had taken and said she planned to tell the story to the whole of London:

> Unless you make an early opportunity for seeing me I shall go
> and see Mrs Keppel who has many times both by word and letter
> assured me of the good friend I have been to Violet.

At the end of May Mrs Keppel gave a ball for the impending marriage. Her old Edwardian friends were there. Denys warned Violet he might tell her mother about the 'unnatural compact' between them. Harold asked Vita if he should give Violet a wedding present. 'I should like to but it may hurt her feelings. Let me know ' Vita gave her an alabaster head of Medusa, a Renaissance copy she found in an antique shop.

By June Denys seemed silent and indifferent to his fate. 'I think he will break it off himself,' Violet wrote to Vita. 'He is beastly to me and made me cry yesterday . . . I think he is beginning to hate me.' And still she believed, or had to believe, that Vita would intervene, prevent the marriage and claim her as Vita said she would do.

But Vita was making other plans. On 1 June she wrote to Harold in Paris. She said she felt like a person drowning. She turned the problem over to him to solve:

> V's wedding is tomorrow fortnight and I know that there will be some disaster if I stop here. I can't be in England or *it will never take place.* If I am in Paris . . . if need be you can keep me under lock and key . . . I tell you about it in order to protect myself from myself. I'm not afraid of anybody but myself. I shall do something quite irretrievable and mad if I stay in England. I shall probably try and do it even from Paris, at the last moment, but there I shall be prevented by just sheer distance.

On 3 June Denys was formally awarded the Military Cross for bravery. He was not pleased with the honour for he thought he merited better. Postwar civilian life was to tax him more than his time in the trenches. Harold replied that day to Vita's letter,

> you must come over at once and let me know by telegra; 1. I shall get a room for you and meet you . . . come at once my poor shattered Viti – and I shall be with you, and help.

Vita did not let Violet know she had reneged on their plan to elope. She told Harold she would arrive in Paris the day before the wedding so as to rule out any chance that she might return. On 9 June she wrote to him:

> Violet thinks I will save her from this bloody marriage. How

much astonished would you be if I did? I shouldn't be astonished in the least. It would be great fun anyway.

It was disingenuous if Vita supposed she was easing matters for Violet by going to Paris. Violet and Denys were to go there immediately after their wedding. It was, as her biographer Victoria Glendinning said, an act of provocation for her to be there at all. But she was out of control. She seldom made demands on Harold, but here, in an incoherence of emotion, she asked him to save her from herself.

On 12 June, three days before the wedding, she told Violet she would not go away with her. Violet, terrified, looked ill and changed and implored her to think again. She said she would wait for her up to the very last minute. 'I was,' said Vita, 'obdurate'. On 14 June Harold met Vita at the Gare du Nord, took her to Versailles and stayed with her the following day, a Sunday.

On Monday 16 June Violet sent her a pencilled note, 'You have broken my heart, goodbye.' She was then driven to St George's Church, Hanover Square. She wore a wedding gown of old Valenciennes over chiffon. The train was gold brocade with a raised pattern of velvet flowers. Her jewellery included a pearl necklace given to her by her mother. Four children and four adult bridesmaids, including Sonia, attended her. The children were her cousins Crispian and Cecilia, Denys's niece Phyllida Walford and David McKenna. The bridesmaids wore yellow chiffon with sashes of blue and silver and blue wreaths in their hair.

Mrs Keppel chose the wedding clothes and flowers. She wore silk chiffon in lapis-lazuli blue with 'oriental colourings' and long russet silk tassels and a matching hat. George arranged the transport, allocated pews, chose the music in church, the champagne for the reception. Purcell's 'Trumpet Voluntary' was played before Violet arrived, the Wedding March from *Lohengrin* as she walked down the aisle, Dame Nellie Melba sang Gounod's 'Ave Maria' during the signing of the register.

Edward VII's intimates were there: Soveral and Sir Ernest Cassel.

'ARE YOU GOING TO STAND BY AND WATCH ME MARRY
THIS MAN? IT'S UNHEARD OF, INCONCEIVABLE'

Violet engaged to Denys Trefusis
Cover photograph of The Sketch, *2 April 1919*

AT THE TREFUSIS—KEPPEL WEDDING: PEOPLE—AND DRESS.

A COUSIN OF THE BRIDEGROOM: THE HON. MRS. ARTHUR CRICHTON.

THE EVER-PRESENT: MR. AND MRS. ASQUITH.

—AND WHITE TOPPER! LORD AND LADY SAVILE.

MOTHER AND DAUGHTER: THE DUCHESS OF BEAUFORT AND LADY DIANA SOMERSET.

Mrs. Arthur Crichton is the wife of the second of the Earl of Erne's uncles, and was Miss Katharine Trefusis, daughter of the late Colonel the Hon. Walter Trefusis.——Lord Savile is the second Baron. His uncle, the first peer, was Minister to Saxony, to the Swiss Confederation, and to Brussels, and Ambassador to Italy. Lady Savile was Miss Gertrude Violet Wolton, daughter of Mr. John Wolton.——Lady Diana Somerset is a younger daughter of the Duke of Beaufort.

Violet's wedding at St George's Church,
Hanover Square. 16 June 1919

AT THE TREFUSIS—KEPPEL WEDDING; NOTABLES PRESENT.

ON HER WAY TO THE WEDDING: LADY DROGHEDA.

ATTENDANTS ON THE BRIDE: BRIDESMAIDS AND TRAIN-BEARERS.

THE HAPPY PAIR: CAPTAIN DENYS TREFUSIS AND MRS. TREFUSIS.

MOTHER OF THE BRIDE—AND FRIEND: THE HON. MRS. GEORGE KEPPEL AND LADY DESBOROUGH.

The wedding of Captain Denys R. Trefusis, M.C., son of Colonel the Hon. John and Mrs. Trefusis, and Miss Violet Keppel, elder daughter of Lieutenant-Colonel the Hon. George and Mrs. Keppel, took place last week. The children in attendance on the bride were the Hon. Crispian Keppel, Miss Phyllida Walford, Master David McKenna, and the Hon. Cecilia Keppel; while the grown-up attendants were Miss Sonia Keppel, the Hon. Joan Poynder, the Hon. Olive Paget, and Miss Myrtle Farquharson.

'HE HAS CEASED TO BE
ANYTHING BUT MY JAILOR AND
I LOOK AT HIM AND THINK:
"YES, IF IT WASN'T FOR YOU".

*Right: Major Denys Trefusis,
Royal Horse Guards*

Left: 'MOTHER OF THE BRIDE —
AND FRIEND. THE HON. MRS
GEORGE KEPPEL AND LADY
DESBOROUGH'

'THE HAPPY PAIR:
MAJOR DENYS TREFUSIS
AND MRS TREFUSIS'

*On the morning of her
marriage Violet sent Vita
a pencilled note,*

'YOU HAVE BROKEN MY
HEART, GOODBYE.'

'VITA BELONGED TO KNOLE, TO THE COURTYARDS,
GABLES, GALLERIES, TO THE PRANCING SCULPTURED
LEOPARDS, TO THE TRADITIONS, RITES AND
SPLENDOURS'

*Vita Sackville-West and the Sackvilles' family home,
Knole, Sevenoaks, Kent*

'THIS IS THE BEST ADVENTURE'

Sketch by Violet of her as Eve and Vita as Julian, 1918

The King and Queen gave Violet a diamond brooch bearing the royal cipher. Mrs Keppel gave her a pearl and diamond bandeau, George a gold-fitted dressing case and a writing set, the Earl and Countess of Albemarle an emerald and diamond brooch, the servants at 16 Grosvenor Street a silver inkstand. Vita sat in her room at Versailles, her watch in her hand, as the hour of the wedding ticked past. 'All that time I knew she was expecting a pre-arranged message from me which I never sent.'

TWELVE

Violet arrived at the Paris Ritz with her husband and maid on the evening of Tuesday 17 June. Her honeymoon was to last a month. She wore new clothes but no wedding ring. Mrs Keppel had supervised her trousseau: a satin peignoir trimmed with ostrich feathers, travelling coats with matching hats.

Harold did not keep Vita under lock and key. Tuesday was a working day and he was busy with the Peace Conference. She left Versailles and booked in alone at the Hotel Roosevelt in Paris. On 18 June, she met Violet at the Ritz, went back with her to her own hotel and had sex with her. 'I treated her savagely. I had her, I didn't care, I only wanted to hurt Denys,' she wrote. She then assured Violet that, come autumn, they would go away together.

Next day they confronted Denys with facts that were terrible to hear. Violet told him she did not care for him. She had planned to run away with Vita instead of marrying him. Marriage to him was only a cover for this elopement. The plan had gone wrong. Neither she nor Vita made any effort to spare his pain. 'Don't you know, you stupid fool, that she is mine in every sense of the word,' Vita said she wanted to say. Denys went white in the face and looked as if he was going to faint. It was a moment of ghastly awakening. For Violet was not Vita's in every sense of the word. She was hers in the sense of sexual possession. In the eyes of the world and the law she was Denys's by the contract of their marriage two days before.

Of all the players in the drama it was Denys who now knew the plot. The true relationship between his wife and Vita was clear. It was not loving friendship as he had, perhaps, liked to suppose. He had been used, tricked. His marriage was not a marriage at all. He was not going to have the consolation of peace after war. To compound his humiliation, that

164

evening Vita dined alone at the Ritz. Violet, with Denys in tears behind her, watched her from an open window in their suite.

In subsequent letters to Violet he referred again and again to that day. If he had hopes that was when they drained away. He cried but could not find words for the mess. He was a man for whom the expression of emotion was a luxury denied. He was volatile, unsettled and in trauma from the war. This was his chance to define civilian life; he needed help not domestic tragedy.

Vita, her point made, booked out of the Roosevelt. She went for two days to Geneva with Harold and, when back in Paris, booked in with him at the Majestic Hotel. The reparation of their love and marriage is well documented.

Violet and Denys began their honeymoon and married life. Their schedule was to spend a week in Paris and then to go south to St Jean de Luz. Violet spent the Paris week crying in the Ritz. She told Denys he got on her nerves and mattered no more than a fly on the wall. Everything she said to him made him wince. She counted the number of cigarettes he smoked and they argued about money. He was devastated and at a loss to know what to do. He agreed that if Vita came on to St Jean de Luz, he would leave them together. But Vita went back to Long Barn to write her poems and to garden. She wrote to Harold, 'everything else is ephemeral but not you'.

In St Jean de Luz the newlyweds took separate rooms in the Golf Hotel and had frequent variations on the following conversation:

Denys: What are you thinking about?
Violet: Vita.
Denys: Do you wish Vita were here?
Violet: Yes.
Denys: You don't care much about being with men, do you?
Violet: No, I infinitely prefer women.
Denys: You are strange, aren't you?

Violet: Stranger than you have any idea of.

He teamed up with a Basque poacher and went off on muleback into the mountains to shoot vultures. Alone in the hotel Violet got drunk and talked to the patron about Monte Carlo and being in love. She bought Vita a stone for a ring. She wanted an emerald to signify jealousy but settled for blue agate, 'exactly the same colour as the most wonderful sapphire'. She asked Vita to wear only her ring and no other and to burn all letters she sent her.

Some days four letters came from Vita. If there was none or only a short one, she felt 'frenzied' and suspicious:

> If only I knew the truth about you and H! If only I knew for *certain* that you weren't playing a double game! . . . Oh God it is *degrading* to trust you so little.

At the beginning of July she and Denys moved to the Grand Hotel Eskualduna at Hendaye in the Basses-Pyrénées. 'Here our rooms aren't even next door to one another.' They went for long uncompanionable walks together in the hills. Some days they argued without stopping, on others he was 'silent, taciturn, unresponsive'. At night Violet wrote to Vita:

> O God another whole week of this. It seems I have never wanted you as I do now -
> When I think of your mouth . . .
> When I think of other things all the blood rushes to my head and I can almost imagine . . . If ever anyone was adored nd longed for it was you.

In one letter Vita suggested meeting Violet in Italy. Fear of her mother, not concern for Denys, held Violet back. Mrs Keppel had rented a house for her daughter and son-in-law, Possingworth Manor in Uckfield, Sussex, the tenure of which began on 15 July. 'Men chinday would be frantic if I didn't go to the house' Violet wrote to Vita.

Possingworth Manor was about twenty miles from Long Barn. Denys, still in the army, spent most of the week in London. Violet and Vita spent most of the week with each other. Gossip spread. On 20 July Vita sacked her children's nanny who spoofed her by walking in the village dressed in a suit of Harold's.

Violet fought with her mother and pleaded to be released from her marriage. On 21 July she went to bed in tears after an extravagant row:

> All this will probably end in my being quite penniless, she already seems to think that I should 'support myself' but I won't, no I won't let things like being jewel-less and impecunious distress me! . . . I shall have to become a governess or something!! When I think that men Chinday has at least £20,000 a year.

Denys, a month into marriage, also wanted a separation. He asked Violet to try to give up Vita and burned some of Vita's letters. His hopes for a workable relationship faded. He said if Violet went abroad with her he would sub-let the house, that her parents would have nothing further to do with her and neither would he. Moreover he was ill. He had what is now called post-traumatic stress disorder endured by many who survived the First World War. He also had symptoms of tuberculosis and needed nursing. He was advised to go to Brighton for the sea air. Pat Dansey said Violet would be 'abysmally selfish' if she did not go too.

'Men Chinday', with all her genius for society, who excelled in making people happy, needed more than discretion and charm to sort this lot out. This was incoherent feeling, emotional disaster, passion wrecking everything in its path. It needed candid scrutiny, wise disinterested counsel, intervention to avoid more pain. And Mrs Keppel had another worry. Sonia wanted to marry. She was 'unofficially engaged' to Roland Cubitt, heir to the Ashcombe title and to the huge building firm founded by his grandfather.

The Cubitts had built much of Belgravia, Pimlico and Eaton Square and had rebuilt Buckingham Palace. Lord and Lady Ashcombe lived at Denbies, Surrey, and were very rich. According to Denys they disapproved of Mrs Keppel's past relationship with Edward VII and of what they knew of her elder daughter's heart. They wanted a pretext to squash their son's marriage. 'Rolie' was the fourth in a family of six boys. His three elder brothers died heroes' deaths in the war. It mattered that he should marry well, fulfil the promise of his brothers, fly the family flag.

The driveway to Denbies was long, the furniture late Victorian, the butler old. In the hall were life-size portraits of Rolie's dead brothers, a stained glass heraldic window and, in a glass case, part of the skeleton of a brontosaurus. Ladies wore gloves indoors and no one smoked in the drawing room or played cards on Sunday. Lady Ashcombe referred to Sonia in the third person: 'Will the young lady have a scone?'

In the dining room, which was the size of a boardroom, hung a large Landseer painting of a horse, a mule, a donkey and a St Bernard. Lord Ashcombe held family prayers every day, was a chronic dyspeptic and carved the meat precisely. Menus, in English, stood on white china stands and followed a daily formula. Sunday lunch was roast beef, a cream pudding and cheddar cheese.

In church at eleven Lord Ashcombe wore a surplice and read the lesson. On Sunday afternoons there was tennis and tea and in the evenings jigsaws, games of patience and bed at ten. Their world was one of propriety, order, family values and time-observed rules on how life should be lived. Violet's recalcitrance unsettled it all.

Mrs Keppel rose to action. She would hear no news of separation between Violet and Denys, forbade all mention of Vita and dismissed reference to Violet's state of mind. When Violet was in London she did not let her out of her sight:

> I see no one, Mitya, not a soul except Chinday's friends. Pat sometimes and Loge [her name for Denys, after the fire god in Wagner's *Das Rheingold*] for perhaps an hour every evening. I never go anywhere. When I am not with Chinday, who makes life Hell for me I am alone ... My thoughts are past describing. I am ashamed of them ... I asked Loge the other day if he would be surprised if I committed suicide and he said, 'No, not in the least. I think it's a very natural thing to do if one is very unhappy. If

one is very wretched and making everyone else wretched it is the most decent thing one can do.'

There is something superhuman and terrifying in Loge's indifference to all the things that most people cherish such as life etc. It is not theoretical either . . . O Mitya what *are* you making of four lives . . . Are you happy? Is H.N. happy? Am I happy? Is Loge happy? I expect the Moral Being is though and that apparently is all that matters.

Instead of four utterly miserable people you could have two flawlessly happy ones. The other two would be wretched for the time being, but *believe* me they would eventually get over it & find two worthier objects of their affection.

She might have been right. But Vita could neither commit herself to Violet nor reject her. She was never other than equivocal; 'when you are not with me I feel and suffer uncontrollably on your account,' she wrote to her, but 'think what would happen if I were to lose you again – I do not think I could bear it . . . I *could* not remain with you *en rocamblo* [as gypsies] . . . and I *could* not let you go again.'

Violet hoped she would choose her, feared she would not. 'Every time I see the gates of Paradise opening in front of me you close them again,' she wrote. Vita perhaps loved Violet equally, perhaps was in an equal emotional dilemma. But she cared for Harold, was drawn to convention, felt an affinity with England, an allegiance to her class. Violet disdained convention. When Vita and Harold went to the wedding of a friend she voiced her essential scorn:

Tomorrow you will go to a charming wedding. You will blend facetiousness and sentimentality most suitably. You will be reminded of your own – damn you – and of mine – damn me. Somebody will say 'Ah six years ago' – damn him . . .

Darling, I wonder if you noticed the parson scratching his head the whole time as though a fly kept tickling it? I wonder if you saw the bridegroom trip as he was walking down the aisle? I wonder if you saw the choir boys titter and I wonder if you

heard the organ play a few bars of its own accord in the middle
of Mendelssohn's Wedding March? Did you? Did you?

Because I tickled the parson's head, I gave the bridegroom a
push, I made the choir boys giggle, I played the few bars and I
even tweaked the Lady Alberta's nose and snatched away her
hassock just as she was about to sit down on it.

That was what she thought of marriage — the King's, her mother's,
Vita's and her own. It was an institution of deception, a meretricious
parade, a declaration of status. What mattered was true love through
whatever door it came.

But she was isolated by her rebellion, in her rented manor house
in Sussex; sustained only by Vita's letters and visits and their scrambled
plans again to run away. She spoke of herself as 'dumped down in a
jungle of entirely foreign and soul-shattering emotions and left to
cope with them alone'.

She and Vita planned to leave England on 19 October for their next
escape. Denys began not to care where Violet was or with whom. He
simply wanted to know when she was going so as to arrange his own
affairs. They saw each other only at meals:

I had another frightful row with D. I haven't seen him since. He
went to London this morning without saying goodbye. I am a
pig to him. If I were him I would never come back. If only you
could come here today.

She told him she would never care for him, criticized his appearance,
was glad when he was unable to get leave from the army.

Harold, in Paris, had a new lover, the couturier Edward Molyneux
— twenty-seven, good-looking, with a shop in the rue Royale and a
smart flat at the Rond Point. Vita told her mother, who kept no
secrets, of Harold's inadequacies as her lover and of how there was
now no sex between them.

On 17 October, two days before they went away again, Violet asked
Vita to weigh her own intentions:

I can't impress upon you sufficiently that this time it is more in the nature of a tragic undertaking than an adventure (like last year). And once again I must absolutely implore you not to go unless you are unmovably sure. Think over it very seriously and weigh everything in your mind ... This time you would absolutely do me in and I swear I don't deserve it at your hands.

Vita was not unmovably sure. The day she left for Paris with Violet, she wrote to Harold that she loved him 'immutably, sacredly and rootedly', nothing in the world could ever alter her love for him: he, the house, the children were all she loved best.

For two months she left all she loved best. She and Violet went again to Paris and Monte Carlo and lived the life of cafés, theatres, of Julian and Eve. They had the same rooms at the Windsor Hotel, the view of the harbour, the liberation from the expectations of home, the same sense of being happy.

It was difficult to dismiss their relationship as a torrid affair. They had loved each other for more than a decade. But in London Harold squirmed when he heard his sexual intimacies turned to gossip and more reports of Julian and Eve. 'It drives me from the haunts of man and woman,' he wrote, and was glad to get back to Paris. He spoke both of divorce and of forgiving Vita everything.

Mrs Keppel was angry with Denys. Violet was his responsibility. She bought a house for them called Stonewall Cottage, at Langton Green, Tunbridge Wells, fifteen miles from Long Barn. She directed that when Denys got leave, on 15 December, he should go to the South of France, collect Violet, take her to this cottage and keep her there.

Violet wanted to leave him stranded on the Riviera and flee with Vita to Greece, Africa, anywhere. Vita would not do this. She said she must sort matters out with Harold. When that was done in six weeks' time, at the beginning of February 1920, she and Violet would elope together for real and start their new life, the choice made, the wavering over.

But to Harold she wrote on 5 December that, though it was impossible for her to have sex with him, she loved him so deeply it could not be uprooted by this other love, 'more tempestuous and altogether on a different plane'. The whole thing was, she said, the most awful tragedy. A 'very great force' had made her risk going away with Violet, she could not bear to think of her as married to Denys, but she was going to give her up 'for ever'.

'Vita is back with her hair short,' Lady Sackville wrote in her diary on 18 December:

> . . . I said nothing as she looked lovely all the same, and I was glad to have her back. She has been so nice to Harold all day and stayed with him all the time. She told me of her gambling in Monte Carlo and we hardly talked of VT. She does not look a bit sad, which surprises me.

Vita returned to Long Barn, to finding a new governess for her children and to seeing her publisher, Collins, about the publication of *Challenge*.

Violet spent Christmas at Crichel and Polesden Lacey with her husband and mother. On 6 January, sustained by the secret plan to fly away with Vita at the beginning of February, she moved with Denys into Stonewall Cottage. She felt guilty at the thought of only being there three weeks. Mrs Keppel had paid for the furniture and servants. 'I feel I ought to give her back the money. Mercifully she got it very cheap – *Quelle triste farce!*'

A week later Violet told Denys of her elopement plan. He asked for a meeting with Vita, who felt like a young man wanting to marry, being interviewed by the father. He was 'very quiet and business-like and looked like death'. He asked her how much money she had to keep Violet. He and Mrs Keppel would provide nothing. He asked Violet if she wanted to renounce 'everything' – marriage, relationship with her family, house, income, place in society – to go away with Vita.

Violet saw that she was trapped between three perils: the life her mother had chosen for her which she did not want; the life with Vita which she had no conviction Vita would sustain, and social isolation if she chose to be alone. She did not give an answer but asked for a week to think it through.

Four days later she asked Vita if they could leave at once. Vita told Harold. He had had an abscess on his knee and was on sick leave from Paris at his parents' house in Cadogan Gardens. He wept. His mother, Lady Carnock, who looked troubled and wispy without her false hair-piece, begged Vita to think again. 'I felt blackened,' Vita wrote, 'and felt my alienation from them and my affinity with Violet so keenly that I wanted to fly where I would not pollute their purity any longer.' So it was Violet who was black and evil. But she sent white lilac to Vita of the sort they had picked in Polperro. Vita went alone to a hotel room. The next day she told Violet she would be spending a fortnight with Harold at Knole. At the end of that time she might or might not go away with her.

In the familiar world of Knole with her children and father, no mention was made of feelings or the scarlet adventurer. When she and Harold parted they exchanged letters: 'I know you can do anything with me,' Vita wrote,

> you can touch my heart like no one, no one, no one . . . and I try to *make* you fight for yourself, but you never will; you just say, 'Darling Mar!' and leave me to invent my own conviction out of your silence . . .
>
> If I were you, and you were me, I would battle so hard to keep you.

And Harold replied from Paris that he missed her all the time, wanted her all the time, would despair without her, could never love or be happy with anyone else, that he could not formulate in words how much he loved her, let alone express it.

So Vita reaffirmed her family life and then, with Harold back in Paris, continued the adventure. She and Violet were to visit Lincoln because Vita was writing a book about the Fen country. From there they would cross the Channel, go to Sicily, buy a house and live together for ever. Or so Violet liked to think. Though the fantasy was wearing thin and Vita's divided allegiance plain, she put all her desperate and disorganized hopes into this frail plan.

The night before she parted from Denys, in what she intended as a permanent separation from him, they had some kind of desperate sexual exchange. 'It was a sort of price to pay; I don't know, but I think he looked upon it as such too.' The following day in South Street, Lincoln, she tried to tell Vita about it. But Vita did not want to hear. For Violet this journey was to be her allegiance to and defence of love, the flouting of marriage, convention and society's ties. She took great risks for it. 'Test after test is applied to my love and test after test is vanquished triumphantly,' she wrote.

They prepared their luggage. Violet gave Vita the money she had saved for the Sicilian house. On 8 February, the evening before they left, Denys delivered a letter to Violet at their Liverpool Street hotel. In writing he advised her of the social destruction her plans would cause. Vita tried to persuade her to cancel the journey and stay with him. Violet refused.

At Dover, at Vita's instigation, Violet went on ahead across the Channel. 'She seemed to think he would mind that less,' Vita wrote. Violet was afraid of making the journey alone. She had never travelled without at least the company of her maid. She was to go to Amiens and Vita would join her the following day. On shore, Vita watched the boat sail out of sight. She then booked in at the Kings Head Hotel and called for help from all those who wanted her affair with Violet to end. She sent telegrams to Harold, her mother, her father, wires that led to a rescue network.

Denys arrived soon after Violet had gone. He and Vita agreed to cross the Channel together the following day. Vita then wrote to Harold saying she had done everything she could to make Violet return to Denys:

> she refused so positively; she said she would never live with him even if I did not exist. I will try to make her, I will, I will, I will;

I will only see her in front of Denys and he shall see that I will try.

... O God, O God, how miserable and frightened I am - and if she refuses, he says he will never have anything to do with her again ...

If she consents and goes with him I shall come to you ... I want so dreadfully to be with her and I cannot *bear* to think of her being with him, but I shall try to make her.

How terrified she will be when she sees me arrive with him ...

How worried you will be by all this ...

O darling, it's awfully lonely here.

I must write to BM [her mother] now and Dada.

By so doing Vita extricated herself from responsibility for Violet and forced Harold and all of them to fight for her. At Lady Sackville's urgent call Harold left Paris for London. George Keppel 'in a white rage' went to Sir Neville Macready, head of Scotland Yard, and asked him to have all the ports watched and to detain his daughter.

Vita and Denys crossed the Channel together. They got on curiously well. Denys said they could not complain that life was dull. The weather was stormy. At Calais they went to the buffet for lunch. Violet found them there. She was trembling, pale and had not eaten or slept for twenty-four hours. She had been to Amiens, left her luggage at the Hôtel du Rhin, then returned to Calais desperate to meet Vita off the boat. They all ate chicken and champagne, booked in at a hotel and next day motored to Boulogne and took the t...in to Amiens.

On the train Denys wrote on a scrap of paper that he knew Violet's mind was made up and he would leave her at Amiens. Vita moved to an adjacent carriage. Denys cried. It was for him another exercise in humiliation. At Amiens he took the next train to Paris, then returned to London. Violet and Vita went to their hotel and Vita spent more time telephoning and telegraphing, so that everyone should know precisely where she was.

Next day, while she waited for rescue, they looked at Amiens and the devastation of war: stained-glass windows in the cathedral broken and boarded up, windowless houses, shelled roads. First to arrive was George Keppel. 'He was pompous, theatrical and unimpressive. He stormed at us and it was all we could do to keep from laughing.' He stood guard and wired to Denys to come at once.

At Grosvenor Street it was arranged that Denys, who was perhaps tired of trains and boats, should pilot a two-seater plane back to Amiens at 7 a.m. on the morning of 14 February. He was to keep Violet out of England. He must take her to Vichy, Nîmes, Toulon, Nice, anywhere away from scandal, Vita, Sonia's marriage chances and society's gaze.

Harold arrived at his mother's house from Paris. Lady Sackville called at Grosvenor Street, 'interviewed' Denys and asked him to take Harold to Amiens too. The drama caught her imagination. She wrote in her diary:

> Denys was very cool and collected, and fully determined to bring
> Violet back or have done with her. I have been thinking all day
> of those two husbands flying to Amiens to try and each get his
> wife back; quite like a sensational novel.

The two husbands got to Amiens in a couple of hours. Harold, in an endeavour to be assertive, ordered Vita to pack which at his order she refused to do. Denys looked pale and ill. Violet told him she loathed him. He stared at her in silence. She then went to the restaur:..t and ordered coffee for herself. Harold, up in the bedroom, asked Vita, 'Are you sure Violet is as faithful to you as she makes you believe? Because Denys has told your mother quite a different story.'

At that point Vita lost control. Here was both her excuse for liberation from Violet and the focus of her obsession. The idea unleashed her rage about sexual possession. 'Violet is *mine*,' she had said. She scarcely cared whether her mother's testimony was true or false or what the question implied. She raged at Denys: 'have you ever been really married to Violet?' – meaning had he had sex with her? He gave an evasive reply.

She went into the restaurant and challenged Violet. There was a scene and screaming. Colonel Keppel could not have liked it and the hotel staff must have wondered about English aristocrats. Denys held Violet while Vita rushed upstairs and packed not at Harold's request but in response to the betrayal by Violet she chose to perceive. She had her justification for leaving with Harold.

She kissed Violet publicly, though Harold and Denys tried to stop her, then she and Harold took the train to Paris. George Keppel was on the same train. His mission seemingly accomplished, he was going on to St Moritz to join Alice for a winter holiday. Harold and Vita booked in at the Paris Ritz and, while they ate their evening meal – Vita could only manage the soup – Violet and Denys arrived.

Harold did not want another public scene and asked Violet and Vita to talk upstairs. There, Violet described such sex as had occurred between her and Denys. She said it had been against her will. Denys came in. Vita questioned him. He replied, 'This must never go further than this room; I promise you that there has never been anything of that kind between Violet and me.'

But Vita needed her excuse to leave with Harold and not be responsible for Violet. She told her she could not bear to see her for two months. 'Two months and what then?' Violet was to write. The answer was more of the same if she could take it. To Harold Vita said she would have killed her unless she left. 'She calls it banishment – it is not. It is simply the impossibility of bringing myself to see her or the present.'

To Denys Vita gave Violet's money for the house in Sicily. He passed it back to his wife: 'How *could* you give it back to him? It kills me to see it in my purse' Violet was later to write.

Thus the affair, though postponed, could continue. Vita would not have to live with Violet but nor had she let her go. She kept Harold, the children, Long Barn. Violet stayed married to Denys. She was his responsibility. This context, reinforced, was anguish for Violet and

Denys. They were again in each other's sole company, all the fraudulence of their marriage clear, ostracized from society, with nothing in common and nowhere to go. That night Violet wrote a despairing letter to Vita:

I am simply dazed and sodden with pain . . .

There has NEVER never never in my life been any attempt at what you thought from that person. *Never* — He said his pride wouldn't allow him to say more, and he particularly doesn't want anyone to know, but O Mitya, I do swear — may I die tonight — that there has never been anything of that nature and scarcely anything of the other. I loathe having to write this, but what I told you this evening is exactly true down to the minutest detail . . . O my beloved, I feel there has never been sorrow or pain or suffering for me till now.

Next day she and Denys motored south on another journey to nowhere. 'Every day L telephones to me from various provincial towns in France on her way south,' Vita wrote, 'and every day her voice is a little fainter.' Violet wrote again and again on the issue of sex with Denys:

Oh my darling, my darling, you *mustn't* call me faithless, you mustn't — *it's not that*. O my God, if only I could tell you the circumstances very fully of that horrible evening . . . It was a sort of price to pay; I don't know, but I think he looked upon it as such too; he was *never* like that before, and O Mitya, it *wasn't* consummated — I know how awful it is for me to tell you all this, but the reality was so very far from you — what you shrink from — if only he could have brought himself to tell you more, namely that he desisted . . .

She wrote to Lady Sackville saying she was heartbroken. Vita wrote too. 'I try so hard to understand,' Lady Sackville wrote in her diary. 'If VT was a man I could understand. But for a woman, such a love beats me.'

Such a love beat Vita's readers too. In Paris she received proofs of *Challenge*. When she returned to London, her mother, Mrs Keppel and the writer Mrs Belloc Lowndes were adamant that publication should not proceed because it would provoke gossip. 'I *can't* give it up. BM asks too much,' Vita wrote. 'Vita is plucky about her bitter disappointment when Mrs Lowndes told her about the scandal it would create,' Lady Sackville wrote in her diary. Violet was disbelieving when news reached her that the book was to be pulped. It had been printed but not bound. This was another betrayal, another capitulation:

> You can't seriously mean it. It would be idiotic. The book is quite admirable. Ten times better than *Heritage*. Don't relent, sigh or soften. It's absurd, disloyal to me, and useless.

Vita told Collins, her publisher, that she was unhappy with the book's literary quality. Her mother paid them £150 to cover costs. 'I hope Mama is pleased,' Vita wrote in her diary. 'She has beaten me.'

These Mamas were hard to defy. Though their example was not always wise, nor their counsel always clear, they had power over their daughters' lives. The book had variously been called *Rebellion*, *Endeavour*, *Enchantment*, *Vanity*, *Challenge*. But *Conformity* won the day. It, like the whole affair, was suppressed. The 999 out of every thousand need hear no whisper of noxious practices.

Life went on, in Paris, London and Long Barn. In March, Harold gave Vita a cocker spaniel for her birthday. Sonia became formally engaged to Roland. She gave him cufflinks, he gave her a ruby and diamond ring and a little diamond star to pin in her hat. Lady Ashcombe allowed them now to dine alone together and to motor unaccompanied to stay with friends.

THIRTEEN

Violet and Denys were spinning in a circle of despair. Events now had a momentum of their own. A year on from their marriage they re-enacted their honeymoon: jilted elopement, the Paris Ritz, joyless travel and separate hotel rooms, all financed by Mrs Keppel.

They alternated between rows and silence. For two days they did not speak to each other except about the luggage. 'I would sooner be with Men Chinday or Papa than with him,' Violet said. Denys wept, destroyed the novel he was writing and longed equally to be elsewhere.

She thought she would drive to Toulon, leave Denys and meet up with Pat Dansey. 'Pat is a powerful ally,' she wrote to Vita. 'Pat will take me away. But if everything fails and you won't come to me I must kill myself.'

At Fontainebleau Denys was ill with chest and joint pains and fever. He was breaking down. Violet told him she could not look after him, he must go to his sister Elizabeth. Mindful of the carnage of the war he said his life now was worse than anything that had gone before. At the Hôtel du Rivage, Gien, he cried at dinner then went to his room. The chauffeur went out for quinine and aspirin. Denys's tuberculosis, undiagnosed, was exacerbated by being gassed in Flanders, ...dless cigarettes and the ghastliness of his emotional life. His vulnerability made Violet despise him more,

> he does nothing but cry and whimper: it fills me with repulsion, and I can't conceal it. My obsession is to get away from him *côute que côute*. . . . He has ceased to be anything but my jailor, and I look at him and think: yes, if it wasn't for you.

If it was not for Denys, Violet liked to suppose, she would be with

180

Vita. As they drove through France she sat in the back of the car, staring from the window, never speaking to him, urging the driver to go ever faster. 'We crash over impossible roads, this morning we killed a dog – poor thing! After that we went faster than ever.' They drove south via Allier, Vichy, Le Puy. On 19 February, at the Hôtel de Beaujolais in Vichy, Denys told her he hated being with her and when he had handed her over to Pat Dansey, or whoever would have her, he would extricate himself from this hell and go away for good.

At Nîmes next evening Violet pleaded a headache and said she must sleep. In bed, she wrote – as ever – to Vita. Denys saw the light, put his head round the door and accused her of lying. She said what she did was no business of his:

> He yelled: 'I hate you. I hate you! I'm going to get even with you for all your deceit. I'm going to make you as unhappy as you've made me. I'm going to ruin your life as you've ruined mine!'

He could not cope with this chaos. Without telling Violet he wired to Mrs Keppel. Five days later when they arrived at Toulon she was there. She had travelled with George from St Moritz and now she held hectic interviews with them both.

Both told her they wanted an annulment. That was out of the question, she said. A façade of marriage must be kept intact. They must go away together, she would pay for it all. They could go round the world for a year, or to Jamaica, or Ragusa, or she would arrange for them to stay in Tangier with the painter Sir John Lavery (who had been at the Knebworth house party with Harold and Vita in 1918). Violet, she said, could stay only a fortnight with Pat Dansey, who was at the Villa Primavera at Bordighera with her partner Joan Campbell. Then she must travel with Denys.

Denys persisted. He felt he had been tricked and he wanted divorce. His terms, he said, would be an unconsummated marriage and the 'undue influence' of Vita – terms likely to cause a social hum. Mrs Keppel passed responsibility to him. She warned that if he separated from Violet she would give her an allowance of £600 a year and have nothing else to do with her emotionally or financially. She was going to write to Vita but would not say what about. She would call her lawyer in England. Violet would need a medical examination to prove she was a virgin. (Given her history with Vita it is unclear what such scrutiny would have shown.)

Next day, 25 February, Mrs Keppel was more determined, less concessional. She saw Denys alone. If he insisted on annulment she would not speak to Violet again, or let her inside the Grosvenor Street house, or give her any money at all. Denys had no money of his own and was to leave the army at the beginning of April. At first he insisted he wanted an annulment whatever the consequences. Under pressure he capitulated and said he would take Violet away rather than see her punished so entirely.

He must, her mother said, take her to Tangier for two months while gossip cooled. It was arranged with Sir John Lavery. After that he could return to England with her only if they lived in a house out of town. She then saw Violet who told her that she loathed Denys. Mrs Keppel conceded the marriage had been a 'hideous mistake', but it was done, it was an agreement, it was binding and necessary.

Things were done much better in her day. Her main concern was to keep Violet married, out of England and away from scandal while Sonia's marriage plans were sealed. Despite the engagement, Lord and Lady Ashcombe, were still dismayed about their son's choice of wife. They hated the marriage 'because of Little Mrs George and a¹. that'. They were, said Vita, 'very old-fashioned and apt to cut up rusty at any provocation'. This latest débâcle would, Mrs Keppel feared, spoil Sonia's chances.

Maggie Greville, Sonia's godmother, had already intervened. Friend to royalty, statesmen, foreign ambassadors and all true aristocrats, she went uninvited to Denbies, the Cubitt estate, two miles from Polesden Lacey. Formally dressed and in her Rolls-Royce with footman and chauffeur, she asked to speak to Ashcombe but refused to go into the house. When he came out she said, 'I only called to tell you that I do not consider that your son is good enough for my god-daughter.'

Ashcombe asked for a meeting with George Keppel to discuss the marriage settlement. He arrived at Grosvenor Street to find Mrs Keppel alone. Unused to financial acumen in women – he gave his wife 'pin money' and paid all household expenses himself – he was off guard. Mrs Keppel said, 'If we give Sonia a certain figure, will you give Roland the same?' Stung by the amount she proposed, he said he hoped this expensive marriage would last. 'My dear Lord Ashcombe, neither you nor I can legislate for eternity,' Mrs Keppel replied.

But she could legislate for the present. Her instructions given to Violet and Denys, she returned to St Moritz and the bridge tables. 'She can't ever have been in love herself or she wouldn't treat me like that,' Violet wrote to Vita.

Alone with Denys, Violet made as if to jump out of a window but he restrained her. He saw that she was no more than her mother's child, felt sorry for her and the mess she was in. He apologized for having summoned her mother and for not annulling the marriage. He said he had agreed to her mother's demands for Sonia's sake. He felt he had betrayed Violet and he wrote her a note:

I know that just lately I have not deserved your trust. I will not undeserve it again.

Don't take *that* away too. Even if you must hate me, try just now to be a little generous and give me back the last vestige that remained to me of anything I cared for.

I will not fail you again in that way. I will try and earn your trust again anyway – even if it comes with your hatred.

I know there is nothing *immediately* that I can do for you. But if you feel that in future you can at least *trust* me – it may help a tiny bit.

He would, like George Keppel, have been a complaisant husband had Violet done things in her mother's style. But she scorned him

and spun like a moth into the flame of her obsession with Vita. She
asked if he thought Vita loved her or Harold more. He shrugged, said
he did not know, but that in his view Vita had shunned the elopement
pact not because of Violet's 'infidelity', but out of a primary commitment to Harold.

Pat Dansey did not want to be held responsible for Violet. She was
going to Venice with Joan Campbell. Each year they went on long
holidays financed by Joan, whose father was the fourth son of the
eighth Duke of Argyll. Joan was scholarly, gentle, published volumes
of verse, won the *Country Life* crossword several times and lived with
her mother in Strachur Castle in Scotland and in Bryanston Square
in London. Pat disliked the idea of Violet tagging along with her and
Joan, pining for Vita. She sent telegrams and letters to Vita on Violet's
behalf, urging her to come and sort something out. 'I am afraid this
constant telegraphing is leading to bad muddles,' she wrote. 'What on
earth you both will arrange in the future beats me.'

Violet was on her own. 'I could not be more maligned and shunned
than I am at present,' she wrote to Vita. 'I am really just as cut off
from my family now as I would have been if I had run away with
you.' Unable to look after herself, unused to doing so and ever more
distracted, she had her money stolen and lost her jewellery — frequent
occurrences throughout her life. Most people, including Sonia, cut
her dead. Former friends would not be seen in public with her. One
received a letter from Lady Sackville saying 'that arch-fiend Violet has
been trying to upset the Nicolsons' marriage'.

'There is no Phoenix,' Violet wrote to Vita. She said her contempt
for compromise, her ambition to dedicate her life to Vita, art and
beauty was the best part of her and it had all turned to ashes:

> I am sick with longing for our old life. I don't think we shall
> ever be allowed to be happy again, ever in our lives.

She and Denys had rows at the Villa Primavera. He burned Vita's
letters, she burned the book he was trying to write. He found the pact
between them impossible and moved out to a hotel in Monte Carlo

where his friend Nancy Cunard was staying. She had short hair, wore short skirts, frequented nightclubs, drank, danced, wrote, had an affair with Henry Crowder, a black pianist. Mrs Keppel spent her days at the casino. It was as if she was gambling for a more abstract luck than money. Denys told her he returned to the villa in the evenings but she did not believe him. Violet felt guilt at her mother's distress. Pat Dansey wrote on 15 March:

Darling, I saw your mother in the Casino yesterday – she does look so ill – worried and sad. And she is quite miserable over the whole beastly business. Cannot anything be done to arrange things without this horrible disgrace? Won't Denys change his mind?

Darling, I was so sorry for your mother. She does mind quite dreadfully.

Oh, Violet, what a hash you have made of things *and all for one person.* You fling all your real friends to the wind – not to speak of your wretched family. How often, darling, have I told you no good would come if you persisted in your downward path. I know, child, you are miserable. So are your friends . . .

Your mother is a brave woman and I admire the courage she displays amongst this fire of hateful gossip. She is a proud woman, and it is hateful for her.

Make Vita promise that her mother shall never tell tales to your mother.

Wanting some kind of reparation, Violet drove to St Moritz to see her mother. Mrs Keppel would not speak to her, told her she planned to go with Sonia to Spain, said she did not give a damn what Violet did provided Denys safeguarded the money she had invested in the marriage. Violet gambled flamboyantly, lost ten thousand francs in one session, five thousand in another. Her mother had managed the roles of mistress and wife with profit and style. Violet managed none of it. She saw the chaos she was in, and worst of all that Love, which she called 'the greatest prize' had become

a debased crippled crafty thing of furtive pleasures and false
generosities, of mean impulses and starved understanding. But to
my mind the worst thing of all is its flagrant, its crushing hypocrisy.
Under our skilful perversion – *not only ours but other people round us* –
cowardice becomes prudence, selfishness is called love, misleading
evasions are supposed to be 'kindness', meanness, blindness and
jealousy are all different manifestations of 'love'. Mind you, I blame
myself every bit as much as I blame you – and I blame our circumstances more than anything. It is impossible for any love to expand
healthily under such circumstances . . . How can one make the
best of anything that revolves on lies and deception?

Behind her obsession and panic she tried to keep a clarity of feeling
and intention, a single-minded belief in the indivisibility of sex, love and
commitment. 'I am singularly pure, uncontaminated, and high prin-
cipled,' she wrote to Vita. 'You will laugh *but it is true*.' She was also, on
her own admission, unable to see anyone else's point of view. Pat Dansey
urged her to seek reconciliation with Denys. But Violet could not extricate herself from Vita, who only sometimes answered the barrage of
letters, phone calls and telegrams she received. She wrote that she was
'not in a state to consider anything now'. For herself, she said, she 'craved
solitude'. She dwelt on Violet's perceived infidelity:

Before I had always buoyed myself with the thought that
although she might hold no other moral precept, at least she
was whole-hearted and true where she did love.

In her love for Vita, Violet was whole-hearted and true, though
unrewarded for it. And it was never a 'moral precept' Vita held. Her
sexual jealousy persisted – towards Denys and Pat Dansey – and her
demand that only by sexual fidelity to her could Violet be of worth.
She implied Violet was jealous of Denys being with Nancy Cunard,
but Violet could not have cared less who he was with.

Vita wanted to see her but spoke no more of a shared life. When
Violet became histrionic, Vita was dry and impatient. When Vita was

dry and impatient, Violet became histrionic. She answered neither yes nor no to Violet's obsession about meeting. Violet accused her of being 'up to her old game' of equivocation. 'How delicious it would be' Vita said in one taunting letter, 'to spend a few days in Italy together.' Her preferred option though would be for Violet to come to England, as Harold was in France, which was forbidden except in Denys's company. 'You have told me all along how you *hated* me being with DT and now you are deliberately suggesting I should return to him.'

She said Vita had played her a 'dirty trick'. She could not tolerate the thought of going back to Grosvenor Street, 'that poisonous Grosvenor Street, that hated, watched and restricted existence'. Her other option was to be with Denys. He had to go to England in late March to finalize his discharge from the army. She would return with him simply to see Vita,

> but if ever you dare say one word of jealousy, or attempt one single row with me because *owing to your own silly fault* I am with Denys, I will clear out of that pestilential country and you shan't set eyes on me again . . . I *hate* England, I hate that life with all my heart and soul. If I wasn't such a fool as to *love you as I do* wild horses wouldn't drag me there . . .
>
> Never say I don't love you, if I have to travel across Europe sitting bolt upright, to England which I detest, braving the fury of my mother, merely to catch a glimpse of you! *Je t'adore* . . .

At the end of March, after a six-week separation, Vita joined Violet in Avignon. Within hours they were quarrelling about commitment and its meaning. They motored to the Villa Primavera, there were rows all the way. Violet had jaundice, 'a most unromantic complaint' Vita said. They travelled on to Italy with Pat Dansey and Joan Campbell and there were, said Pat, 'scenes and storms'. At San Remo Vita promised Violet, wearily and without conviction, that they would stay together:

L. [Lushka] horrible to me all day and makes me very miserable and exasperated. After dinner I lose my head and say I will stay with her. Paradise restored.

It was a hollow promise and a fetid paradise. A week later Vita told her it was all impossible. She would be followed and brought back if she tried to stay with her. 'It is horrible,' Vita wrote in her diary. 'She is in the depths. So am I. I feel the Grand Canal in spite of slime and floating onions would be preferable.'

A complicity grew up between her and Pat Dansey. Ostensibly Pat was Violet's 'powerful ally', a 'saint to them both' in their trials. But she was attracted to Vita and to the passion she inspired in Violet. She switched allegiance. 'All through those scenes and storms at Bordighera and Venice I was working entirely on your side,' she wrote to her some weeks later. She urged Violet to stay with Denys, asked Vita to trust and confide in her:

My dear, I worry for you as much as for Violet, more perhaps for you than for her . . . I would be gratified to feel you knew you could speak about anything which troubles you in tangles with Violet . . . all I shall ever want is to see you both happy.

After three weeks Vita returned to England. Violet, entirely distressed, wanted to stay abroad alone. Vita said she could not allow it, that she would not be safe from thieves and that they must travel back together. 'I saw the sort of life she would lead, ranging from hotel to hotel, quite irresponsible and horribly lonely.' By mid April, Violet was back in Grosvenor Street. She wrote of feeling terrified. Her mother's world closed around her: the world of Grosvenor Street, where a king might come for tea and politicians for supper, where it was as *de rigueur* for a daughter to have a husband as it was for husbands to shoot grouse and deer, play bridge, have titles, fields and servants. 'In the Middle Ages,' she wrote to Vita, 'when people did things that the community didn't understand they were instantly burned at the stake for being sorcerers and witches.'

The injustice of their twin positions oppressed her.

How can you expect me not to find it unjust? It's as though two people had been caught stealing, but one is put in prison and the other is not. The one who is in prison can't help feeling the injustice . . .

Vita, she saw, would not change. Sex was exciting and essential, 'a very great force', but she was not going to live openly with a woman. After Violet she always had women lovers. They stayed in the wings, a private matter, and did not disturb her writing, marriage, gardening, house renovation or reputation.

Violet for her part struggled alone with Vita's equivocation and a society that required her to conceal her love. She was ostracized and panic-smitten. Her mother stayed abroad a further month with Sonia. When she returned she would not speak to Violet. George Keppel wanted Violet out of Grosvenor Street and to go there only by invitation. In letters to Vita, Violet returned to her key theme of social hypocrisy. 'What a dreadful thing is marriage,' she wrote:

I think it is the wickedest thing in the universe. Think of the straight, clean lives it has ruined by forcing them to skulk and hide and intrigue and scheme, making of love a thing to be hidden and lied about . . . It is a wicked institution . . .

It has ruined my life, it has ruined Denys's – he would give his soul never to have married. It has ruined – not *your* life, but our happiness . . .

Ever since I was a child I have loved you. Lesser loves have had greater rewards – you don't know what you have been – what you are to me: just the force of life, just the *raison d'être*.

She moved with Denys into the Dower House, Sonning-on-Thames, but described the house as small, claustrophobic and haunted. Vita hated it too. 'Hate seeing her in her own house – hate the hypocrisy of it.' Denys told Violet he intended to please himself in all things, she had done nothing to please him, he would do nothing to please her. She feared if he left her she would be entirely alone and that if she angered him he would 'estrange me from my mother for the rest of my days'.

Harold did not want Violet at Long Barn. Denys did not see why, if that was so, Vita should visit the Dower House. When Violet banished him so Vita could spend the night with her, he stayed at Grosvenor Street and threatened to give Mrs Keppel the reason. Vita lost the ring Violet had given her and felt miserable and superstitious about it.

She went sailing in mid-May with her father and Harold on the Sackville yacht *Sumurun*. 'I can't bear to think of you in a boat on the sea with Harold,' Violet wrote. 'It makes me quite frantic — the enforced intimacy.' Harold went back to Paris and Vita booked in with Violet for two nights at a hotel in Sonning, near the Dower House.

Denys talked to Violet of killing himself. Mrs Keppel criticized him, so he kept away from her. He again wrote to her saying he wanted to end the marriage. Violet called him a 'mercenary humbug', accused him of saying awful things about her mother but when confronted by her 'making up to her for all he was worth'. To Lady Sackville he said Violet was a liar, terrified of her mother, fond of money and social success. At a dance given by Lord Farquhar of Castle Rising, Kings Lynn, in June, he told Violet her mother had put a clause in her will disinheriting her unless she had a child. Mrs Keppel, he said, had willed most of her fortune to Sonia and the residue to him. In front of guests Violet called him 'the most ill-mannered swine that ever walked the face of the earth', asked for the key to the Dower House, which he refused her, and rushed out in her evening clothes.

She felt continually unwell, suffered palpitations, fainted at the Ritz and had all the symptoms of acute anxiety. Her doctor said she had an 'irritable' heart, advised rest, giving up smoking, a cure at Evian. She craved sleep in the day and at night woke bathed in sweat. On her birthday, 6 June, she received no card from Vita, no present from Denys. 'I am twenty-six, *passée*, futile, pointless and — letterless.' She still pleaded with Vita to choose: 'You can't do "*la navette*" any longer. We must have a "*situation nette*".' But she knew Vita had chosen.

Vita said their love had become 'debased and corrupt' and she could not trust her. Violet replied,

> O Mitya, you can trust me, you must have seen what is at the bottom of everything – an incorrigible, insatiable longing to be with you – no matter where, no matter when.

In mid-July Violet had 'a momentous interview' at Grosvenor Street with Denys and her mother. Mrs Keppel insisted she stop seeing Vita until Sonia was married. Denys said that after that unless she lived with him as his wife 'in the fullest sense of the term' he would dissolve the marriage. There was a scene and Violet left the house. Vita was on holiday in the Beacon Hotel, Hindhead, longing to go home to Long Barn and peace, but Violet 'was so distressed and seedy' she felt she had to be with her.

There was no way out for Violet. All her relationships were in chaos. Pat Dansey said gossip had reached its pitch, no decent person would have her in the house. George Keppel maintained his refusal to speak to her and always went out of the room if she entered. He burned letters to her from Vita. Her mother wrote to say that if she tried to separate from Denys

> I fear the scandal would be very great and you would be the laughing stock of the country, becoming Miss Keppel again . . . Even if you went for 6 months with Mrs Nicolson I could have nothing more to do with you.

Provided Violet did not go off with Vita she would agree to an nnulment after Sonia's wedding. She would have to stay away for five or six years 'to live it down'. Mrs Keppel would take her to Jamaica and leave her there with a small allowance and Moiselle as a maid.

Violet lost all hope of continuing to live in England. 'I know you realize how intensely and devastatingly I mind about my mother,' she wrote to Vita:

> I could not live in the same country as she was, to say nothing of Sonia, knowing that by living either with you (which would

191

end in disaster) or near you, I will be insulting her more and more irrevocably, and making her hate me more and more each day. There is nothing to be gained and everything to lose by remaining in England.

Vita longed for peace. She wanted to go to Albania with Harold in August but Violet made such a fuss she cancelled. She finished her novel, set in Lincolnshire, *The Dragon in Shallow Waters*. Harold worked in Paris on the Treaty of St Germain and a biography of the poet, Paul Verlaine. He was having an affair with Jean de Gaigneron, a socialite who painted pictures, said witty things, had sex with lots of men and introduced him to Proust and Cocteau. 'Jean is a nice friend for Hadji,' Harold wrote to Vita, 'as he knows all the clevers'. In late July he came with him to England. 'Can you arrange with BM for Jean to sleep at Hill Street with me (!!) on Friday night?' he wrote to Vita.

While Harold was with Jean de Gaigneron, Vita began her autobiographical 'confession', published fifty years later by her son as *Portrait of a Marriage*. She began writing lying in the grounds of Long Barn 'in the margin between a wood and a ripe cornfield':

Having written it down I shall be able to trust no one to read it; there is only one person in whom I have such utter confidence that I would give every line of this confession into his hands, knowing that after wading through this morass — for it is a morass, my life, a bog, a swamp, a deceitful country, with one bright patch in the middle, the patch that is unalterably his — I know that after wading through it all he would emerge holding his estimate of me steadfast. This would be the test of my confidence, from which I would not shrink. I would not give it to *her* — perilous touchstone! . . .

Neither the bright patch nor the perilous touchstone ever got to read it. And though actions showed how swamp-like and deceitful a country her relationship with Violet now was, she still did not say, emphatically and categorically that no, they would never be together.

They planned another 'escape' for after Sonia's wedding and snatched five days when Harold was in Paris and Mrs Keppel away. Vita wrote to say how this time together disturbed her and how she despised herself for shillyshallying. 'Darling, it's true I'm afraid what you say,' Violet replied. 'You are neither fish, fowl, nor good red herring.'

At times Violet and Denys made the social effort. Sonia and her fiancé called at the Dower House. Roland Cubitt found Violet alarming and teased her to conceal his apprehension. He and Denys talked of horses. Sonia thought Denys impossibly reserved and felt 'submitted to some form of kit inspection' by him.

In private the Trefusis marriage grew worse by the day. Denys checked Violet's alibis about going to the ballet or being alone, twisted her wrist to make her say, 'Goodnight darling', hit her on the side of the head for saying she was devoted to Pat Dansey, took more of Vita's letters from the drawer of her writing table and burned them. Violet told him she could not stand living with him any more and was looking for a flat for herself. He went out with other women, but she said she did not mind his 'Jeannes and Yvonnes'.

He became ill and was put to bed in the blue room of the Dower House with a temperature of 103°F, an infected throat and visits three times a day from the doctor. His sister Betty, a theosophist with golden hair who was writing a novel, came to stay and look after him. His condition alarmed her. Her own husband had been killed at Gallipoli leaving her to care alone for their small children. He was posthumously awarded the Victoria Cross for his courage.

Mrs Keppel worked to give Sonia a dashing start to married life. The wedding was fixed for 15 November. They shopped for clothes:

> three dozen nightgowns, petticoats, bodices, chemises, knickers, stockings, handkerchiefs, gloves. A dozen pairs of evening and day shoes; six pairs of stays . . . a pink satin peignoir trimmed with ostrich feathers for summer, a quilted blue velvet dressing-gown with a real Valenciennes lace collar, for winter . . . two evening dresses . . . a black velvet square-necked ball dress and a

pink velvet ball dress trimmed with silver lace . . . two tea gowns, one trimmed with Chinese embroidery and the other of billowing chiffon; three day dresses and three afternoon dresses; and three tweed suits and a travelling coat with matching hats and jerseys and shirts . . . a going-away dress of pale blue marocaine, with a skirt cut into petals, topped by a black velvet coat with a grey fox collar, and a grey velvet cap trimmed with ospreys.

In late summer Violet joined her mother at Duntreath. They had a week's remission from their woes. Away from Vita and Denys and in the perfect setting of her childhood Violet was restored. Her mother was happy too, freed from scandal and gossip:

She has been gardening such a lot and cutting down so many trees, she is quite brown and sunburnt. She says she has been so happy here away from everybody. She was so attractive like she was yesterday no one could help loving her.

Instead of being 'hard and inquisitorial and menacing', she was 'kind and humorous and gay'. It was as if the social disaster of the past three years had not happened. She walked the dogs, charmed the neighbours, tended to a dove wounded by a rat:

I couldn't bear Mama a grudge for anything in the world. Whatever she did, she could always be forgiven. There are some people like that. She laughs and jokes . . . Oh! The charmers of this world, what an unfair advantage is given them!

At Duntreath Violet felt calm and free. 'the moment I get away, how gloriously emancipated I feel. I shed certain aspects of my life as easily as a garment . . .' She, too, began to write 'an undraped chronicle of things that actually happened'. It soothed her to write this chronicle, though she had no belief in its merit and it has not survived.

She slipped into the fantasy of her childhood with Vita, the childhood which she could not leave:

You haunt this place . . . How young and happy we were − as

'THINGS WERE DONE MUCH BETTER IN MY DAY'

Mrs Keppel in 1932

‘OH VIOLET WHAT A HASH
YOU HAVE MADE OF THINGS, *AND
ALL FOR ONE PERSON*’

Left: Pat Dansey, Violet's friend — and Vita's

‘HER FACE WAS MORE LIKE A LAND-
SCAPE THAN A FACE, CLOUDY OF HAIR,
BLUE OF EYE, RUGGED OF CONTOUR’

*The Princesse de Polignac,
Violet's lover, after Vita*

Violet in 1932 in the garden of Mrs Keppel's Villa Ombrellino

free as the sparrow hawks that nest on the hill, as shy as the roe
deer that feed on its slopes.

. . . The place is inviolably yours, the lanky, awkward, adorable
you that wrote historical novels and had no sense of humour.
You have changed more than I have, for I haven't changed at
all.

She would have benefited from a long stay there, away from the
muddle she had made. But after a week she sailed with her mother
and Sonia for the Baroness de Brienen's house, Clingendaal, in The
Hague. All the provocations returned. Denys was so ill he had been
sent on ahead. He was to stay in a cottage on the estate. Violet was
not to be out of her mother's sight until Sonia was a bride.

On the Channel crossing Mrs Keppel appropriated Violet's cabin
saying she must not be disturbed. Violet shared with Sonia who snored.
Vita wrote caustically that she supposed Denys would be waiting
impatiently for her. In fact he went for a walk when he knew she was
about to arrive, did not return until lunchtime and evinced no interest
at seeing her. He took all meals except lunch alone in his cottage.
Violet visited only once, when he was out, to borrow a book. He
befriended a guest called Ruby who asked Mrs Keppel if Violet was
going to divorce. Out riding, he lamed one horse and killed another
'by making them jump impossible obstacles'.

He looked emaciated: 'like a wraith, there is nothing of him'. Mrs
Keppel tended to him. 'She fusses far more about him than she has
ever about anyone in her life.' George continued to leave any room
Violet entered and did not address a word to her. 'In some extraordi-
nary way he seems to think that I am responsible for D's complaint.'
Sonia told Violet she could not help despising her both for missing
Vita so much and for the way she had treated and continued to treat
Denys.

Mrs Keppel took long solitary walks and could not, for a moment,
be civil to Violet. 'She is diabolical in her intuitions . . . She knows
exactly what to say to hurt me.' She was scathing to and about her

in front of the guests. The atmosphere of the house was ghastly. Violet felt like a pariah. 'Men Chinday displays the greatest ingenuity in finding fault with me. It amounts almost to genius.' Daisy de Brienen took her cue from Mrs Keppel. Other guests were beloved Archie, the Alingtons, the Harry Lehrs, Lady de Trafford. In the evening they played bridge. Violet stayed alone. There were, she said, no temptations of any kind.

With her mother's party she trailed the sights of Amsterdam and Gouda 'trying to persuade myself that I liked stained glass'. She stayed in the grand hotels of Bruges and Brussels, Ypres and Antwerp, gambled her money, complained about the architecture, cathedrals, brassware, carillons, the Memlings and Van Eycks, the Rubens and the Brueghels. It all sickened her, she said. 'If I can't be a peer of the future, I won't be a vassal of the past.'

She lived with depression, self-dislike, and the failure of love:

This time last year, what a lot there was to look forward to. And now . . . Across my life only one word will be written: 'Waste' — Waste of love, waste of talent, waste of enterprise . . .

She tried to write a novel but felt she had no talent:

I can only feel things. I can't express them. I don't know English well enough, I can't analyse . . . But my chief handicap is that I *cannot* argue! I can only see my side of the question: I am blind to the other person's . . .

In her despair she tried to keep her love for Vita alive. Without this life was too bleak to contemplate:

I love nothing in the world but you . . . not the slightest inflexion of your voice, not the subtlest nuance of your letters, escapes me . . . I got one yesterday that was cold, almost impersonal.

She still wanted to believe that, after Sonia's marriage in November, they might go away together for ever. One morning she tried to talk a little to her mother about her feelings but did not get far.

Mrs Keppel was 'nice on the whole'. She made clear that it was the prospect of scandal more than the relationship itself that affronted her.

The day Violet returned from Holland she met Vita at Paddington. 'It was like two flames leaping together,' Vita said. They drove to the Dower House and spent 'four absolutely unclouded days'. Violet then joined Denys in Brighton. They stayed at the Royal Crescent Hotel but did not speak to each other. She had 'the most *horrible* kind of hallucination' which she said she could not describe on paper. She visited Lady Sackville, who gossiped, which led to a 'scene' between Violet and her mother. 'I know your mother will never ask me inside her house again,' Violet wrote to Vita. 'And I suppose the old antagonism will revive.'

Lady Sackville tried to come to terms with Vita's unorthodox marriage:

she *seems* absolutely devoted to Harold, but there is nothing whatever sexual between them, which is strange in such a young and good-looking couple. She is not in the least jealous of H. and willingly allows him to relieve himself with anyone if such is his want or his fancy. They both openly said so one evening when I was staying at L. Barn and Reggie Cooper was there too. It shocked me.

And Reggie Cooper — a schoolfriend of Harold's — confounded Violet's tarnished fantasy of true escape after Sonia's wedding when he told her of a statue Vita and Harold had bought for £300. 'I know you wouldn't dream of being so foolish as to spend £300 on a statue that you were never going to set eyes on,' Violet wrote on 13 November:

How I wish I was Harold Nicolson! I envy him with every fibre of my body. He can be with you as much as he pleases. His words come back to me 'I have always had everything I wanted' — and I am as the beggar at your gate.

Two weeks before Sonia's wedding the 'royal photographer' Bassano asked to take Mrs Keppel's photograph:

> We have been asked by the Editors of several papers for a new portrait for this purpose and should esteem it a favour if you would give us a complimentary sitting at our studios at an early date . . .

The camera showed her grand appearance. The following week Sonia had an asthma attack and feared Rolie would get impatient with the smell of camphorated oil and Himrod's Inhalation Asthma Cure. Her mother filled her bedroom at Grosvenor Street with flowers. Her father brought her Charbonnel & Walker chocolate peppermint creams. Bessie cleaned her room quietly. Janet drew the curtains and made up the fire. Perriat, the cook, dressed in a white tunic, brought her the menu book and recommended the cream of chicken soup. Frances, the kitchenmaid, suggested pommes soufflés with the pheasant. Rolie brought the weekly illustrated papers and magazines and news of who had phoned and called. Nannie packed for the honeymoon.

Dr Bevan told Sonia she would have to wrap up well for the ceremony. Her 'bachelor girl' party was cancelled, the afternoon gathering to view the presents, organized by her mother and Violet, took place without her.

Her mother gave her a diamond tiara, an emerald and diamond pendant, an eighteenth-century diamond brooch in the shape of a sheaf of wheat and Nannie, who was now to be her maid. Her father gave her a piano and a Georgian writing table. Sir Ernest Cass l gave her a fat cheque. Mrs Keppel said this was vulgar so, to Sonia's regret, it was converted into furs. Violet and Denys gave her two crystal and diamond hatpins, Lord and Lady Ashcombe a turquoise and diamond pendant, Uncle Arnold and Aunt Gertie a Georgian sideboard, Uncle Archie and Aunt Ida nineteenth-century gilt candlesticks, Maggie Greville an emerald ring, the Grand Duke Michael and Countess Torbay a Fabergé snuffbox, Marjorie Jessel and eighty girlfriends a Spode china breakfast, dinner and tea service, Rolphe the butler and the servants at Grosvenor Street a silver salver, Nannie two toast racks in silver plate, each strut forming the letters ROLIE and SONIA.

Her wedding dress was silver lamé. Mrs Keppel wore plum velvet and fox furs, Nannie a black plumed hat and white kid gloves. 'What am I going to do without my Doey?' her father said to her on the way to the church and Sonia silenced him to keep back tears. Ten brides-maids and pages held her train and the band of the 3rd Battalion Coldstream Guards played 'Oh! Perfect Love' as she and Rolie walked down the aisle.

At Christmas Vita sent Violet a fur coat, but her voice was cold on the phone. In January 1921 Violet and she left for two months together in the south of France, in Hyères and Carcassone. Mrs Keppel thought Violet was meeting Pat Dansey and Joan Campbell in Algiers. Violet went on ahead alone to Nîmes so London society would not know that yet again she was travelling with Vita.

FOURTEEN

It was their last journey together. At Carcassone they rented a house with a garden. 'Do you remember our garden in Carcassonne with its enormous latch-key?' They planned to go on to Andorra but were prevented by snow.

Denys packed his possessions, left the Dower House and went home to Devon to be looked after by his mother and sister. In a letter to Harold he said he was seeking legal separation and would have nothing to do with Violet when and if she returned. 'Damn,' Harold wrote in his diary, fearing more scandal, more onus on Vita to be responsible for Violet. Lady Sackville was fearful for Ben and Nigel's sake: 'I don't want them to blush when their mother's name is mentioned.'

Early in February 1921 Harold wired Vita asking a definite date for her return. She wanted 'to stay on a bit', she replied and again as in January 1919 said writing to him was indecent when she was with Violet. He compared her to a jellyfish addicted to cocaine and with equivocal insistence told her to return on Friday 25 February:

> On Saturday we shall go down together to the cottage. So please take your tickets at once. And please also realise that this is definite. I shall be more angry than I have ever been if you do not come back on that date. Don't misunderstand me. I shall really cut adrift if you don't. It is a generous date, it is longer than you promised: but it is a *fixed* date and you must keep to it.

It was not in his nature to be so stern and he added a rider that if the date was inconvenient, then let him know and he would change it. Vita reassured him that though she felt responsible for Violet, which was why she was away, she only really loved him and that would always be the case. 'Wild oats are all very well, but not when they grow as high as a jungle.'

There was no breach in her affection for him. She arrived back on 9 March, her twenty-ninth birthday. Harold thought she looked well. They and the children went to Knole reunited as a family. A few of society's doors, but not many, closed: Mrs Mary Hunt, sister of the lesbian composer Ethel Smyth, asked Lady Sackville not to bring Vita to her house, Hill Hall, because 'the whole thing horrifies me'. Such social snubs were tiresome but made no impact on their lives.

But Violet was in deep trouble. Wild oats had choked her life. She went alone to the Dower House. Mrs Keppel was wintering on the Riviera and in North Africa. Violet asked if she might join her in Tunis but received no reply. Denys did not answer her letters. Mrs Keppel instructed her brother Archie to supervise Violet. He had a three-hour meeting with her. Violet described it as 'simply disastrous'. Her mother and George had said they wished to 'disown' her. Moiselle her governess since childhood, then maid, was to 'act as a sort of gaoler'. Violet was to see no one. All letters from Vita were to be destroyed. Moiselle was to intercept Violet's post and to report back to Mrs Keppel on her every move:

> M'elle never leaves me for one instant. She knows exactly when I go out, when I come in; in fact she nearly always goes out and comes in with me – when I write a letter, when I go upstairs. I might be a criminal . . . I can't have five unspied on minutes even in my own house.

Denys spoke freely in social circles of having left Violet. The Cubitts were said to be furious. Sonia was expecting her first baby in August. Mrs Keppel apprised Violet of the disgrace she had brought to her family. 'Another letter from Men Chinday that simply breaks my heart,' Violet wrote to Vita.

> You are the only thing that stands between me and dissolution.
> How lucky you are to be with somebody who cares for you

201

and is anxious to spare you and shelter you as much as possible.

Socially her position was now impossible. On 11 March she tried to see Denys to see if they could work out some *modus vivendi*. She went by train with Moiselle to Exeter. They hired a car to take them across Dartmoor. It was late, the road was crude, the light dark. A mile from the Trefusises' house, Mitty, Denys's mother, 'with a red lantern, suddenly sprang up from nowhere, barring the road'. She said she had been warned by telegram of the time of Violet's arrival and told the driver to take her back to wherever she had come from. Denys, she said, would have nothing whatsoever to do with her. The driver sniggered, Violet felt humiliated and hit Moiselle who, she felt, goaded her. She believed Vita had sent the telegram. 'You see you were the only person who knew.' If so, it was another of Vita's curiously cruel games.

Denys applied for legal separation. Violet heard from a 'disinterested third person' that he disliked her, that nothing would induce him to set eyes on her, he would not read any communication from her, it was entirely because of her involvement with Vita that he had left her. He said he had the Nicolsons, Keppels and Sackvilles all 'in his power and that if he wanted to he could ruin all our lives'.

On 17 March, at her uncle's insistence, Violet saw a lawyer. He said if he was to act for her she must not communicate with Vita. Vita he had been assured wanted nothing more to do with her. She had returned to family life. Even without Denys's legal proceedings she wanted the relationship to end. It was Violet who made this difficult with her phone calls and letters. These must stop.

Violet panicked at the news, felt faint in the taxi home, was stunned and disbelieving. On 18 March Mrs Keppel travelled back reluctantly from the Riviera to sort out this latest scandal. Violet was remorseful:

My poor mother . . . I would far rather she hadn't come, as at least she would have been spared a little by being abroad. It will break her heart . . . I expect she will want to sell the house and all my things. Of course I shall let her if she wants to sell them.

For a week Violet went on writing to Vita, despite the lawyer's caution: letters of anger that her own life was blighted and Vita's not. 'You have all you want – a lovely place to live in, love, affection, understanding. How can I help feeling bitter?' And it was true. Vita's life was intrinsically intact. She had Harold, Long Barn, her children, animals, possessions. 'And what should I have?' Violet wrote:

NOTHING.

> No one who loves me and lives with me, no possessions, no reputation, no hope, nothing.

> I ache with the sense of the appalling unfairness ... what a proof, that in spite of it all, I still manage to love you above everything!

Nor could she again exact from Vita the promise that it was hope deferred and that some day they might again be together:

> If only you would map out some sort of existence for me, with some sort of reward at the end – something to pin my hope to. *One cannot live without hope.* You said: 'None for the present' – but is there any in the future? That's what I want to know ...

The answer was that there was not. For a time Vita continued to send letters – for Violet to collect at the Connaught Hotel. But if she still felt involved, she could no longer show it. The price was now impossibly high. Violet needed help, a context for her life, a channel for her feelings. Denys's defection spoiled the balance. Mrs Keppel was furious with him as well as with her daughter. The social graces, charm and concealment she held so dear were all flaunted in her face.

She battled on for Sonia, the Cubitts, the unborn baby. The family name must not be tarnished more. Violet could no longer live in England. Her mother said she would take her abroad until after the birth of Sonia's child and after that she could live in Paris or some other foreign city. She told her to make an inventory of what she wanted from the Dower House. Violet took with her two photographs of Vita, a Persian painting of a fish, some Egyptian beads, the head of

Medusa Vita had given her. Her paintings, rugs, writing desk she put in store. Mrs Keppel sold the rest for £200 which she kept 'to pay for the carpet'. Violet claimed she had herself spent £3000 on the place.

All contact with Vita was forbidden. Violet was to receive no calls, no letters from her. At Grosvenor Street Rolphe the butler checked her mail. Nor was she to see Pat Dansey — Mrs Keppel feared they would scheme. On 26 March Violet wrote her last direct letter to Vita. Her battle for love was lost: 'You have chosen my darling; you had to choose between me and your family and you have chosen them.'

Vita tried to conceal her unhappiness from Harold. Two days later she wrote a postscript to her account of her affair with Violet:

> It is possible that I may never see Violet again, or that I may see her once again before we are parted, or that we may meet in future years as strangers; it is also possible that she may not choose to live; in any case it has come about indirectly owing to me, while I remain safe, secure and undamaged save in my heart. The injustice and misfortune of the whole thing oppresses me hourly.

She went to see Pat Dansey who counselled her to make a complete break — 'no writing no communication'. It had to end, she said, for both their families' sake. Vita should make no promises and exact none from Violet. If she kept in touch Violet would hope that they would go away together. 'It would be far wiser and better for you both not to prolong the misery.'

Vita went sailing with Harold on her father's yacht, saw the publication of *The Dragon in Shallow Waters* which she dedicated to 'L' and which sold well, cultivated her garden and sowed the seeds of a new affair — with Dorothy Wellesley whose marriage to Gerald, Violet's former admirer, was going wrong. Dorothy Wellesley was, said Vita, a born romantic and a natural rebel, with fragile build, 'blazing blue eyes, fair hair, transparently white skin'. Her poetry was admired by Yeats. She lived in Sherfield Court, a moated Georgian mansion near Basingstoke, with furniture inlaid with lapis lazuli and paintings by Caravaggio.

Harold welcomed the signs of transference. The Nicolson children and the Wellesleys' son Valerian could play together. Vita and Dorothy went to Tintagel in Cornwall, played tennis and stayed with Lord Berners at Faringdon Hall in Berkshire. Harold did not object: 'Tell Dottie she is an angel and very good for us both.' Lady Sackville had her doubts: 'I don't like at all that friendship either,' she wrote in her diary.

Mrs Keppel kept Violet on an emotional leash. In April she took her to Pisa to 'a sort of mediaeval fortress flanked by four towers'. It was quiet and Violet would like to have recuperated there, but her mother preferred Florence. Violet was wry at being taken to Florence to have her character reformed. She spoke Italian, French and German, her mother did not. The rich cosmopolitan set of Florentine villa life, the expatriates and aristocrats, were, she said, 'the most corrupt I have ever run across'.

She lost weight, was lonely, unhappy and adrift. Her mother ignored her socially, said her affection for her was dead and cut her allowance. Violet sent letters to Pat Dansey intended for Vita. She asked that Julian write to her Poste Restante, but he did not do so. She took stock of her life:

> It seems so odd to have lost V and D, my freedom, my home, my money, all at one fell swoop. I begin to think the sort of reckless, exorbitant love I gave is the one unjustifiable crime in this world. One should love prudently, reasonably, comfortably; not dash one's glove in the face of the world . . .
>
> Mama made me cry and cry last night. She said if she had been me she would have killed herself long ago! Will you tell — he can telegraph anything he likes in Italian if he signs himself Scovello?

Like Julian and Vita, Scovello did not telegraph. Pat was seldom long at one address and these *cris de coeur* were forwarded to her. 'I am really losing my mind over these telegrams and missing letters . . .'

she wrote to Vita. 'In what a fix she plants one.' Pat was for a time Violet's ally, gave circumspect replies knowing letters were opened, transferred money to Thomas Cook's in Florence when Violet said she had not a penny in the world and had been 'swindled by the cook', sent cigarettes and press cuttings of Vita's poems and stories.

At the end of May Violet went with her mother to Rome and stayed in a villa on a hill with a 'beautiful garden with fountains that play day and night beneath my window'.

Men chinday now completely ignores me. It's as though I didn't exist. She says that her affection for me is dead and that after Sonia's baby is born I may do as I like. I have only one preoccupation. Chepescar. [Escape.]

She met Rebecca West who agreed to take a large, framed, coloured photograph of her to London and give it to Pat who would pass it to Vita. On her birthday she received via Pat an unsigned telegram from Vita, a mute reminder of past times.

In July her mother took her to Clingendaal. Violet disliked the room she was given. She tried to write a novel which, she said, was now 'everything to me inevitably: Lover, Husband, Child, Friend'. She felt, she wrote to Pat, 'out of everything; I am never asked to take part in the numerous expeditions, dinners, dances, etc. that the others get up. I am always left out.' Her mother said that if she ever gave   party again she could not ask Violet to it. 'It is a small thing but it hurts my feelings.' The guests treated her with condescension or were openly rude. 'Julian and Denys between them,' she wrote to Pat, 'have completely ruined my chances of respectability for ever. Whatever I become it would be their fault.'

She urged Pat to come out to Clingendaal. Mrs Keppel was going back to England while Sonia's baby was born. Pat declined. 'I honestly don't want to go,' she wrote to Vita:

I have a lot of visits to pay in July and I hate old Daisy [de Brienen] as much as she hates me! Surely if she [Violet] is coming back in September, she can bear two more months?

Violet went often to the doctor, scrutinized herself in the mirror, feared she had lost her looks, dreaded the approach of age. She was twenty-seven, her chin seemed to sag, her throat looked wrinkled. 'I look ten years older than when you saw me last year,' she wrote to Pat:

My whole life seems ruined. I see only too clearly that it would be impossible for me to live in England. I cannot bear being snubbed and mortified. I am too proud.

It was too problematic. She was *déclassée*. 'I can count the pleasures that remain on the fingers of one hand,' she wrote to Pat, 'sleeping, smoking, a hot bath.' She read D.H. Lawrence's *Women in Love* and said there were beautiful things in it, 'like jewels in a manure heap'. She asked Pat to send her more novels as writing and reading were her only resources and there were no books at all at Clingendaal.

In her role as go-between Pat moved closer to Vita though her ostensible concern was Violet. 'I would gladly do anything to help her,' she wrote to Vita on 15 August:

But what can I do? I have written her a most urgent appeal to give you up in *all ways* — for as long as there is any connection between you two the world will never allow the scandal to be forgotten. *Curse* the malicious tattlers who did all the harm, curse them. I have done my best to impress Violet that there can be no future for her as long as people are not made to understand that the mad friendship between you two is over and not to be revived.

Poor child, I am afraid she has not much future ahead. O Vita, Vita, why didn't you leave her for the first 6 months after she was married? Now the harm is irretrievably done. Doubtless you can be strong, but it is too late. I am sorry. I did not mean to upbraid! The tragedy was that in those days you looked upon me as an enemy. I wasn't and never have been. *You* were the enemy, but the point is, how can Violet be helped?

I think it is cruel the way she is being treated and that sort of treatment is not going to make people forget the scandal − is it? I simply don't know what to do. Shall I go and see her mother and try to make her see that treating V as a pariah does more harm than good? . . .

Vita, will you put all feelings aside from your personal point of view, and tell me quite candidly and truthfully what you consider would really be the best for V in the future?

Neither had an answer. Both feared Violet's return to London, scheduled for late August. 'I do really really want to evolve some plan by which to regulate my life,' she wrote. Lonely at Clingendaal, she invited Denys's sister, Betty, to visit. From her she learned Denys had dropped legal proceedings because of her separation from Vita. He too was adrift, without occupation, and living unsatisfactorily with his mother. He felt 'caged up' in Devon. Travel, the war and the trials of marriage had 'upset the old ideas' he used to hold. Betty advised Violet to repair what there was, told her the mess was of her own making.

Sonia's daughter Rosalind was born in August. Mrs Keppel stayed with her and Roland at their house Hall Place in the village of West Meon, Hampshire. Rosalind was in her turn to be the mother of Camilla Parker-Bowles, Favorita of a future Prince of Wales.

After the child was born, Violet was allowed to return to London and to her room in her mother's Grosvenor Street house. Vita wrote L for Lushka in her diary, underlined it three times and, within a week, left for months of holiday in Italy with Dorothy and Gerald Wellesley. They were to be joined in October by Harold.

Within a week, too, Violet was on her way to Paris with Denys. Their reunion was a convenience. It was, Pat told Vita, at Violet's suggestion. 'Her mother *refuses* to advise her one way or the other.' They stayed in the Paris Ritz, then moved to a flat in the seventeenth *arrondissement.* London society was unperturbed; Violet had relinquished her place in it.

She continued to send Pat letters asking if Vita cared. Pat told her Vita 'would *never* lead the mad life of the past 3 years again'. But to Vita she wrote in November, 'Beyond that I have said nothing. Personally, I would not bet 6d that in less than 3 months' time you are not again on the same footing with V!!' She would not have lost her sixpence. The old footing was gone.

Less than three months after Violet's exile Pat switched loyalties. 'I do wish, Vita,' she wrote in December, 'that when you come to see me you could manage to look ugly. You always make me forget all the important disagreeable things I want to say.' Pat now read Vita's poems in bed at night and dreamed of her. By December she told her she could not 'serve two masters' and was beginning to dislike Violet. 'Of course she is bound to say I am in love with you; however that won't do you any active harm as she will only *dare* say it to me.'

On 10 January 1922 some kind of lovemaking took place between her and Vita. 'Dine Pat' Vita noted in her engagement book. Next day Pat wrote to her: 'You had struck something in me that has not been struck but once before – ten years ago.' She pined to see her, called her DM which stood for Dark Man, planned a ring with the letters DMPAT inlaid in diamonds, pearls and topaz, but feared it would make an ugly mix. When Vita, stooping to kiss her, jabbed her eye with a hatpin, Pat said she did not mind how many hatpins ran into her eye under similar circumstances for she was, she declared, in love.

As for the Nicolson marriage, Violet had discomfited it but no worse. Sex had found its marginal place. After Violet both Vita and Harold had affairs, she with women, he with men. These did not disrupt the form and fabric of all that made their marriage. If at times other hearts got hurt or even broken that was not a moral issue or a groundrule for change. Vita called her relationship with Harold 'odd, strange, detached, intimate, mystical'. There was freedom in it and acceptance. She was unconcerned by his sexual relationships. He referred to the wreckage hers caused as the 'muddles' of his 'little mar'. 'I only feel that you have not got *la main heureuse* in dealing with married couples' was as near as he got to criticism.

Later lovers learned their place with less display than Violet made. 'After all,' Harold wrote to Raymond Mortimer, 'half a loaf is ever so much better than a whole one.' He would, he said, like to go away with Raymond for weeks on end: 'But I can't and that's the fly in the ointment.' In December 1925 Raymond Mortimer wrote to Vita of his anxiety at not joining Harold in Teheran:

> I do not remember ever having been so much disappointed over anything . . . everything now seems unutterably dreary . . . I felt childish and wanted to break things . . . of course the sickening thing is not to see Harold for so long. There is no one else I in the least want to go abroad with.

Vita wrote to Harold and tried to help them both.

Like Edward VII and Alice Keppel, Harold and Vita believed that the best life was marriage 'plus liaisons'. Vita conceded a 'smug satisfaction' over the way they resolved what she called the claustrophobic contract of marriage. 'It is only very, very intelligent people like us who are able to rise superior.'

Violet did not rise superior. She found it too difficult to be in love with a woman and to pretend to be married to a man. For her, marriage was a wicked sham. 'It has ruined my life, it has ruined Denys's . . . It has ruined not *your* life, but our happiness.'

She was the only one of Vita's liaisons whom Harold truly loathed. 'I do so dread that woman . . . I think she is the only person of whom I am frightened.' In November 1922 when he heard she was visiting London he worried Vita might be mesmerized by that 'panther sneaking about, waiting to pounce . . . and you my darling are so gullible and weak'. Vita sent him a telegram, followed it with a letter, gave him all the reassurance she could:

> I curse myself for having told you she was coming to London, and so having given you even a moment's anxiety.

Darling, my own darling, *not for a million pounds would I have anything* to do with V. again; I hate her for all the misery she brought upon us; so there . . . *don't worry*, oh don't, my little boy; word of honour, padlock [their word for 'promise'], don't. I wish I could convince you.

And above all, I would *never* have anything more to do with her; the boredom of it . . . and the lies . . . and the rows . . . oh no, no, NO. Even if you didn't exist, you whom I love so fundamentally, deeply and incurably.

Oh yes, I know you will say, 'But you loved me *then*, and yet you did.' It's quite true, I did love you, and I always loved you all through those wretched years, but you know what infatuation is, and I was mad.

So Harold as he travelled could safely write to Vita about the bonds of marriage and home:

And with it all a sense of permanence so that as you sit in your room tonight I shall think of you there, I dashing through the Île de France in a train. And I shall think of the Rodin, and the blue crocodile and the figure of St Barbara – and the London *Mercury* upon the stool. And it will be for both of us as if I were there, and love still hangs, as well as smoke, about the room.

. . . And please don't run away with anybody without giving me time to get my aeroplane ready.

And Vita could reassure him that he was the one and only person for her in the world and give him news of the polyanthas, the roses, the chicken run, tennis court, strawberry beds and Irish yews.

FIFTEEN

'How black is my future!' Violet wrote to Pat Dansey. 'I can hardly bear to think of it.' She felt guilty and self-critical at the trouble she had caused:

> I feel I am such a trial to everyone, a sort of drag on the family who are so different. Heaven knows I am trial enough to myself.

She took stock of what she described as a Greek tragedy, checked her feelings, made reparative moves toward her mother and, to salvage a vestigial social position for herself, kept the front of her marriage to Denys.

This marriage was a screen riddled with recriminations and scenes, but without it she was on her own in a foreign city. She and Denys shared what she called a 'tiny flat' in the rue Fourcroy but led separate lives. They made no attempt at partnership. Anti-bolshevik, absorbed in Russian counter-revolutionary politics, Denys mixed with Russian emigrés, even spoke French with a Russian accent, went to night clubs, had love affairs. Most nights Violet dined alone:

> Denys would frequently ring up late in the day to say that he was not returning for dinner ... I awoke to the fact that the wasp-waisted Caucasian dancers had more in common with him than I had.

When she asked if he was having an affair with a Russian model at Coco Chanel's he said yes, he loved Ludmila, she 'was exquisite and had suffered' and he was not made for marriage.

On 17 March 1922 Mrs Keppel summoned Pat Dansey to lunch at 16 Grosvenor Street with an aunt of Denys's, Daisy de Brienen and 'two or three other old Grosvenor Street haunters'. She instructed her to arrive early, stay until all other guests had gone, then drive George to the City. The purpose of the lunch was to discuss a dinner party Mrs Keppel was to give for Denys in Paris. This was to be her 'touching reunion' with him, their first encounter since his defection the previous year, her public sanction of Violet's relaunched marriage.

The party took place in April and went off 'fearfully well much to V's disgust,' Pat told Vita. Denys, after a technical hitch, was again Violet's husband. The *status quo* was restored. Violet, who had always loved Paris, was there, living in a smart apartment, speaking flawless idiomatic French, married to Denys Trefusis. Occasionally they 'gave makeshift dinner parties'. Sometimes they travelled together to Amsterdam, Brittany, Venice, Monte Carlo.

Mrs Keppel's money eased the day. She found him a remunerative office job and financed his and Violet's move to an apartment at 7 rue Laurent Pichat in the sixteenth *arrondissement*. Pat's brother Henry helped Violet find it. He said it was 'extremely nice'. At Mrs Keppel's request he supervised the financial arrangements. Pat retrieved Violet's dispersed pictures, tapestries, rugs, furniture and sent them from Folkestone by van. Sonia thought such things of Violet's as she had acquired were now hers and was annoyed at parting with them.

'I have to go and see Mrs K.,' Pat wrote to Vita:

> Ugh! All the things that V wants she thinks may be at G. Street. So 'will you go and ask Mama'. Why hasn't the silly said where they were before? It would have saved endless unnecessary bother. Mama won't want the bother of finding them.

Pat Dansey was still ostensibly Violet's friend, ally, confidante, her link with the past. Through her Mrs Keppel kept check on her daughter's affairs. When Violet wired Pat that she was in debt and low on funds, Pat conferred with Mrs Keppel who made the necessary transfers of cash. 'I *do* hate these tangles,' she wrote to Vita on 10 March from the flat in Bryanston Court that Joan Campbell had given her:

The part I hate most is having that old terror George Keppel here for hours on end. I do dislike it so . . . Darling, please treat what I have told you about V's difficulties as private. It is all a curse but only to be expected.

Pat, courier, counsellor, go-between, reassured Mrs Keppel that she was a true friend to Violet, doing all she could to help. Violet could always rely on her, always stay with her in London. Thus Mrs Keppel was free to cruise to Greece, Italy and the East without more stigma from her daughter, more fear of scandal, bubbling back home.

Neither Mrs Keppel nor Violet knew that Pat now wrote Vita daily declarations of love on stationery stamped with her seal — a witch on a broomstick captioned 'All Have Their Hobbies'. Nor did they know that by her bed was a framed photograph of the painting of Vita by William Strang and a copy of her poems *Orchard and Vineyard* inscribed 'with love from DM'.

Violet, cuckolded again, confided to Pat her problems with Denys, his affairs, their debts, her loneliness. She longed, she said, for the old happy days when she had stayed as a young girl with Pat at Berkeley Castle. She asked if they might go there for a summer holiday:

I will go as your maid, secretary, chauffeur, anything. Alas! Alas! In any case, even if we can't go there couldn't we go somewhere lovely? I long for the country and peace!

'Well! I'm damned!' wrote Pat to Vita:

Darling, she might have second sight and have guessed you and I were planning to go to Berkeley. I suppose she would kill me with anger if she knew.

Pat was 'fearfully careful' to keep Vita's letters out of sight when Violet visited. 'I even burn the envelopes so as she should not see your handwriting.' When Violet accused her of taking Vita's side she denied this but next day wrote:

Darling if V was not so conceited, so wrapped up in herself, she
might have guessed last night that I had more than affection for
you! . . . O my darling DM . . . I simply must see you . . .

Vita was, Pat told her, only 'the second person ever who has really
attracted me in a way which I cannot describe'. She 'missed her dreadfully' when separated, was jealous she might return to Violet.

In a game of whispers and deceptions she derided Violet. To increase
her own standing with Vita she implied Violet schemed and deceived
in promiscuous relationships:

Surely from old days Denys knows the trick of V saying she is
with me when she is not. Her falseness simply appals me . . . I
saw Henry [her brother] in London and his description of V in
Paris is positively alarming.

She stressed Violet's impracticality. 'All Violet's and Denys's things
were stolen in Venice . . . I think we've heard the same story before
. . . She's a hopeless woman . . . Mrs K wrote me an awfully funny
letter on the subject . . .' She let Vita know when Violet travelled to
Munich with Gerald Berners and someone referred to only as 'M'. She
told her when Violet asked to borrow £100. 'I am sure it is blackmail
money . . . If it was bills she would tell me I think. It is probably
blackmail to do with M.'

She had, she said, received from Rebecca West a letter about Violet
'too dangerous to send through the post'.

She bought Vita a Burberry mackintosh, sent her crates of Mumm
Cordon Rouge, said she had seen 'such a nice Daimler' coupé she was
'crazy to get' for her, told her to order – on her account – anything
she wanted for the Long Barn garden, flattered her writing talent, 'you
can leave future generations a legacy,' she said.

She gave her a diamond ring, an emerald ring, a gold keyring, an
exquisite copy of the *Arabian Nights*, sent her oranges when she bought
an orange farm in South Africa, flowers from the Riviera – 'you shall

have all the flowers in Monte Carlo sent to you' − and tempted her with money:

> I was fearful that you wouldn't realise how *desperately* shy and nervous I should be of daring to ask you to give me the joy of lending you any money you wanted . . . you know that I would do any mortal thing in the world for you.

Pat bought a kite and carpentry set for Ben, found letters for Harold for the book he was writing on Tennyson, shopped for, lunched with and listened to Lady Sackville, who viewed her as Vita's true friend, preferable to Dorothy Wellesley. She wished Vita would travel abroad with Pat instead of Dorothy.

Pat kept Joan Campbell as her constant companion, her equivalent of the dependable marriage partner. In London Joan lived with her mother in Bryanston Square a minute away from Pat. They always phoned each other first thing in the morning while still in bed and socially did most things together. Pat wrote to Vita from the Ritz in Paris and Madrid, the Hotel Inglaterra in Seville, from Lisbon, Madeira, Singapore, Panama, California, Hawaii, from 'somewhere up the Amazon', from various ocean cruisers. 'The sea is blue blue blue,' she told her, 'and there are flying fish.' Joan, like Harold, felt insecure when Pat cut short their holidays, cancelled meetings and dithered over dates. 'I have palpitated at every footstep thinking it will be a telegram from you to say you can't come,' she wired from Strachur Castle in summer 1922 on a day when Pat sent a dozen bottles of Veuve Cliquot 1906 to Long Barn.

The Dansey affair was a pale parody of Vita and Violet's relationship. It held faint echoes of their drama: jealousy, manipulation, insecurity, secrecy. But Vita was not interested in Pat except as a link with Violet, a symptom of her pain at parting, a way of punishing Violet more. As for Violet, she knew scant details and this, from her 'powerful ally,' her one true English friend, her mother's appointed messenger, was simply a postscript to the death of trust.

In December 1922 Pat told Vita she would, in her will, leave every-

thing to her. From the Berkeley Castle wine cellar she gave her all
the remaining champagne and 'some delicious Sauterne'. 'So Hadji
better hurry up and come home,' Vita wrote to Harold who was in
Lausanne.

Violet visited London for the Christmas holiday and stayed with
her mother at Grosvenor Street. 'Apparently her mother is keeping
an eagle eye on her,' Pat wrote to Vita,

> and demands an account of where she spends every second. This
> is *quite* intolerable for V. But though I have not said it to V it
> may be done because her mother thinks she is trying to see you.
> V told me that when she had said she was coming round here
> last evening her mother had said 'Why now so late?' The Keppel
> lot may know you come here and are afraid of a meeting. You
> remember Sonia did come one morning and went away again! I
> also told old G myself I frequently saw you and that often you
> came to the flat. V is coming here this morning . . . I must warn
> CD [the novelist Clemence Dane] somehow not to mention Long
> Barn in front of V . . . Have you any idea of how terribly I miss
> you?

'I shall turn her down properly if she *does* telephone to me – beast',
Vita wrote to Harold on 2 December. Six days later Violet phoned.
Vita asked Dorothy Wellesley to stay in the room while she told Violet
nothing would tempt her to see her. Pat spent Christmas in Brighton
with Vita, her children and Lady Sackville and was a 'howling success'.
Lady Sackville referred to her as 'beloved Pat'.

Like Violet Pat knew that Vita valued devotion and fidelity in her
lovers, but if they asked the same of her she quit, pleading her marriage
to Harold, her need for a quiet life. Knowing, too, that Vita's faltering
attention could be fanned alight by hints of sexual competition from
any man, she fed the flame even while sensing it came not from Vita's
desire for her, Pat, but from 'your obsession' as she put it 'that you
are a romantic young man who treats women badly'.

In July 1923 Vita seemed jealous of a man called Anselm whom Pat was seeing. Pat reassured. 'I loathe being touched or kissed by anyone unless I love them or they physically attract me . . . I *don't* want it except from you . . .'

Men were a social convenience, a cover for appearances' sake, of no emotional relevance. 'Would it,' she asked, 'be easier for you if I produced a husband?'

> Would that lighten the position? I know that it is not for yourself but fear of talk. If a husband would make it as easy as it is with anyone else, I will produce one instantly. I don't say I want to produce one, but at the same time I will make the sacrifice for you.

She shared none of Violet's scorn of hypocrisy and volunteered the usual adulterous formula: give society — the drawing rooms of Grosvenor Street and Mayfair — the 'values' it said it respected. That done, have secretive sex with whoever you please. 'Three perfect days', she wrote in summer 1923 when her driver, Burley, took her to Long Barn on Wednesday and collected her on Friday before Harold arrived from London. 'I *cannot* think about them — hot waves rush all over me. Little electric needles of sensation prick all through me.'

Less manageable sensations followed in autumn. Vita and Harold stayed in Florence with the writer Geoffrey Scott and his wife Sybil. Scott, author of *The Architecture of Humanism*, was writing *The Portrait of Zélide*. On Saturday 24 November Pat received a letter from Vita saying she had fallen in love with him. This love, Vita said, was intense and spiritual and left no room for Pat.

Pat fainted when she read the letter, then sat until 5 a.m. in her sitting room with what she called a broken heart. Then she turned nasty. 'I centralized on you for 3 solid years *as my life*,' she wrote, 'and you just shut me off bang! stranded.' Vita was, she told her, vile, contemptuous, a coward, a bully, base and awful. God would, if he existed, one day punish her. She herself felt picked up, used and dropped. She called their three years an 'episode', accused her of motives of lust and money and returned such presents as Vita had given her – 'I would sooner die than be beholden to anyone for a $\frac{1}{2}$d stamp who has treated me as you have.' She wanted the immediate return of all gifts bestowed – books, jewels, fountain pen, vases and more.

She had, she declared, always shown the greatest interest in Vita's life, 'your dogs, cats, garden, books, children, husband and mother!' She had given her money and deep affection and was now on the edge of a nervous breakdown. She intended to shoot herself or jump out of a window and she asked Vita to look after her myrtle tree when she was gone. Worse, she threatened to appear at Long Barn in the small hours of the night and make a scene. Harold, she felt sure, was a just man who would discern the truth in all she had to say.

Scenes took place when Vita tried to placate her. 'My darling,' Pat wrote:

> I do apologise for the hitting scene in the flat! I simply saw red when you talked to me of honour! I wasn't going to have murdered you. Also sweet, let me warn you that you must *never* try to take a pistol away from anyone in that rough way! If it had been loaded it was *bound* to have gone off . . . I will show you the correct *Daily Mail* survival way of taking a pistol away from someone.

She sent reply-paid telegrams to Vita which went unanswered and she parodied Violet's plight. 'You have,' wrote Pat, '*always* only considered *your* feelings, *your* wishes, *your* wants.' Now, she said, she intended taking Vita to the Law Courts to 'thrash the thing out there'. It would, she hoped, mean 'ruination to your self and family'. She consulted a lawyer called Dixon and contrived a plan to make a public apology to Vita for having made her feel under 'a great obligation' toward Pat. This apology would, Pat said, rouse curiosity, require explanation from Vita and involve 'washing much dirty linen' in public:

> I am going to tell my story. I shall tell the despicable way in which you treated me throughout, the way in which you played

me off against DW [Dorothy Wellesley]. How you dropped me when it suited you. How miserable you made me and after my unhappiness you cruelly took me up again and then dropped me last summer with *no fair explanation.*

She threatened scandal on a scale to dwarf anything caused by Violet. She had, she said, heard from Lilly, a servant of Vita's, that Vita and Dorothy Wellesley had been seen 'in a very amorous position, D. with no clothes on' and that when Dorothy acquired a black eye, Vita said she got it from walking in her sleep.

She made specious threats, tried peculiar bribes. She said the newspaper *Morning Post* had changed hands and she was now a principal shareholder. She offered to send her chauffeur round to Vita with £10,000 in cash, realized from these shares. Vita's acceptance of the money would console Pat and dissipate her feelings of bitterness and hatred. Vita, disconcerted, wrote to Lord Northumberland, owner of the *Morning Post*, to see what was behind this convoluted story. It was, he replied, a fabrication:

She never bought any shares in the *Morning Post* nor sold any. I can't imagine why she has told you this story . . . she has endeavoured to impose upon you in the most shameless way. I believe (but am not quite sure) that some years ago a lady of that name wrote to me in regard to anti-Bolshevik propaganda and I am informed by a friend that she was not quite right in the head.

Many women went through passion, anger, suffering in vain pursuit of Vita's love. The strength of her pact with Harold meant lovers were marginalized and kept in place. Pat's letters showed tense and unresolved conflict between propriety and desire. Sex − hot waves and electric needles − she maintained, as do many when jilted, should carry with it obligations of commitment.

With this idea Vita did not concur. Her sexual partners came then went − usually in anger, often with broken hearts and homes. Dorothy Wellesley's marriage broke up in 1923. 'I do *not* want to be dragged into this,' Vita wrote to Harold, 'either for your sake or my own. We have had quite enough of that sort of thing, haven't we?' Geoffrey Scott's wife, Sybil, was 'completely broken' by his desertion. He gave up his job at the embassy in Rome in June 1924 telling Vita, 'It was just one more barrier separating me from you.' Dumped by Vita after a week or so, he was then adrift. Lady Sackville saw him at Long Barn and recorded he was 'trembling all over'.

Harold was not threatened by this wreckage. It was Vita's business how she behaved, he said, but he did not want to be drawn again into a 'vortex of unhappiness'. Only Violet, 'absolutely unscrupulous . . . waiting to pounce' had the power, he believed, to do that.

All doors were closed against Violet. For a while she nudged at these then turned away. Paris was her second love. Paris had compensations. 'I surrendered all my links with the past and began again in Paris' she wrote in her autobiography:

> Paris would make up for everything: failed friendships, the measures necessary for making new ones . . . In a half-hearted way I tried to pick up the threads of the life I had lived as a *jeune fille*.

These threads were thin. Paris in the 1920s offered a context for artistic talent, same-sex relationships and experimental thought. But though she loved the city, emotionally she was on her own in it and without the romantic optimism of her youth. 'I was unhappy . . . I had no intimate friend.'

In Paris she turned her disappointment into fiction. She wrote equally cleverly in French and English, her style witty, polished, concealed, sharp. The themes she chose for her novels were betrayal, marriage for gain, malicious matriarchs, love versus possessions.

She did not seek publication for her first novel. It was in English, a *roman à clef*, not witty or fast but sad. It was about her plight. She called it *The Hook in the Heart*. On the first page of her manuscript she wrote, 'Less voluntary than grief or death is the choice of desire.'

She appeared in it as Cécile, innocent and young. Vita, she as ever masculinized. She was both the Spanish duke whom Cécile is forced to marry and Kalo the gypsy with whom she falls in love. Mrs Keppel and Lady Sackville she merged into the controlling persona of the duke's grandmother, a dowager duchess who lives in a tower in her Spanish castle, 'a smile of malice on her lips'. She manipulates her grandson's fate.

Marriage between Cécile and the duke is a loveless tryst arranged by his aunt:

> Every night they made love, in married fashion, without prelude or subtlety. Cécile did her best to respond but could not repress, every night, the same reflection: So this is what makes people torture themselves, fight each other, kill each other. Incredible!

The newlyweds travel to Spain to visit his grandmother. On a terrible honeymoon journey Cécile writes to her mother the letter of disappointment Violet might have sent:

> How could she make her understand that her marriage . . . that aim and object of so many girlhood dreams, seemed to her to have no emotions, no ecstasies to divulge? When once the first shock was over . . . Cécile might have summed up her reactions in one short phrase: 'So that's all there is to it?'

The duchess in her grotesque Spanish castle appears at supper dripping with jewels. She hates Cécile, thinks her not good enough for her grandson, claims her with a diamond necklace 'the ice-cold necklace slipped round her throat like a snake'.

To escape the castle, its lovelessness, manipulation, materialism, Cécile goes alone to the Spanish countryside. She meets, falls in love and has sex with a gypsy, Kalo, who lives in a cave. But Kalo betrays her. His trade is to catch songbirds, put out their eyes to make them sing better, then sell them. He does not tell her he has a wife. Cécile finds them in bed planning to steal her necklace. Disaffection makes her ill:

> Her love of love had bred disgust of love . . . with all her soul

she cursed passionate love, the hook in the heart that you cannot
tear out without tearing out the heart also.

The duke rejects her for her infidelity. She sells the offending necklace
and runs away:

Disowned by her own class, disowned by the gypsies, forsaken by
all, she found herself face to face with an unknown quantity.
Solitude.

It was a romantic yarn of no great worth but it was how more or
less she felt. All her trouble with Vita was because her heart was
caught. Though her links with the past were severed, her personal
tragedy was acute. She could not live with the woman she loved, her
marriage was a disaster, she had offended her family, she was on her
own.

Violet, without a heart, could not be hooked though she would do
her share of netting. In 1923 Denys, aware of her needs and wanting
his own freedom, introduced her to Winnaretta, Princesse de Polignac,
the eighteenth child of Isaac Singer, inventor of the sewing machine. In
her autobiography Violet described Vita as tall, graceful and beautiful.
Winnaretta de Polignac she described as remarkable, imperturbable,
inscrutable, infinitely intimidating, immensely rich and given to
making dry, caustic utterances:

People quailed before her . . . her face was more like a landscape
than a face, cloudy of hair, blue of eye, rugged of contour . . .
her rocky profile seemed to call for spray and seagulls; small blue
eyes, the eyes of an old salt – came and went.

It was not a face to inspire love and passion. But the Princesse de
Polignac provided Violet with patronage for her novels, emotional
protection, dazzling society and a lesbian relationship rich and discreet
enough to impress Denys Trefusis, the elite of Paris society and Mrs
Keppel.

PART THREE

Chacun Sa Tour

SIXTEEN

The Princess talked through her teeth, wore high-necked gowns, spoke French without concession to accent, taught herself ancient Greek when she was fifty and willed that her personal papers be burned when she died. Jean Cocteau said she had Dante's profile. James Lees-Milne, Harold Nicolson's biographer, called her 'very Faubourg Saint-Germain'. Virginia Woolf described her as like a 'perfectly stuffed cold fowl'. Thirty years older than Violet, reserved, controlled, she gave her a place in Parisian life.

Her biographer, Michael de Cossart, recorded a sartorial penchant for riding boots and hunting clothes, a preference for sexually submissive women and relationships with a sado-masochistic undertow. She married two princes without sexual interest in either. The first marriage, in 1887 when she was twenty-two, was arranged by her mother. Prince Louis de Scey-Montbéliard, was aristocratic, short of money and masterful. Winnaretta refused sex with him, accused him of cruelty and petitioned the Vatican for annulment. Being very rich helped. She was granted a civil divorce in 1891. The following year the papal court, the Curia, declared the marriage null in the eyes of the Catholic Church.

Pope Leo XIII on 15 December 1893 gave his blessing to her union with Prince Edmond de Polignac. Homosexual, sensitive to draughts, a composer of an avant-garde sort, Polignac was thirty years older than she. Edmond de Goncourt described him in his journal as having the air of a drowned dog. Winnaretta he said had 'a cold beauty, distinct, cutting'. The marriage was agreed

on condition that the husband does not enter his wife's bedroom and on the payment of a sum of money which might permit him to mount his music which the opera houses do not want.

227

The Princess bought a fifteenth-century Lombardesque palace in Venice, renamed it the Palazzo Polignac and spent consecutive summers there until, as she put it, 'the hideous Hotel Excelsior was built on the Lido . . . and before the invasion of fashionable visitors from every Continent during the bathing season.'

Before such spoiling times hers was *la dolce vita*. Her neighbours were 'the lovely Lady Helen Vincent whose Palazzo Giustimani was perhaps the most beautiful in all Venice'; the Countess de la Baume whose Casa Dario was, 'a marvel of comfort and good taste, filled with the finest pictures and the most precious books and musical instruments'; the Marchesa Casati at the Venier de Leoni, who at one of her own fancy-dress balls appeared wearing a costume designed by Bakst, a drugged tiger at her feet.

The Princess revered culture and was a formidable patron of the arts. Cosmopolitan in a way Violet admired, if she liked what she saw, heard or read, she bought it. Her vast Paris house at the corner of the avenue Henri-Martin and the rue Cortambert was a temple to art. Reconstructed in eighteenth-century French classical style, she fitted it with public galleries and concert rooms and filled it with priceless things. She had a Renaissance tapestry in her bedroom. She liked the paintings of Goya, Edouard Manet, Claude Monet, Sisley, Renoir, Boudin, Degas, so she bought them. Her *grand salon* resembled the *galerie des glaces* at Versailles. In it, she held concerts and exhibitions of paintings including her own. She commissioned the Spanish artist José Maria Sert to paint the pilaster capitals with 'sapphic scenes' of naked ladies cavorting with bunches of grapes and each other. In the oak-p nelled music room she installed a full-sized organ on which she played Bach. In the library, which led to a raised garden, she commissioned a ceramic tabernacle from the sculptor, Jean Carriés, to house a Wagner manuscript she valued. From the engraver, Paul Helleu, she commissioned an album of etchings of her lovers, then bought and destroyed the plates so no copies could be made.

Music was her particular love. From her earliest years as a child at her mother's house at 27 avenue Kléber near the Bois de Boulogne she

constantly heard all the great works of Beethoven, Mozart or
Schubert, including the last Quartets of Beethoven, Nos 10 to
17, which were then considered almost incomprehensible . . . I
remember that on my fourteenth birthday although I was offered
a little watch from Boucheron's or a fan painted by Chaplin the
famous portrait painter, I chose as a present, or 'birthday surprise'
a performance of my favourite work by Beethoven – the Fourteenth Quartet.

The quartet was played on her mother's collection of Stradivarius
stringed instruments.

Denys's friendship with the Princess evolved from their shared interest in avant-garde music:

Together they would attend concerts and rehearsals, the score
under their arm; together they would curtail elaborately prepared
dinners so afraid were they of missing any part of the programme.

Each year the Princess went to Bayreuth. She was a devotee of
Richard Wagner. Ravel dedicated piano pieces to her. Stravinsky,
Debussy, Nadia Boulanger, Erik Satie were commissioned by her. She
knew Diaghilev, Nijinsky, Pavlova, Karsavina, Ida Rubenstein. Gabriel
Fauré, when her guest at the Palazzo Polignac, composed Melodies de
Venise on her portable yacht piano on her boat on her lagoon. Janet
Flanner heard the first performance of Oedipus Rex by Stravinsky at
the avenue Henri-Martin: 'The Latin was sung, with Italian pronunci-
ation, to the French audience by Russians.'

At the Princess's salons Violet socialized with 'names to conjure
with': Jean Cocteau, Anna de Noailles, Colette, Jean Giradoux, Misia
Sert, Paul Valèry, Francis Poulenc, Marcel Proust. Proust wove dialogue
and impressions of her salons into A La Recherche du Temps Perdu. Winnaretta corresponded with him but said it was impossible to endure his
company for long because he took offence all the time, assuming
slights where none was intended. She said his life was governed by

unrequited romantic attachments to men and that she found this wearisome.

She lived as she pleased, arranged life carefully and, like Edward VII, was too grand for scandal to stick. When she took Violet as her lover in 1923 her 'inner circle' was comprised of gay or lesbian artists. Though she had no contact with the Left Bank – Gertrude Stein at the rue de Fleurus, Natalie Barney and her Temple of Love, Sylvia Beach and Shakespeare & Company – she too was a lesbian who lived for art in the city where modernism was born, where the climate was accepting and the spirit free.

Oscar Wilde and Lord Alfred Douglas had attended the Polignac salons. Prior to Violet the Princess's lovers included her husband's niece, Armande de Polignac (married to the Comte de Chabanne la Palice, she used her maiden name and never mentioned him), the painter, Romaine Brooks and Olga de Meyer. Bertie was rumoured to be Olga's father. Her middle name was Alberta, after him. Her mother, the Duchess di Caracciolo, left her husband at the altar steps to live with her lover Prince Josef Poniatowski in a villa near Dieppe. Bertie was a frequent visitor. In 1901 Olga married his friend Baron Adolf de Meyer, the fashion and society photographer. Olga filled her bedroom with paintings of nude women and was Winnaretta's lover from 1909 until the start of the First World War. She and her husband were opium addicts. Violet called them Péderaste et Medisante 'because he looked so queer and she had such a vicious tongue'.

The surface quality of the lifestyle of Mrs Keppel and her daughter began to elide. The Princesse de Polignac was not quite King Edward VII, but she was rich, large, hugely influential, entertained lavishly, had royal connections and lived in undoubted splendour. Such credentials were unimpeachable in Mrs Keppel's eyes. She connived at this new relationship of Violet's. It was pragmatic and rewarding and this she could admire. It had none of the domestic reference of the affair with Vita. Passion did not fly. The French were unperturbed and it was away from the Cubitts' eyes and the hypocrisies of home. The Princess ruled, with status and authority, at 57 avenue Henri-Martin as Mrs Keppel ruled at Grosvenor Street. Each had the same hauteur and unwavering selfconfidence.

In 1923 Violet moved to a house in Auteuil, in the rue de Ranelagh. It was large, peaceful, had a woodland garden and the view of a huge chestnut tree from her bedroom window. She furnished the house in her eclectic style, helped by her new lover's wealth. The materialism she deplored for controlling and restricting her life became her security. She alluded to a gift from her mother of symbolic significance. It was of a painting on glass:

> It represented a Chinese lady smiling at a small grey parrot perched on her arm. She attempts nothing to detain it. Its cage is in her eyes.

In such glancing remarks Violet told the world of her own captivity. The glass picture, bought by Mrs Keppel on her trip to China, allied with the photograph Violet kept on her desk of herself as a child looking into her mother's eyes.

She entertained extravagantly. Mrs Keppel complained to George of the bills. Through her mother and the Princess, Violet 'maintained an exceptional position in Parisian society'. The painter Jacques-Emile Blanche, who did a portrait of Violet, described the house at Auteuil as like 'a miniature Ritz'. He asked her why, when she was so evidently privileged in her own country she preferred Paris. She replied, 'because here one is freer to say and do what one pleases without conventional restrictions.'

She was not now the rebellious gypsy of her fantasy. Few people knew of her broken-hearted past. She was not going to get hooked or hurt again. Though she scorned hypocrisy she stopped being open. She could not break her attachment to her mother and began to mimic parodically her mother's style. She told trite lies but everyone knew they were lies. Like a child testing virtue she teased at the truth:

I am always – being a liar – seeking passionately for truth, TRUTH
in people, real people, not shams and sycophants and humbugs.

At Christmas 1923 the Princesse de Polignac took her on a cruise
up the Nile to Egypt. Denys was in the party too. So were Mrs Keppel
and George. For evening soirées the Princess took along a new protegé,
the pianist Jacques Février. Above board Violet flirted with him, below
deck she answered to the Princess. This was the acceptable face of
infidelity without family rifts or jealous scenes. Husbands, lovers,
mothers, observed civilities in high Edwardian style. Winnaretta and
Denys were the best of friends. There were concerts, excursions to
archaeological sights, games of bridge:

> Sometimes Mrs Keppel would interrupt the game and spread out
> a map: 'Look Georgie, that's ours,' she would say, pointing to
> the location of some lucrative investment Sir Ernest Cassel had
> advised her to make.

Such travel featured in French *Vogue* for its style and expense. The
next year they all went to Greece. Photographs of a Polignac cruise
show the women in hats and gloves viewing the Parthenon and riding
on donkeys on a Greek island.

Rumours of unorthodox sex were the confection of gossip. The
diplomat Duff Cooper relayed to his wife Diana what his friend Mrs
Blew-Jones saw when she delivered furs to the Princess:

> She went round to Polignac's house at eleven in the morning.
> She was asked by the servant at the door whether she was the
> lady who was expected. She said she was and was immediately
> shown into a large room where she was greeted by the old
> Princess in a dressing gown and *top boots*. On a sofa in another
> part of the room she saw Violet Trefusis and another woman,
> both stark naked and locked in a peculiar embrace. She ran from
> the room in terror. It sounds incredible, may be exaggerated but
> can't be quite invented.

'In love' said the Princesse de Polignac to Charlotte Wolff, author of *Love Between Women* and *The Human Hand*, 'there is always one who suffers.' 'I suspected it was *not* she who did,' Dr Wolff wrote in her autobiography.

Violet perfected her French, learned Paris slang, went to lectures at the Sorbonne and tested her ambition to write fiction in French. She called her first novel, *Sortie de Secours* (*Emergency Exit*). In her memoirs she derided it as

a mediocre little book, a patchwork affair, aphorisms, maxims, annotations, loosely woven into the shape of a novel. It served its purpose, it was a loophole, an outlet, above all a piece of blotting paper which absorbed my obsessions.

These obsessions were jealousy and faithless love. Most of her fiction was an attempt to make sense of her past. The emergency exit she described as 'self-love in all its various forms'. The exit was there for when obsessive love threatens to destroy the person it consumes. It allows them 'when some obsession becomes too violent to vanish away with a mocking laugh'.

In French she wrote with a mocking laugh, a comic irony to shield past pain. In French she joked about games of the heart. This was her adopted language which her mother's society could not claim. The tone she found, caustic and defended, contrasted with the rawness of her letters to Vita.

In *Sortie de Secours* Laure loves Drino, a charmer. Because she loves him so much he withdraws. Because she waits for letters they do not arrive. Because she fears betrayal she finds it. She falls ill, leaves Paris for Provence and starts a seemingly safe relationship with a painter, Oradour. Because she has someone else Drino is jealous. She visits him in Paris and he tries to 'claim' her as his. The gamesmanship of it all frees her and she travels back to Oradour. On the train she overhears two middle-aged women talking of love. One speaks of jealousy, the other of her attachment to . . . Oradour.

Love, Violet suggested, is a merry-go-round of betrayal. There is no freedom in it. Its manipulations, declarations and reversals form repetitive patterns.

~'

Mrs Keppel moved from 16 Grosvenor Street in 1924. She bought the Ombrellino, a huge villa overlooking Florence at the top of a hill called Bellosguardo (beautiful view). She had tired of London, her social dazzle tarnished by the war, the first Labour administration, Violet's scandal, middle age, the English climate which she loathed. Sonia was ensconced in Hampshire. Henry, a brother for Rosalind, was born in March 1924. George had no occupation to keep him in England.

She kept a furnished suite at the Ritz for when she was in town. The Ritz, created at the turn of the century with Bertie's tastes in mind, was her spiritual home. The Palm Court with its panelled mirrors, gold trellises, glass roof, little gilded replica Louis XVI arm-chairs made by Waring and Gillow, was an Edwardian haven in a changing world. Its marble fountain was known as 'La Source'. Her suite with marble basins and gold candelabra looked out over Green Park and had servants' rooms attached.

The Ombrellino was her palace in the sun, financed by the King's bequest. Here she could spend, indulge and enjoy her wealth. Every room and terrace gave a stunning view — over the Duomo, Baptistery, Palazzo Pitti, Ponte Vecchio, over olive groves, the river Arno and 'the greenest of pastoral landscapes'. Harold Acton wrote of it and her:

In London she had been on parade, as it were, but in Florence she could lead, comparatively, the simple life. The food at L'Ombrellino was conspicuously more lavish when a Rothschild was being entertained on the principle of 'unto everyone that hath shall be given, and he shall have abundance'.

She never learned the language but this proved no impediment to her Italianate life. Bellosguardo, studded with monolithic villas behind stone walls and surrounded by olive groves, was an ex-patriate colony. English was spoken. Mrs Keppel's neighbours composed, painted,

collected works of art, travelled and entertained. There was the art
historian Bernard Berenson in the Villa I Tatti (for many years he
worked for Joseph Duveen), Mabel Dodge 'presiding over Bohemia' at
the Villa Curonia, Sir George Sitwell at the Villa Montegufoni, Harold
Acton at La Pietra.

Rich English and Americans bought these huge Tuscan villas at low
prices from the late nineteenth century on. The Villa Ombrellino was
on a heroic scale. It served Mrs Keppel's status fantasies. From the
terraces Violet said, it was like being on the deck of 'some great ship
about to sail'. The villa, she said, had

> quality, beauty, spaciousness, but not intimacy . . . large, hand-
> some rooms leading out of each other . . . a mere cupboard
> assumed the proportions of a cathedral organ, an armchair can-
> not forget that it is distantly related to a throne.

Galileo had lived there and his bust was on the loggia. Monumental
rooms and a great staircase led to the *piano nobile*. There were three
drawing rooms to every bedroom. The servants' rooms filled the third
floor. There were walled gardens with purple bougainvillea, an iris
garden, baroque statues, cypress trees.

Into the Ombrellino Mrs Keppel imported all the Grosvenor Street
furniture and more. The Chinese pagodas given her by Bertie, Chinese
porcelain, eighteenth-century portraits, tapestries, Chippendale chairs
and Regency settees. No one, Harold Acton, said, could compete with
her glamour as a hostess:

> A fine figure of a woman as they used to say, more handsome
> than beautiful, she possessed enormous charm, which was not
> only due to her cleverness and vivacity but to her generous heart
> . . . Altogether she was on a bigger scale than most of her sex.

She presided aware of past times. Queen Alexandra's signed photograph was displayed, feathers stuck to a card were captioned in Bertie's
writing 'shot by me', a sapphire the size of a duck's egg was a gift from
the King of Persia. Presents she gave had a history. A diamond owl

hatpin for the Countess of Listowel was once a trinket for Little Mrs George from Bertie.

Expatriate European princes and queens, Florentine, English and French aristocracy gathered on her terraces. Group photographs taken by George show Princess Irene of Greece, Queen Helen of Romania, Prince Paul of Yugoslavia, Count Raben of Denmark whom Violet resembled. Violet, her social status restored, posed in these photographs with the Princesse de Polignac, with Denys, Sonia, Mrs Keppel, the Princesse Bibesco, the Princesse de Chimay.

The English aristocracy summered at Ombrellino or travelled there from the casinos of the Riviera, the spas of Montecatini and Arles. The talk was of 'so and so's liaison with a chauffeur or the rumour of some Casanova's impotence — variations on the sempiternal themes'. The Earls and Countesses of Rosebery, Abingdon, Kimberley, Ilchester and Listowel, the Viscounts and Viscountesses Knollys, Ellbank and Chaplin, the Dukes and Duchesses of Wellington and Westminster, Lord Stavordale, Mrs Hwfa Williams, the Marchionesses of Curzon and Crewe, Ambassadors from the Netherlands and Chile, French Generals, Admirals of the Fleet and Masters of the Realm, signed the visitors' book, admired the views, praised the food, played bridge and tipped the butler, who was, said Harold Acton, 'insatiable of tips especially from the bridge players: he had an intuitive knowledge of their winnings'.

'Winston was so happy staying with your Mother at l'Ombrellino', his wife Clementine Churchill wrote to Violet some twenty years later from Montecatini Terme where she was taking a cure:

> & I think it was at the beginning of his painting career ... I remember he tried to do a Panorama from the Terrace. He wanted to take everything in, but I think & hope he was persuaded that the human eye can't take everything in at one focus. I am enjoying the mud baths but Alas to-day they are not functioning because of the Strike.

Hedonism was obligatory. Luncheon in the huge dining room with its marble floor, frescoed walls, glass doors opening to the terrace, took three hours. George's niece Lady Cecilia, daughter of the 9th Earl of Albemarle, and her husband, David McKenna, visited the Ombrellino when they married. There was a lavish dinner in their honour. David McKenna got sunstroke, felt ghastly and needed to be in bed. Mrs Keppel told him he was well enough to dine. It was his honeymoon, he would appear, the dinner was for him, the show must go on. Persuasion, as Violet said, was her mother's hallmark.

George got himself an early Lanchester, red and very sporty. He liked to drive it fast with the roof down and a 'little darling' from the Ombrellino at his side. He kept an apartment in Florence for his personal use. And he became an author. He privately published a series of *Aids to Memory* by Colonel Keppel. These dealt, in columns, lists, indices and addenda, with 'Contemporary Dates between the 13th and 18th centuries of the Medici in Florence and the Renaissance' and 'French Painters (1400–1900) And Their Times'. The Colonel's readers could ascertain that in the year Charles X died at Goritz, the first electric telegraph was erected and that Manet 'was an attractive personality, and had an exquisite sense of paint, as well as great decorative charm'.

Previously, Violet said, George had 'scarcely glanced at a picture in his life'. Now he could tell his visitors that the 'Tribuna' was added to the Uffizi Picture Gallery during the reign of Ferdinand I, or that Ghiberti's Baptistry Doors were finished in 1424.

In Paris on 3 December 1924 after a gap of three years, Violet and Vita met briefly. Vita was there for the sale of remaining pieces from Seery's flat in the rue Lafitte. She stayed at 53 rue de Varenne home of the American lawyer Walter Berry. He arranged a dinner party for her and invited, among others, Violet and Gerald Berners. 'Oh my God. What am I to do?' Vita wrote to Harold in panic. She said she was frightened out of her wits. He wired urging her to be careful. 'You are always so opty about things and so weak.' Next morning she said curiosity had replaced her agitation. 'If V does not know I am here she will get a nice jump – and anyway it will be great fun for Berners.' Violet, Harold replied, had the evil eye, was a fiend of destruction and all she wanted was to destroy their happiness, 'do do be careful and not get mesmerized by that devil. I know she will try to do us harm.' But Violet and she were no more than guests at the same table. The fiend of destruction did no damage that day.

Denys freed himself from being accountable to or for his wife when he matchmade between her and the Princesse de Polignac. He accompanied her if a husband was required but she saw him less and less. Unencumbered, he travelled. He was drawn to Russia, had been working as a tutor there in 1914 and left only to fight in the war. In 1926 and again in the winter of 1927, he returned. Violet wanted to go too but he discouraged her. He was gone for months at a time. 'I realised I was married to Lohengrin,' she wrote.

In an unpublished book, *The Stones of Emptiness*, he alluded to business appointments and curiosity as to what he would find 'after a disastrous European war' and eight years of Bolshevik rule. He was emphatic he was not a spy. 'Above all I have never taken any part whatever in espionage of any sort or kind.' But he was undoubtedly an English aristocrat averse to egalitarianism, socialism, trade-union rule.

He found a changed country. He called it a wilderness now with the stones of emptiness stretched out on it. His prewar Russian friends shunned him. He was shadowed night and day, arrested, fined 500 roubles for contravening the Labour Code and half a rouble for getting off the wrong end of a tram. His book was a polemic against communism. He marshalled antipathetic arguments: it rewarded the unskilled and inefficient, sapped ambition and energy through lack of material incentive, encouraged widespread unemployment, exported goods in short supply at prices below production cost.

He wrote of street hawkers, 'careworn faces', queues for food, no well-dressed people, and emblems of hammers and sickles replacing crowns and eagles. 'Wealth has flown but poverty lingers.' He complained that British royalty was mocked, as were Ramsay MacDonald, Winston Churchill and Austen Chamberlain. In the street, people fingered his clothes in envy. At a Trade Fair there was nothing to buy. The state monopoly on vodka was a third of the national budget.

Theatres were full, he said, only because free seats were given to the Unions. The audience wore muddy boots, ate oranges, made no attempt at evening dress. State theatre conveyed the 'ravings of an unbalanced mind tempered by hideous Bolshevik propaganda'. Ballet dancers were kept on long after they should have retired. Opera singers and sportsmen were second-rate.

He did though enjoy his favourite sport, shooting capercailzie – a sort of wood grouse – in the spring:

> For $1\frac{1}{2}$ roubles – 3 shillings – anyone can shoot throughout the
> USSR from the Baltic to the Pacific, from the Black Sea to the
> Arctic . . . I have never had the good fortune to kill a bear though
> I went after a fine specimen on one occasion.

He also shot foxes, hares, blackgame, snipe, ducks and wild partridges.

In March 1926 when Denys was getting away from his wife, deriding Bolshevism and shooting creatures, in Paris the play *La Prisonnière* by Edouard Bourdet at the Théâtre Femina caused ripples of interest. It was about the triangle of love of a young wife, Irène, her lover – an older woman – and her husband. The characters were said to be Violet, the Princesse de Polignac and Denys. Through the Princesse, Violet had become friendly with Bourdet's wife, Denise. At the play's end the lovers part and the older woman sends Irène a bunch of violets. Irène presses these to her lips and weeps. Lesbians in the audience showed solidarity by pinning violets to their lapels.

Denys went back to Russia early in 1927. At a dinner at the British Embassy in Moscow he met Vita, travelling to Teheran with Dorothy Wellesley to see Harold. 'Lord bless me!' wrote Virginia Woolf. 'Think of meeting your paramour's husband. What did he say?' Later that year he joined the Princesse de Polignac, Violet, Mrs Keppel, George and a 'large party' for a trip to the USA. 'Denys vaguely toyed with the idea of finding a job there,' Violet said. They had tea at the White House, went to Palm Beach, Florida, were guests of Winnaretta's brother Paris Singer at the Everglades Club.

In 1928 Denys made his last visit to Russia. 'He went there' Violet said 'at the risk of his life. He was fundamentally restless ... Russia never left him in peace for long ...' He travelled back to England via Vienna, Florence, Cannes and Avignon. With his sister Betty and his niece, in rain and mud he revisited the battlefields of Belgium, now fields of white crosses. In England he stayed with his other sister, Beatrice, a musician, at Buxted in Sussex. His tuberculosis was chronic. He had a permanent cough, was extremely thin, suffered from insomnia, mood swings, disturbing dreams that made him shout in his sleep. She nursed him while he completed his book.

Back in Paris

he continued to go to bed as late as ever, sometimes even neglecting to take an overcoat on the wildest winter night; precautions were not for him ... Then, what was bound to happen, happened.

Denys was thirty-nine. He had not tried to avert his death. His decade of civilian life had no particular direction. His scars of war were deep. He had not spoken to Violet of that war and all that he and relatively few others survived.

Violet did not look after him for his last illness. His sister Betty travelled to Paris and arranged his admission to the American Hospital in Neuilly. His mother travelled over too. The Princesse de Polignac gave help to them all and visited. 'I can only suppose they talked about music,' Violet wrote, 'as I was not encouraged to be present.'

Violet, according to Denys's niece, Phyllida Ellis, would

put her head round the hospital door, say 'Hello Denys' in her deep voice. 'Goodbye, I'm off to the south of France.' Part of it was a horror of illness. But she was so selfish. That was a key word. She could never see anybody else's point of view.

He died on Monday 2 September 1929. 'Heard from Pat that Denys was dead,' Vita at Long Barn wrote in her diary. She had spent the day of his death with Virginia Woolf. They had a picnic under pine trees in Ashdown Forest. She visited Pat in London on 19 September and they talked about Denys's death.

Violet in the world's eyes was a young widow, more socially acceptable than a divorcee. Her mother invited her to live at the Ombrellino. Violet preferred the 'less obvious charms' of her own house in France. After the funeral she wrote to Cyril Connolly in a way that circumvented feeling and romanticized the short life of a man whom she should not have married and to whom she had nothing to give:

> By now you doubtless know that Denys – my husband – is dead. He died nearly three weeks ago – and since I have been living in a sort of mist ... My life is going through a series of revisions ... More than anyone I know, he liked to live dangerously, his life was spent in impossible crusades. Russia was his Holy Land. His attitude towards life and towards death was magnificently condescending ... I am writing hard at present with the fervour born of unhappiness.

SEVENTEEN

La Tour de St Loup de Naud near Provins was where Violet wrote after Denys's death. Provins is a medieval town eighty kilometres from Paris, the hamlet of St Loup 'one steep Utrillo-like street, green or blue shutters closed because of the heat, zinnias outside the cottages'. Marcel Proust urged her to visit Provins, its Romanesque church and St Loup in 1922.

The steep street led to a derelict tower which the Princesse de Polignac bought and renovated for Violet. 'Romantic and mysterious', it was a continuation from Duntreath, Berkeley and the romance of childhood. Like Duntreath it was 'half medieval, half exotic'. Set in the ruins of an eleventh-century abbey, it had a monks' refectory, ramparts, twenty acres of park and woodland.

Violet disdained practicalities, derided the ordinary, preferred theatrical effect. Her tower was inaccessible and hard to maintain. The unwary tripped down the narrow stairs. Beneath the dining room were dungeons, the chimneys had so far to draw that fires in the bedroom grates smoked like 'the last act of the Valkyries', waterpipes burst in winter, the place was so exposed.

Alone there Violet half-faced ambition. 'I had been put into the world to write novels,' she said in her self-deprecating way. If the truth was unacceptable she could admit experience in fictional guise. *Broderie Anglaise*, written in French, was her *roman à clef*, the third in a trilogy about herself and Vita. The others were *Challenge* by Vita and *Orlando* by Virginia Woolf. (She did not know of Vita's 'confession', written in 1920 and hidden away.)

In 1924, four years after *Challenge* was pulped in Britain, it was published as a palliative in New York. American readers did not know why it had been previously withdrawn. Reviewers surmised it was

242

'I HAD POISE, EXPERIENCE, FRIENDS, POSSESSIONS.
ROMANCE WAS AT LONG LAST DISCIPLINED'

Violet at the Ombrellino c.1937

'A MERE CUPBOARD ASSUMES THE PROPORTIONS OF A
CATHEDRAL ORGAN, AN ARMCHAIR CANNOT FORGET
THAT IT IS DISTANTLY RELATED TO A THRONE'

*The Ombrellino, Florence, with views over the river Arno, the Duomo,
Ponte Vecchio and Palazzo Pitti*

'ACROSS MY LIFE ONLY ONE WORD WILL BE
WRITTEN: "WASTE" — WASTE OF LOVE, WASTE
OF TALENT, WASTE OF ENTERPRISE'

Violet in 1919

because of risk of libel. Vita changed the original dedication which read 'with gratitude for much excellent copy to the orginal of Eve' to

ACABA EMBEO SIN TIRO, MEN CHUAJANI; LIRENAS,
BERJARAS TIRI OCHI BUSNE, CHANGERI, TA ARMENSALLE

which meant not a lot to most. Translated from Julian and Eve's Romany language it read: 'This book is yours, my witch. Read it and you will find your tormented soul, changed and free.'

Pat Dansey gave Violet a copy of the American edition. Violet underlined passages she believed showed Vita's love. The book was not published in Britain until 1973, a year after her death. Vita's son and executor Nigel Nicolson returned the manuscript to its original publisher, Collins, their schedule interrupted by fifty years. In a foreword he wrote of Eve:

> The subtlety of *Challenge* is that an odious girl is made convincingly lovable. Eve, like Violet, is . . . a seductress who risked time and again her victim's love by indifference, insult, and finally by betrayal. Eve is the portrait of a clever, infuriating, infinitely charming witch.

Eve/Violet makes Julian/Vita lose his upright manly head with her wanton ways. And because she is a witch and full of feminine wiles, she betrays him. *Challenge* was the stuff of Hollywood psychodrama. 'In the end,' said Greta Garbo in 1922 of her role in *The Temptress*, 'I have to fall through the ice so the show can go on.' Similarly Eve drowns so that Julian can shape up, the expedient fate for bewitching sirens.

Through Pat Dansey Violet heard of Vita's burgeoning relationship with Virginia Woolf, Bloomsbury's leading woman novelist. *Orlando: A Biography* was published in 1928, the year before Denys died. Openly dedicated to Vita and about her, it showed photographs of her *décolletée* with ropes of pearls, and with her dogs at Long Barn. Violet knew every allusion, every characterization in the book. By publishing it Virginia Woolf declared intimacy with Vita's life. Violet had lost any such intimacy. Even trivial contact was denied. She was punished, exiled, silenced, for her manifestation of love. 'I ache with the sense of the appalling unfairness,' she had written to Vita. 'You are as guilty as I.'

She is cast as Princess Sasha and rooted in the usual tyrannies of her sex. Orlando calls her Sasha after a white Russian fox he had as a boy 'a creature soft as snow, but with teeth of steel, which bit him so savagely that his father had it killed'. She and Orlando meet on the ice which melts under their passion. She talks 'so enchantingly, so wittily, so wisely (but unfortunately always in French . . . English was too frank, too candid a tongue for her'. 'In all she says and does' there is something hidden 'she never shone with the steady beam of an Englishwoman'.

Her rank is not as high as she would like, she flirts, there is something coarse about her, she is 'deceitful', 'faithless', 'mutable', 'fickle', a 'devil', 'adulteress', 'deceiver'. She abandons *Orlando* on the very day when they had agreed to elope together. By the time she is forty she is fat, lethargic, befurred 'marvellously well-preserved, seductive, diademed, a Grand Duke's mistress'.

Violet had not met Virginia Woolf. This was Vita's account, as fed to Virginia, of her character and part in their relationship. It was as Violet saw it one more distortion, another betrayal, a reversal of what had happened, a blackening of her name.

Vita assured Harold that Violet was 'a madness of which I should never again be capable . . . a thing like that happens once and burns out the capacity for such a feeling'. She confided to him – up to a point – her same-sex affairs with Pat Dansey; Dorothy Wellesley; Mary Campbell, wife of the poet Roy Campbell; Margaret Voigt; Evelyn Irons; Hilda Matheson, Director of Talks at the BBC. Her relationship with Virginia Woolf was of a different ilk.

'These Sapphists love women; friendship is never untinged with amorosity,' Virginia wrote of Vita in her diary on 21 December 1925. She did not consider herself one of 'these Sapphists', though she was interested enough in women who loved each other. She described herself as 'sexually cowardly', 'valetudinarian', with a 'terror of real life'. Mentally fragile, afraid of loss of control, she preferred to hold hands, exchange glances and ideas: 'But what I want of you is illusion – to make the world dance.' She and her husband Leonard had, early on, some sexual endeavour which Vita said 'was a terrible failure and was abandoned quite soon'. She gained her hold on the world by writing things down.

Vita reassured Harold that here was a 'soul friendship. Very good for me and good for her too.' Virginia she said was not accustomed to 'emotional storms':

> She lives too much in the intellect and imagination ... I look on my friendship with her as a treasure and a privilege ... I shan't ever fall in love with her, *padlock*, but I am absolutely devoted to her.

She admired the originality of Virginia's mind, her perspicacity, depth, wit and gift – the excellence of her prose. She deferred to what she perceived as true talent, was flattered and honoured by Virginia's interest in her, found her 'dowdy but beautiful' and was 'scared to death' of any sexual exchange. She did not want to precipitate a psychotic or depressive attack. Sex with Virginia, Vita reassured Harold, was a fire with which she had no wish to play. 'Probably I would be less sagacious if I were more tempted, which is at least frank.' They went to bed together twice which was often enough.

Vita could write to Virginia

> It is incredible how essential to me you have become ... oh my dear! I *can't* be clever and stand-offish with you; I love you too much for that. Too truly.

And Virginia could take it on board for it was on paper, contained, without danger.

Vita's aristocratic 'splendour' inspired Virginia's love and satire and informed *Orlando*:

> she shines in the grocers shop in Sevenoaks with a candle lit radiance, stalking on legs like beech trees, pink glowing, grape

clustered, pearl hung . . . There is . . . her capacity to take the floor in any company, to represent her country, to visit Chatsworth, to control silver, servants, chow dogs; her motherhood (but she is a little cold & offhand with her boys).

In literature, Virginia Woolf had comparable confidence, style and aristocratic splendour. She shines with candlelit radiance on the printed page. Vita, she thought, had a 'pen of brass' and no particular originality of mind ('she never breaks fresh ground. She picks up what the tide rolls to her feet'). But she was, for Virginia, life. She was in awe of the 'central vigour' that prompted Vita to write fifteen pages a day, admired her manner – 'striding; silk stockings; shirt & skirts; opulent; easy; absent; talking spaciously & serenely to the Eton tutor' – the way she dominated the road as she drove her large blue Austin car. In her diary she wrote of the 'opulence and freedom' of Long Barn, 'flowers all out, butler, silver, dogs, biscuits, wine, hot water, log fires Italian cabinets, Persian rugs, books.' And when Vita took her to Knole, as Vita did with all the women she loved, she saw her living heritage, her links with the past:

Vita stalking in her Turkish dress, attended by small boys down the gallery, wafting them on like some tall sailing ship – a sort of covey of noble English life: dogs walloping, children crowding, all very free & stately: & [a] cart bringing wood in to be sawn by the great circular saw . . . They had brought wood in from the Park to replenish the great fires like this for centuries: & her ancestresses had walked so on the snow with their great dogs bounding by them. All the centuries seemed lit up, the past expressive, articulate; not dumb and forgotten . . . After tea, looking for letters of Dryden's to show me, she tumbled out a love letter of Ld Dorset's (17th century) with a lock of his soft gold tinted hair which I held in my hand a moment. One had a sense of links fished up into the light which are usually submerged.

Vita gave Virginia *Challenge* to read in June 1927. The gift stirred memories and on 11 June, she wrote, provocatively:

Do you know what I should do if you were not a person to be rather strict with? I should steal my own motor car out of the garage at 10pm tomorrow night, be at Rodmell [Virginia's house] by 11.5, throw gravel at your window, then you'd come down and let me in; I'd stay with you till 5, and be home by half-past six. But, you being you, I can't; more's the pity. Have you read my book? *Challenge*, I mean. Perhaps I sowed all my wild oats then. Yet I don't feel that the impulse has left me; no, by God; and for a different Virginia I'd fly to Sussex in the night. Only with age, soberness, and the increase of consideration, I refrain. But the temptation is great.

Virginia wired, 'Come then', to which Vita did not respond. Three days later she wrote to Vita:

You see I was reading *Challenge* and I thought your letter was a challenge 'if only you weren't so elderly and valetudinarian' was what you said in effect 'we would be spending the day together' whereupon I wired 'come then' to which naturally there was no answer and a good thing too I daresay as I am elderly and valetudinarian – it's no good disguising the fact. Not even reading *Challenge* will alter that. She is very desirable I agree: very.

But what Vita had of course said was that if Virginia was not who she was, they would be spending not the day together but the night.

Orlando was Virginia's gift to Julian, her way of being Eve. She intended it as a little book with pictures – about 30,000 words. When Vita heard she was writing it – in October 1927 – she was 'thrilled and terrified' and asked Virginia to dedicate it to her 'victim'. Virginia wanted facts for the book. She asked for 'some inkling' of the quarrels Vita had with Violet and 'for what particular quality' Violet first chose Vita. 'I want to see you in the lamplight, in your emeralds'. 'Is it true you grind your teeth at night? Is it true you love giving pain?'

Short of heaven, *Orlando* was the ultimate gift to the aristocrat who has everything. It gave Vita Knole, a masculine and female identity, a lifespan of some hundreds of years. Time and gender are unconstrained. Orlando is a woman one century, a man the next. Knole can be Vita's for she is a man. Violet can be hers for she is a man. Harold — Marmaduke Bonthrop Shelmerdine — can be hers for she is a woman.

No scandal attached to *Orlando* though it talked in its way of androgyny and lesbian love. Virginia Woolf treated the issue of sexual freedom with acceptable obliqueness and irony, acerbic disdain for 'compulsory heterosexuality', and with imagination. She sent the finished manuscript to Vita in a leather binding. Vita said it 'was like a cloak encrusted with jewels and sprinkled with rose petals'. It made her laugh and cry. She read it in a day and was ecstatic, 'completely dazzled, bewitched, enchanted, under a spell'. It was the 'loveliest, wisest, richest' book she had ever read. She said she felt like a wax figure in a shop window on which Virginia had hung 'a robe stitched with jewels. Darling how could you have hung so splendid a garment on so poor a peg?'

Harold loved it too. 'It really is Vita,' he wrote to Virginia on 15 October 1928. 'She strides magnificent and clumsy through 350 years.' He said it filled him with 'amazed excitement'. 'I am deeply grateful to you, Virginia, for having written something so lovely and so strong.' Nigel Nicolson called it 'the longest and most charming love-letter in literature'. But there was something mocking in Virginia Woolf's tone. Orlando/Vita is slow-witted. He/she lives in a place that 'is more like a town than a house'.

Lady Sackville was unimpressed. She regarded the book as an insult, called Virginia 'that Virgin Woolf' pasted a photograph of her in her own copy and captioned it:

> The awful face of a mad woman whose successful mad desire is
> to separate people who care for each other. I loathe this woman
> for having changed my Vita and taken her away from me.

Virginia wrote *Orlando* at a time when Vita's relationship with her mother had reached an all-time low. Lord Sackville died in 1928. Violet wrote Vita a loving note when she heard:

> I know what a flawless companionship yours was, and often as a child was awed by your twin silences which I didn't then realise arose from a perfect understanding of each other.

Lady Sackville became paranoid after his death and quarrelled with everyone. In the family lawyer's office she screamed that Vita had stolen her pearls, she would stop every penny of her allowance, she wished her dead.

The following month Vita went alone to Knole in the evening and let herself in to the grounds with a master key:

> I kept thinking that I should see Dada at the end of the long grass walks . . . But needless to say I saw nothing – nothing but the lilac in the dusk.

'I must' she wrote to Harold in a telling phrase 'try to put Knole out of my heart as one puts a dead love.'

So Virginia's gift of *Orlando* soothed. It took Knole and Violet out of Vita's heart and put them on to the literary shelves. It was published to 'great excitement' in September 1928. Sales were 'amazingly brisk'. By December it had gone into a third edition. In six months 8,000 copies were sold. It was a bestseller.

Publication coincided with the trial for obscenity of Radclyffe Hall's *The Well of Loneliness*. Virginia offered to testify in its favour though she thought it a 'meritorious dull book'. It is the forlorn story of Stephen Gordon a 'congenital invert' who sees herself as a man trapped in a woman's body. Orlando, by contrast, is a free spirit who time and gender cannot constrain. 'Sapphism' was topical. Virginia allied herself with the cause by going away alone with Vita for a week in France.

For Violet the book was a laceration, the perpetrating of a lie the more painful because of Virginia Woolf's reputation. Yet again Vita was the hero and she, Violet, the evil fox. *Broderie Anglaise* was her retaliation. She read in *Orlando* that English was 'too frank and candid a tongue' for her. In French she was frank, candid and disparaging. She took for her title an untranslatable French term for a kind of English embroidery that consists of decorating holes. Her novel, decoded, is a swingeing rebuttal of Vita's version of their affair as published in *Orlando*. In *Broderie Anglaise* Violet tells the world that Vita loved her equally and that Vita, not she, was the one who reneged on the arranged wedding day.

Far from spanning centuries and landscapes of the mind, the entire action of Violet's novel takes place in a single afternoon in the London drawing room of the house where the writer Alexa/Virginia lives with her pipe-smoking literary uncle, Jim/Leonard Woolf. She and Lord Shorne/Vita, who lives with his domineering mother, are having a lukewarm affair. On the day of the novel's action, Alexa is to have a visit from Shorne's former lover Anne/Violet, who now lives in Paris. Shorne does not know of this intended visit.

Alexa is an awkward lover, 'incomplete as a woman', 'an old maid', a virgin, her bed 'so small and shy' you can scarcely find it in the bedroom. Her hair is thin (Violet was often commended by Vita for her 'truly beautiful hair'), she has an 'elderly neck', is of indeterminate age with 'no bloom to lose'.

Everything about her is cerebral, famous, she has beautiful hands, but she is too thin, uninterested in food, wears dowdy clothes, is 'very Oxford'. She is 'a piece of waterweed', 'a puff of smoke'. A fifteenth-century Flemish painter would, Violet wrote, have ' portrayed her with a caged goldfinch and a carnation spotted with dew'.

Shorne is flattered 'to be the lover of one of the most distinguished women in England'. But Alexa lives only in her books, writes with her brain, not her heart, and there is not a prostitute or royal bastard among her ancestors.

Lord Shorne has plenty of prostitutes and royal bastards among his ancestors. Tall, with 'perfect self-assurance', he is attractive to women, has 'languid grace', 'latent fire', is easy with the servants and a Rolls-Royce waits at his door. Despite his foreign mother, his English ancestry prevails. He has that 'hereditary face which had come, eternally bored, through five centuries'. 'Down the years, this face, [the Sackville face], has been painted by Moro, Van Dyck, Gainsborough.' Again and again for her heroes Violet used this description of Vita.

Shorne admires Alexa's mind but does not desire her. They are awkward together when they travel abroad. 'Alexa admired the wrists and ankles of the Medici Venus, Shorne admired those of the chambermaid.' He pursues Alexa only because she is unavailable. A formula underpins all his love affairs: 'I advance, you retreat. You retreat, I advance.' It was elementary, as old as the hills.'

The true relationship of his life was with his cousin Anne/Violet, 'who knew everything without having had to learn anything, and who had been as expert at fifteen as Alexa was at thirty . . .'. Shorne, on his nineteenth birthday, told Anne he loved her. Love, for him, is possession. He said it 'as if he were handling some familiar object'. All other women are passing fancies. Anne was the one who mattered. She now lives in France, is witty, has a tendency to put on weight:

> Would he never manage to banish that ghost? Never have done with that slow unfurling love which had sapped his youth, taking root in every recess of him like a perennial plant that blooms without any help from the gardener?
>
> Alexa — what was she but a makeshift? A wearisome substitute, founded on renunciation. 'From the ruins of my palace have I built my cottage.'

In bed with Alexa, Shorne imagines he is with Anne. He has a recurring dream of piercing her heart with a sword. As this buries into her flesh

> it sent up on either side of the wound a little spurt of white foam . . . it was at once horrible and delicious . . . he would wake up feeling cheated and drained.

(Violet had read her Freud.)

He lives with his mother in the ancestral home, Otterways/Knole. Alexa/Virginia is in thrall to the trappings of the aristocracy. The place is a 'whole little town'. Even pats of butter on the breakfast tray are stamped with the family coat of arms. Shorne shows her portraits of his ancestors: 'one who wrote a sonnet to Queen Elizabeth, another who died of wounds at the battle of Agincourt'. Alexa is overwhelmed. Her own family

> consists of nothing but respectable middle-class citizens, much too learned and rather sexless. Our only flirtations have been with theses and all we've ever carried away is an audience.

In comes Lady Shorne, fat and fifty, with a cruel mouth and beauty in decline. She wears a dirty old flannel dressing gown pinned with the family jewels – rubies, diamonds and emeralds galore. On her head, 'pushed slightly askew by her curlers', is her tiara. There is 'something not quite right about this great lady'. Not quite right at all. She alludes to intimate matters with a mixture of clinical curiosity and prudishness, talks in *non sequiturs*, waits for no answers, makes malicious asides and inventories of her jewellery.

She is a wicked old courtesan, her fists in the money bags, obsessed with power, a caricature of Mrs Keppel, Lady Sackville and all matriarchs who undermine their children's lives. Shorne is afraid of her. Under her spell he is the Cheshire cat's smile, the bird on the painted-glass picture caged by her eyes. When pregnant she viewed his birth as an immediate pleasure and a distant threat: a pleasure because she 'could bring him up according to the sacred principles of her antique dealer's heart'; a threat because he would one day challenge her power.

Safe in French Violet was as rude as she liked. All that she dared not say to or about her own mother, or mothers in general, she levelled at Lady Shorne. Her materialism and lust for power destroys her young. Her huge property is her passion:

> Her exclusive and fanatical nature, hungry for a 'mission' embraced the cause of Otterways with a fervour which in earlier

times would have been directed towards religion and heavenly rewards.

Otterways, like Knole, the Ombrellino, Grosvenor Street, is the forbidding palace, the status fantasy that accords grandeur to its owner but excludes intimacy and love. Shorne learned from an early age 'not to touch glass cases and to be careful with petit-point chairs'. In Paris he was left alone in his mother's huge apartment in the rue St Honoré. His childhood was lonely, sumptuous and punctuated by the appearances of this big spider who dispensed refusals and permissions, 'the second even more frightening than the first'. His compensatory relationship is his love for his cousin which mother destroys. She spies on him, tells lies, pieces together letters he has torn up, throws away Anne's photograph.

In a disconcerting scene, whether fiction or fact, Shorne seduces Alexa in the Charles II bedchamber at Otterways. The room is cold, musty and smells of camphor. Objects in it come ghoulishly alive. The Mortlake tapestry shows Joseph trying to escape the caresses of Potiphar's wife. The figures have swarthy faces and fair curls and 'looked sinister, like victims of the plague wearing wigs'. Shorne lights all the candles and tells Alexa to lie down on the bed:

fainting with pleasure, she obeyed. Shorne lay down beside her, impatiently brushing aside the little bags of camphor on the bolster.

Soon he was muttering incoherent phrases she could scarcely understand: 'I'm the master here! I'll show her! How dare she ...'

With a frankness and candour not equalled by *Orlando* Violet implied Vita had a sexual score to settle with her mother: that she used women sexually to be revenged on her, that materialism and possession extend to people, too. The scene echoes the sexual exchange between Vita and Violet in that Paris hotel the day after Violet's wedding in June

1919 when, Vita wrote in her Confession, 'I had her, I didn't care, I only wanted to hurt Denys.'

Mother spies through the keyhole while her son has sex. When Shorne wakes in the morning he does not know where he is or with whom. Pinned to the bedcover is a note from his mother: 'Don't worry – you won't be disturbed. I'll explain to the servants.'

Alexa/Virginia sets the scene for Anne's/Violet's afternoon visit. Shorne has told her Anne is 'ravishingly pretty' but overweight. Alexa hopes she will be huge, peroxided and painted. She rehearses topics of conversation, rejects gardens, sport and clothes and decides on cars. Buicks. (Cars, according to Violet, were talked about by her own mother and Virginia Woolf on the one occasion when they met for lunch in March 1932. 'Neither knew a thing about motors; both thought they were on safe ground discussing a topic on which they could bluff to their hearts' content.'

Alexa has used Shorne's version of his affair with Anne in her bestselling book, *Conquest*. Anne, Shorne told her, was false, flighty and only wanted the opposite of what she had. Shorne wanted to marry her. 'Everything was signed and settled.' Anne was affectionate, ardent. Shorne suspected nothing. And then, without warning, she left him in the lurch, because of her horror of anything irrevocable, her inability to commit herself.

Anne arrives. She is of medium height, plump, her eyes small and mocking, her mouth too big, her hands small, square-fingered, slightly stained by nicotine. Her voice is her best feature, 'soft, full of hidden depths, crepuscular'. That and her thick springy hair 'curly as vine tendrils'. She has herself written two well-received novels. 'Where was the siren Shorne had described?'

They talk, as prescribed, about gearboxes, shock absorbers and servo-brakes. It transpires that the fictional Violet has a husband and a little boy in Paris. She lives in a very old house by a stream and an old local woman cooks for her. 'I'm so happy in France,' said the languid voice. 'If I hate England it may be because I've always been unhappy here.' She tells Alexa she had not enjoyed *Conquest*, that the character of herself in it is 'psychologically false', 'why make her into an intriguer, someone false and treacherous, when really she's only an impulsive little animal?'

Violet retaliated against the portrait of herself in *Orlando*, the account of her relationship with Vita that the book broadcast, her chagrin that *Challenge* should have been censored by their mothers. Through Virginia as briefed by Vita she is described, she says in *Broderie Anglaise*, as

a brilliant, volatile, artificial creature, predictably unpredictable,
a historical character, a du Barry who behaved like Lola Montez.
In short a king's mistress.

She had been turned by their combined efforts into 'a family portrait worthy to hang in the Long Gallery beside Lely's Nell Gwynne and Kneller's *Louise de Kéroualle*'. It was, she implied, a portrait of a courtesan more fitting to her mother's life. The very opposite of this portrait fitted herself. This was the role she had sought to avoid. She had wanted with Vita a life together, a marriage of the heart.

The public, with its taste for the romantic, loved *Conquest/Orlando*. It won enthusiastic praise from the critics and literary prizes. But it distorted Violet's life.

Anne/Violet gives Alexa/Virginia her version of the broken 'marriage'. The wedding was fixed for 11 April. Their cases were packed. Anne was waiting for Shorne to arrive. Shorne sent the chauffeur with a message: 'The dreadful lying letter he wrote me! He didn't even have the courage to tell me face to face.' Lady Shorne has intercepted all their letters and forbidden him to marry. John Shorne is a coward with no assertion of his own. Anne was his victim, not the other way round. She asks Alexa if Shorne is still afraid of his mother. She ends the meeting by saying that, though betrayed, she still loves Shorne and always will. It is the abiding theme of her life.

Too late for *Conquest* Alexa sees Shorne through Anne's eyes. She sees his character as torn between his mother and father, 'fatally divided ... between two kinds of atavism'. Because of his mother he has 'paltry affairs', plays the role of libertine, wants to feel strong, masculine and brutal. But the other side of him is repressed, kind, solitary, lives for his dogs and fields.

Alexa sympathizes with Anne, and is contrite at having written ineptly about her using false information from Shorne. As Anne leaves she gives her all the flowers in the room and says she will read her books. She then confronts Shorne with Anne's accusations. He defends himself, blames Anne, says she is 'cunning personified'. Alexa then asks him one question:

> 'Were you or weren't you afraid of angering your mother by marrying Anne?'
> 'Yes, but . . .'
> 'That'll do.'

It was on an autumn afternoon in November 1932 that the real Violet, over from Paris, called for tea in the London drawing room of the house where the real Virginia lived with her pipe-smoking literary husband, Leonard Woolf. Curiosity made her visit her rival — and she wanted impressions for her *roman à clef.* 'Who d'you think came and talked to me t'other night?' Virginia wrote to Vita

> Three guesses. All wrong. It was Violet Trefusis — your Violet. Lord what fun! I quite see now why you were so enamoured — then: she's a little too full, now, overblown rather; but what seduction! What a voice — lisping, faltering, what warmth, suppleness, and in her way — it's not mine — I'm a good deal more refined — but that's not altogether an advantage — how lovely, like a squirrel among buck hares — a red squirrel among brown nuts. We glanced and winked through the leaves; and called each other punctiliously Mrs Trefusis and Mrs Woolf — and she asked me to give her the Common R. which I did, and said, smiling, 'By the way are you an Honourable, too? No, no,' she smiled, taking my point, you, to wit. And she's written to ask me to go

and stay with her in France, and says how much she enjoyed meeting me; and Leonard: and we positively must come for a whole week soon. Also Mrs Keppel loves me, and is giving a dinner party solely for me in January. How I enjoyed myself! To be loved by Mrs Keppel, who loved, it is said – quite a different pair of shoes.

In the new year of 1933 Violet sent her 'a vast nodding bunch of lilac'. 'No, I'm not spending the New Year between her and Mme. de Polignac,' Virginia wrote to Vita. 'I wave the banner of chastity and cry upward.'

Violet hoped that Virginia Woolf, through the Hogarth Press, would publish her novel *Tandem*, written in English, about the relationship of two Greek sisters from 1900 until an imagined 1962 (the year Vita was to die). This did not happen. The doors of Bloomsbury and Kent were closed to her. She was not to be acknowledged seriously. She was Eve, Sasha, fox, squirrel, siren, panther.

Broderie Anglaise was published in France in 1935. In March that year Virginia perceived her love affair with Vita as over:

Not with a quarrel, not with a bang, but as ripe fruit falls. No I shant be coming to London before I go to Greece, she said. And then I got into the car.

Neither Virginia nor Vita read Violet's book. It was not mentioned in their correspondence. There was no copy of it among Vita's books when she died. Virginia Woolf did not read in French. It was not dedicated to either of them or translated into English until 1968 when both were dead. It caused no stir, offended no one, its truths and half-truths curtained by fiction, a foreign language and the passing of time.

EIGHTEEN

Violet's account of herself in *Broderie Anglaise* was fictional too. A refutation not a correction. She was not Princess Sasha in *Orlando*, Eve in *Challenge*, nor the straightforward Anne of her *roman à clef*. She did not have a husband, child and peace of mind in France. *Toute vérité n'est pas bonne à dire.*

Within five years of her exile she created a distinguished life. In Paris she went to first nights of concerts and plays, to private views of exhibitions. In her novels, light malicious commentaries on aristocratic preoccupations, she wrote with equal style in French and English. She was invited to the supper parties of Jean Cocteau and of Anna de Nouailles. Francis Poulenc was a friend. They shared a liking for beautiful houses and good food. She would visit him at his house beside the Loire, he was often at St Loup. Colette called her Geranium, not Violet, thought her tower at St Loup beautiful in a gothic way 'and the cushions in all kinds of pink. And the woods full of wild strawberries.'

St Loup was the home Violet would like to have had with Vita whom she called 'the tallest feather in my immodest cap'. Vita visited twenty years later and said the place gave her a 'queer feeling . . . almost as though I belong there'.

But alone there Violet's vulnerability and identity became masked by façade. With satirical flourish she adopted the values of the world she had said she despised. As time passed she seemed more her mother's camp understudy than the bohemian spirit to which she had aspired. She was châtelaine, and hostess, with a butler, chauffeur, cook, a maid who dressed her and did her hair.

In her twenties she had written to Vita: 'I have shown myself naked to you, mentally, physically and morally . . . I have added curtains to

my manners for other people's benefit, but for you there are no
curtains, not even gossamer ones.' The curtains became embroidered,
her manner strange. To many she seemed quirky, unknowable. The
diarist Peter Quennell wrote of her:

> the relationship between Violet and the truth was always a flirta-
> tious, loosely knit alliance rather than a firmly faithful bond. She
> did not conceal or distort facts as much as lightly play with them,
> doing her best to redeem their intrinsic banality by adding a touch
> of fiction here and there. What *should* have happened interested her
> far more than the humdrum march of real events.

To furnish St Loup she brought statues from Italy, blackamoors,
elaborate silver. The place seemed geared for grand romance. Visitors
were told to ask at the Paris Ritz and the concierge would arrange a
car. Those not on private incomes felt deterred. Guests slept in can-
opied beds in turret rooms with chandeliers, mottled mirrors in magnificent frames, wall hangings of coats of arms or mythical birds. One
bedroom she called 'chambre Louis XIV. It boasted a fourposter bed
of that period, some high-backed tapestry chairs'. She gave extravagant
attribution to pedestrian antiques, appeared not to care what was real
or imitation, the truth or a lie. The Louis XIII dining-room chairs were
upholstered in mauve velvet. The vermeil dessert spoons had belonged,
she said, to Catherine the Great. The faïence lions either side of the
Gothic fireplace had belonged to some king.

For her library she collected books of royal provenance. She bought
them if they had belonged to Mme de Pompadour or bore the coat
of arms of Henry VIII or Elizabeth I. From them she constructed royal
genealogies for the Keppels and Edmonstones. She was Mrs Keppel's
daughter and, so she said, Edward VII's too. As time passed she put
on weight, cared overmuch about food, was outwardly sparkling and
sharp while her eyes stayed sad.

In her novels she mocked the attitudes with which she seemed to
collude. She contrived slight plots, used brittle dialogue, took for
her themes betrayed lovers, dominant mothers, mercenary old ladies

making inventories of their jewels. When one of her characters complains her marriage is an empty parody her hostess replies, 'still, you'll be able to entertain.'

> *To entertain* . . . you'd have sworn that doors opened, that a glittering crowd thronged down a staircase out of Tiepolo; that musicians tuned their instruments, while liveried flunkies bowed to the very ground.

'To entertain' was the essence of life at the Ombrellino where Mrs Keppel ruled. She kept alive in microcosm Edwardian high life under southern skies. 'Chips' Channon — Sir Henry Channon, Conservative MP and diarist — visiting in 1934 described her as like a worldly Roman matron without the cruelty. She lived, he said, in a 'super-luxurious villa full of treasures' was 'grey and magnificent and young in spirit,

> but she cannot resist lying and inventing, and saying anything that comes into her Roman head. It is a habit she contracted long ago when, to amuse the blasé King Edward, she used to tell him all the news of the day spiced with her own humour.

From her mother Violet learned to embellish the truth to entertain eminent guests.

Violet did not again quarrel with 'men chinday' over issues of verity. Banishment made her wary. She lost Vita, love, England, youth and was not going to risk losing Mother too. The Ombrellino became her second home. She preferred St Loup but moved between the two and acknowledged her debt:

> If I speak four languages fluently it is thanks to my mother; if I know anything about pictures, furniture, *bibelots*, it is again thanks to her. If I enjoy travel, good conversation, good company.

All the social graces came from Mrs Keppel, if not integrity of heart. Violet seemed to forgive her mother, to concede to her values and style. She filled her time with writing, flirtations, travel, conversation, company. The days of *Rebellion* were over. As in her stories possessions triumphed over love. She was caught in a quest for status, a craving to impress. To her chosen country she brought the hedonism of her mother's world, of the Edwardians whom she satirized but did not reject.

Behind the mask she seemed ill at ease, her flirtations false. She was bright and sparkling in society, depressed in private. Phobic about being on her own, she spent inordinate time on the telephone, would not sleep in a house or apartment alone, yet could not say of what she was afraid. She was a chronic insomniac – 'I am sleep's beggar, grateful for a yawn' – and said that in the small hours of the night the word '*déclassé*' confronted her 'like a gamekeeper'. She panicked about growing old, had her face lifted, her hair permed, coloured, curled, was for ever powdering her cheeks and painting her lips.

She and her mother now wrote letters of devotion. Her mother called her 'darling Titten', 'precious Luna', sent her money, paid the bills. After a stay by her mother at St Loup Violet sent a love letter, cloying, adoring:

> Little love
>
> . . . I could not bear you to go, every minute we spent together was perfection. It is months since I have known such happiness. You can't think how much I admire you, my own precious, you are all the world to me, and I could not live without you.
>
> God bless you and keep you, my sweet.
>
> Your adoring Titten
>
> Best love to Papa and Uncle Archie.

Her mother referred to Violet's novels as 'writing' in inverted commas. Literary and oblique and so often in French, she took scant interest in them. To readers they seemed inconsequential, like the slight relationships of lords and ladies who lived in grand mansions and fooled with love. Philippe Jullian said her characters came straight from her address book, 'the rich and fashionable with their hangers on'. Her novels, he said, were like dinner parties in a rich mansion:

During the evening the smartly dressed and witty guests from time to time let drop a remark that suggests that they too know what it is to love and suffer. But however intense their emotions it is hard not to think that a longish cruise or plans for a party or two would not lighten their mood.

Her style sparkled with cleverness, irritated and concealed. She littered her prose with foreign quotation. Her readers did not know that she coded into her work her experience of lesbian passion, emotional betrayal, self-division, riches as rivals and the leitmotiv of lost love. She dealt in word games, paradoxes, conundrums and parried and played with the lies and truth. 'Trust no one,' she said in old age to her friend and executor John Phillips.

After *Broderie Anglaise* she again wrote in English. In *Hunt the Slipper* her hero has Nicolson names — Nigel Benson. He is middle-aged, 'feminine', married, safely adulterous. Caroline, his lover, wants to break the secret, cause a scandal. 'She had none of the frivolity of the older generation,' Violet wrote with a swipe. 'Latent in her mind was the theory that the world was well lost for love's sake.'

'I *want* to throw everything away for your sake,' her alter ego says:

I could so easily dispense with luxury ... You think that the lover has the romantic part. You're wrong: a lover ... is a convention. But what is *not* a convention is a husband who is also a lover.

Violet knew the convention of infidelity well: from the King despite the pomp and promises of royal marriage; from her mother in her boudoir of flowers, there with the King while her husband was out. With Vita she had hoped for unconventional fidelity, for a partner who was also a lover.

In conversation and writing she switched with facility from French to English and weakened her style by intertwining the two — *Broderie Anglaise* and *Echo* in French, *Hunt the Slipper* and *Tandem* in English. She interlaced her unimportant plots and slight characters with epigrams and apophthegms – a sort of conversational spice:

'I wish we could have children without the mothers. A kind of masculine virgin birth.'

'She is the last representative of a milieu to which she never belonged.'

'Her bones were joss-sticks, her eyes were by Fabergé, her heart, made out of Venetian glass, was a pretty toy.'

But she moved into a cultural limbo, her books not translated, her worlds divided, her print runs small, her readership split. She had no need to make her writing pay. She said she wrote each morning for a couple of hours but as the day passed her brain went woolly. She thought of herself as naturally indolent, without particular talent, deferred to Vita – a bestselling author – as the better writer, though her own style was sharper, her wit quicker, her intelligence more acute.

In 1930 Vita with her mother's money bought Sissinghurst Castle in Kent, a parallel to St Loup. It was a ruin set in seven acres of land. Its single intact fragment was a high square tower with adjoining turrets. The place, said Vita, 'caught instantly at my heart and imagination. I saw what might be made of it. It was Sleeping Beauty's castle.'

The creation of Sissinghurst and its gardens was her shared enterprise with Harold. He stayed the week in London and caught the Saturday train to Kent. In letters to each other they wrote of its reconstruction: moat walls, ponds, Tudor fireplaces, courtyards. But the tower was her citadel, sequestered, closed to her family. In thirty years her son Nigel visited her there twice. '*Chacun sa tour*,' Violet said when she saw it.

'I will not pretend,' Violet wrote after Denys's death, 'that after a year or two had elapsed I was not seriously tempted by the thought of remarriage.' It was one of her teasing sentences, not quite a lie. She was tempted by the thought and display of it, but steered clear of the fact. Her declared suitors were gay, rich, titled and playing the same game. Often they proved spiteful about her in memoirs and letters. One or two had been lovers of Harold's. She went through a charade of wooing, spoke always of who was in love with her, never of whom she loved.

She boasted that Max Jacob proposed to her. He was painter, poet, a friend of Picasso's, had a lover, Maurice Sachs. She met him through the Princesse de Polignac and Jean Cocteau:

> He called on me one afternoon dressed, he imagined, for the part of a suitor. A small dapper Punchinello, he wore a top hat, white spats, gloves the colour of fresh butter. He hung his hat on his stick which he held like a banner between his legs. He was irresistible. I longed to take advantage of his proposal which was couched in terms that sounded as though he had learned them out of a book on etiquette. We examined the pros and cons. St Loup, far from being an asset, proved a stumbling block.
>
> '*Je déteste la campagne*,' said Max, '*tout y est trop vrai!* The nearest I ever get is the Bois, and that is bad enough because it *reminds* me of the country.'
>
> 'What about travel?'
>
> 'That is different, the place doesn't belong to me, there are no responsibilities. *C'est comme si je mangeais au restaurant.*'
>
> A great advantage, he pointed out, was his being about twenty years older than me. 'I have waited forty years before proposing to anyone. I am not likely to propose to anyone else.'

Another great advantage was that it was no proposal at all. It was a way of parodying heterosexual necessity, of attracting attention, of seeming to be sexual, an in-joke for the circles in which she moved. She entertained her conquests at St Loup and flaunted them at the Ombrellino. True partnerships were not revealed and, as time went on, not made.

Gerald Berners was another of her fiancés for a day. He composed, painted, was amusing and liked his lovers young and male. He had a house in Rome overlooking the forum, another in London in Halkin Street and the eighteenth-century Faringdon Hall in Berkshire. On his desk there he kept a little clockwork pig. Wound up, it danced on its trotters. He called it Violet.

In autumn 1933 he visited St Loup. He was taking pep pills bought from a chemist at the Place Blanche in Paris. Violet suggested they marry and pool their assets. By the end of the evening they were engaged. News of it appeared next day in the London papers. Violet received congratulatory telegrams. 'Lord B. is marrying V. Trefusis (whom you once knew) because they both like poached eggs,' Virginia wrote to Vita. Mrs Keppel thought it all in poor taste and published a denial. Berners said he sent *The Times* a note: 'Lord Berners has left Lesbos for the Isle of Man.'

Such games were not the same as being candid. They were a camp version of Edwardian duplicity. Violet dismissed her suitors with a quip and an anecdote. 'Happiness for me lies in things, not people,' she has one of her characters say:

> You could say that my irresponsible and evasive nature can't
> support the heavy trappings of love . . . it becomes as grotesque
> as a little girl dressed in grown-up finery. It knows what's expected
> and wanted; flattered, for a little while it will turn grown-up . . .
> but the result is caricature.

She had told Vita and Denys that she was not attracted to men but she flaunted her quasi-seductions. Mrs Keppel was said to deter some of the fortune-hunting young men who hovered round. Comte Stanislas de La Rochefoucauld 'a witty though fatuous young man' had a title, an actress wife of whom he was tired and a small inheritance. He lost interest in Violet when Mrs Keppel told him English marriage customs precluded a widow receiving money from her parents if she remarried. 'I wonder how much Violet still has,' she is supposed to have said. 'She's *such* a child.'

Comte Jean de Gaigneron, with whom Harold had an affair in 1919, was another of the gay men with whom Violet made a sexual parade.

And then there was Comte Louis de Lasteyrie who knew Proust, owned a medieval chateau and was great grandson of the Marquis de Lafayette . . . And the Marquis de Chavannes who was once married to the Prince de Polignac's niece and to whom Violet proposed on account of his title. He said he resisted because she wanted him to shave his moustache.

The games she played with her princes and beaux were part fantasy, part parody and in part pathological. There was desperation behind the charade. It was as if her mother's warning about not having a husband had frozen her heart.

Like her mother she admired and flirted with men of rank. She had some kind of affair with the statesman Paul Reynaud Premier of France in 1940. In her memoir she wrote of a lunch party with him and her mother at 'Lapérouse, the world-famous restaurant on the Quai des Grands Augustins'.

> My mother chaffed him in a way to which he had certainly not been accustomed; they parted in amused and mutual esteem. After that, I was constantly to meet Paul Reynaud.

It was not clear whether Reynaud wanted mother, daughter, neither or both. 'You have two wives,' Violet is supposed to have said to him, 'it's time you had a mistress,' and offered herself. And then there was Comte Jean Ostrorog, son-in-law of the munitions' manufacturer Sir Basil Zaharof who had propositioned her in London in the 1920s . . . And for a winter in Budapest the Regent's son Horthy Estvan . . . :

> No wonder I fell in love . . . He had eyebrows like swallows' wings, and the figure of a Caucasian dancer. No wonder I took a rococo house in Buda which might have belonged to the Rosenkavalier . . . night after night we would dance . . . Up and down outside the detectives would pace for Horthy's escapade with an English-woman was not approved of. It was lovely while it lasted.

Vita writing of her in the early 1950s called her '*une âme damnée*. Dance little lady, dance dance dance.' She used the same phrase of her own mother who died in January 1936. 'I do wish she had been a happier person,' she wrote to Harold.

Violet was entirely silent about her relationships with women like the Duchesse d'Harcourt and the Princesse Gilone de Chimay – drawn from the Princesse de Polignac's set – the châteaux, the *gratin*, the closed discreet world of the French aristocracy. George Keppel photographed them on the terraces of the Ombrellino. But as in those group photographs of Edwardian weekend parties, with Edward VII at the centre in a Homburg hat, nothing was revealed in their closed faces of intimacy, affection or desire.

For her forty-third birthday in June 1937 Violet hired the Eiffel Tower for a costume ball. She told her guests to come dressed in the period of the inauguration of the tower in 1889:

> People arrived in dog-carts, on bicycles, in bloomers. They had muffs, feather boas, buttoned boots, fans, *carnets de bal*, hats with sea-gulls . . . Jewels were mostly astronomical – crescent moons, comets constellations . . . A contemporary Colette, with a tiny waist and a boater, flirted with a 1900 Boni de Castellane. I made an unrehearsed entry with Serge Lifar; we polkaed round the palms of the first floor where my guests were assembled . . .
>
>   The June night was perfect . . . Multi-coloured balloons floated up from between the iron shafts of the great Tower, which was mine for the night. All summer in a night. My childish wish had come true: I was one with Paris.

'Chacun sa tour'. For a night the Eiffel Tower was hers, symbol of the city she loved:

> I was at the apex of my life. I had poise, experience, friends, possessions. Romance was at long last disciplined, *coups de tête* rationed. Then, as ever, I believed in three things, God, France, my mother.

She had published four novels, three of them in French, created a home, carved a place in the cultural and '*mondaine*' life of the city. She did not dwell on what she had lost — love, looks, youth. She had aged, was overweight, had brittle bones, broke a knee, then an arm. Her mother said she expected a letter saying, 'By the way I forgot to tell you I broke my neck.'

On 26 June 1939 Chips Channon gave a lunch party at the London Ritz for the Prime Minister, Neville Chamberlain. Mrs Keppel was there — her once auburn hair now blue. Regal, charming, she seemed anachronistic. She sat between Chamberlain and Lord Birkenhead, who asked her if she was any relation to 'King Edward's friend' whom he thought was dead.

Two months later and a week before the eruption of war, Sonia arranged a ball at Holland House, Lord Stavordale's home, for her daughter Rosalind, who was eighteen and coming out. 'We were dancing on the edge of a precipice,' Lady Cecilia McKenna, George Keppel's niece, said with hindsight.

Mrs Keppel was staying with Sonia and her family at their house, Hall Place, in West Meon, Hampshire. She was anxious to get back to the Ombrellino. 'I am here till Friday if there is no war,' she wrote to Violet on 29 August. Hitler, she maintained, had lost his 'war of nerves'. 'nothing is calmer than England or France and personally I don't believe in war now . . . I don't think Chamberlain has done badly.'

She was restless in the English countryside and her grandchildren irritated her. Rosalind was eighteen, Harry fourteen, Jeremy twelve:

> Those children! Harry I consider an idiot. Yesterday he said Mummy loves us much more than you love *your* children, you don't love anyone!! All I could do was to clasp my hands *believe* me I love Luna [Violet] and Doey [Sonia] with every old particle of me but *not* Harry.

The exchange riled, for perhaps Harry received his opinion from his mother.

Mrs Keppel prayed for peace and worried about her bank accounts in Italy and France. On 1 September Germany invaded Poland. On 3 September at 5 p.m. Britain declared war on Germany. She changed her mind about Chamberlain. 'Who could help Poland? Impossible and idiotic ever to say we could. It has come out as I always said.'

Violet did not want to leave France. She moved between St Loup and Antoinette d'Harcourt's Paris house in the rue de Verneuil. Antoinette was separating from the Duc d'Harcourt who owned the Château d'Harcourt at Thury-Harcourt in Normandy. She wrote poetry, had two sons, worked for the French Resistance and when the Gestapo arrived in Paris was imprisoned and tortured. At her instigation Violet joined the Ambulance Brigade – though she could not drive – and talked of turning St Loup into a convalescent home for soldiers.

Mrs Keppel worried for Violet's safety and was 'terrified' to think of her still in Paris. 'I must know where you are' she wrote to her on 19 September:

> Are you going to remain with Antoinette? I can do nothing about fetching you to England. No one of course is allowed on the troop ships. Had you only come any time in August when I implored you everything would have been quite simple. Now you can only stay in France or get François [d'Harcourt] to make friends with the harbour master and he could tell you the best way. Its terrible being cut off like this and I can't see how St Loup would be a convalescent home . . . Darling, darling, do be careful. You know you are the person I love best in the world . . . I love you with all my old faithful heart.

She sent Violet £3000 for herself and £10 for the Ambulance Brigade, 'we had *such* a struggle and it can only be done till January'. She had the Ritz searched from top to bottom for Violet's lost *carte d'identité*. 'I have paid unknown sums!! Not a trace, so darling you must have lost it somewhere else.' Beloved Archie and her friend Ria Ponsonby joined her in Hampshire, but the weather was dismal, the daily round 'duller than ever', the food poor. 'There is very little to eat here. (I am sure Berlin has far more) and it is so nasty.' She had bronchitis and persistent back pain but an X-ray revealed nothing. She missed the Ritz a great deal, the Ombrellino more.

At the end of October 1939 she went to London 'for a consultation' with her bank manager. 'I am afraid there will be endless complications . . . I may have to leave England.' She needed to get to her accounts in Monte Carlo and Florence. War was a hectic worry, a financial drain, a chaos of displacement, a cruel contrast to the delights of past times.

At Sissinghurst Vita flew the Sackville flag, 'a dream of gaiety and garishness'. Harold in his daily letters wrote to her of the politics of invasion. 'What fiends are loose over this earth.' She wrote to him of the moon, swans and subsidies on ploughing and feared she must appear 'dull and rustic' in his eyes. She wondered how she would feel if all her male relations were wiped out and she were to succeed to Knole:

> Would I be happy giving up Sissinghurst for Knole? I broke my heart once and for all over Knole and finished with that . . .
>
> How I wish Dr Freud had never existed to explain our deepest feelings to us.

'My word!! The budget!!' Harold wrote to her at the end of September. Income tax was raised to ten shillings in the pound. The House, he said, 'gave one long gasp' when it heard. 'My darling we must discuss our finances. I fear that life is not going to be easy.'

At the end of April 1940 Mrs Keppel and George were at the Hôtel de Paris, Monte Carlo. She had been to the Ombrellino, put treasures into store, seen her bank managers. She hoped to go back there — her luggage had been packed for a fortnight — but the news was 'worse and worse'. She heard a swastika had been hoisted over the villa and she was 'taking advice' from the British Consul: 'the Consul here is charming & so kind'. George was not coping:

> Papa's temper is beyond words' I think his spots make him much worse, & I am sure *mine* is not too good. If only he could make some friends but he wont or cant . . .
>
> all this worry has made him very very ill . . . his heart is very very tired and his nerves are completely out of hand. He is having

Bromide to try to calm him now, but it's very sad to see him
like this, *covered* wih rash and furious with everyone . . . his kidneys
have gone wrong too.

She was, she said on 11 April, longing to see Violet. 'I can't bear to
think of you in Paris and I here.'

Violet was having trouble with her teeth, which had loosened in
her gums. As the prospect of German invasion drew near she closed
St Loup, left her silver with the Duc d'Harcourt, and in a car marked
with the Red Cross travelled with her friend the Princesse Gilone de
Chimay to the safety of the Princess's chateau in the Dordogne. 'Never
shall I forget the exodus from Paris,' she wrote with embellishment,
'the terrified scrutiny of the skies . . . the wild-eyed refugees . . . the
swaying, stinking *camions* . . .'

Her plan was to meet with Mother so that together they could
escape to freedom. On 20 April Mrs Keppel got three telegrams from
her. She replied to her at Gilone de Chimay's house, told her it would
be a joy to see her, not to bring much luggage and to watch what she
spent:

> This hotel is so fearfully expensive — £600 in six weeks, so sweetie
> you will have to try & be very careful here. You left a bill (unpaid)
> in the bar & owed that beastly Nigger some francs!!

Over the next six weeks the Germans took Boulogne, Ypres, Lille,
Paris. Italy declared war on Britain and France, Hitler threatened total
annihilation of his enemies. Mrs Keppel again found protection from
the British Consul and officials in Biarritz, Violet dashed around acquiring visas for Spain and Portugal with the thought of getting a boat for
England there.

They made their exodus in July 1940 in a Royal Navy troop ship
from St Jean de Luz. Places that echoed with memories of regal adultery
and disastrous matrimony for La Favorita and the ill-favoured Lushka
were ports of passage for mother and daughter, both adventurers,
whose romantic days were done. Politics had rushed like a tide into

their lives, taken their houses, riches, freedom, friends and forced them literally into the same boat.

They were three days docked in the harbour while soldiers and British nationals crammed on board. Violet gave her bag of jewels to someone she supposed to be a porter. Mrs Keppel was the only passenger to be given a cabin. Privilege and status are relative concepts and wherever she went she was something of a queen. Each morning from the engine room she collected a jug of hot water for her wash and George's shave. Violet was afraid of submarines, torpedoes, bombs and the Gestapo and vexed by a shortage of good food, privacy and cigarettes. After an arduous journey they arrived unharmed on England's shores with a story to embroider. At Polesden Lacey Mrs Greville remarked, 'To hear Alice talk about her escape from France, one would think she had swum the Channel with her maid between her teeth.'

NINETEEN

They repaired to Mrs Keppel's spiritual home. During the war years she became known as 'Empress of the Ritz'. She presided in the Edwardian lounge with an 'aura of grandeur ... far more regal than the poor Queen of Albania'. Sometimes her audience wondered quite which war she was in. She divulged the latest gossip, professed intimacy with the Prime Minister and the Secretary of State for Air, held 'completely pre-war cocktail parties' and worried about her money.

Violet, dispossessed, was back in the land where she had always been unhappy. She described herself as 'fundamentally sad and homesick', bereaved at being separated from her tower, language, country. 'People were very kind; they forebore from questioning me; it was as though I was in mourning for an unmentionable relation.'

She stayed first at Pat Dansey's London flat then moved to Coker Court in Yeovil, Somerset, home of Dorothy Heneage. Dorothy, in her sixties, lived with an older companion, Miss Darnell, in a regulated atmosphere of fastidious habits, antique furniture, Persian rugs, views of mature gardens. Violet was given the room she first stayed in when she was seventeen. She was grateful but claustrophobic, called life at Coker Court a 'rehearsal of old age' and herself 'a cosmopolissonne if ever there was one'.

She and Vita made contact again. 'Curious how war has drawn the strands of our lives together again,' Vita wrote:

I was so worried about you when France collapsed; I couldn't bear to think of you in danger and distress. One travels far, only to come round to the old starting point. I realised then that we might still be sitting on the leather fire-seat at 30 Portman Square, when I went home to Hill Street saying to myself 'I have a friend. I have a friend.' And thousands of other things as well.

She wrote seductively of Sissinghurst, white owls flying across the orange moon, her garden of green vistas, her pink tower and less seductively of constant air raids and bombs. She wanted Violet to visit but was afraid she would find it painful 'since, as you say, I believe my tower must have some affinity with yours'.

Violet equivocated, turned down the offered dates, agreed to Wednesday 28 August 1940 then phoned without notice to say she had to be in London with her mother and to rearrange for the 31st. 'I am quite absurdly pleased at the thought of your coming here' Vita wrote – while telling Harold she devoutly hoped Violet would not come. She prepared the scene, put out gramophone records they once played together. Violet again cancelled at the last minute and said she was going back to Coker Court. Vita was both disappointed, 'a real disappointment', and relieved:

> The very sound of your voice on the telephone upsets me. I loved you and I think you loved me. Quite apart from our three years of passionate love affair we had years and years of childhood love and friendship behind us . . . It makes you dear to me. It makes me dear to you . . .
>
> We have loved each other too deeply for too many years and we must not play with fire again. We both upset the other's life, we mustn't do that again.

She hoped Violet would come another time, 'yet in a way I don't want you to come'. Both were afraid. Violet, more self-protecting now, hoped to meet on neutral ground, a village in Somerset perhaps. She did not want to arrive at Sissinghurst, dispossessed of her tower, language, friends and way of life. It had always seemed that Vita kept her world intact while she was stripped of hers.

Vita was rooted in her Kent home, 'How horrible towns are . . . they all seem to me a mad system of life,' more hating of confrontation,

cautious with her lesbian affairs, careful never to distress Harold who
had proved such a permanent support. She asked nothing from him
that she knew he could not give, did not complain if troubled or in
pain.

She and Violet delayed meeting, circumvented, cancelled. They
wrote letters of affection – for those at least were safe. They used their
old romantic sobriquets Mitya and Lushka, remembered the gardens
at Carcassone, the owls at Duntreath. In October Violet heard St Loup
was occupied by German soldiers. Pity me a little, she asked Vita in
French. 'I mind for you more than you will believe,' Vita replied. 'I
translate it into terms of my own tower and can't imagine anything
more grievous.'

After twenty years of silence and four months of circumvention
they met for lunch at the Red Lion in Pulborough, Sussex, on Thursday
15 December. As ever despite their towers and castles, they had no
place to go.

Violet was forty-six, Vita forty-eight. It was a quest for the past.
They said that interim loves had been ephemeral. Violet tried to
pick up their love despite its corrosion by time. It had, she said, two
dimensions, 'the Greek tragedy sort and the childhood friendship sort'.
That evening Vita stayed with an aunt nearby and wrote to Violet of
their meeting. She had felt as though 'the wings of the past' were
beating around her:

> Yes it was good to see you – and the absurd happiness of having
> you beside me in the car – even the sudden pain of saying goodbye
> to you was vivifying . . . I told you I was frightened of you. That's
> true. I don't want to fall in love with you all over again, or to
> become involved with you in a way that would complicate my
> life as I have now arranged it. I definitely don't want to become
> involved in the intrigues which 'an affair' with you would entail.
> Besides, it wouldn't be just 'an affair'. It would be a resumption
> of what you rightly call a Greek tragedy and I don't want that . . .
>   We simply couldn't have this nice, simple, naif, childish con-

nexion without it turning into a passionate love affair again . . .
You and I can't be together. I go down country lanes and I meet
a notice saying 'Beware unexploded bomb' so I have to go round
another way. The unexploded bomb is you, Lushka.

It was a love letter that belonged to the past, an echoed renunciation,
fair because Vita knew that life as she had 'arranged it' excluded
Violet, sad because of passion denied, unfair because Violet was not an
unexploded bomb or a fox or witch, but the woman who had loved
her with single-hearted obstinacy. The last part of Vita's letter scrawled
across the page as her biographer Victoria Glendinning put it, 'in
the jerky, spidery way she wrote only when blurred by drink or
tears'.

Violet knew that it was over, but in a spoiling war she sought to
repair her past. She wanted friendship at least. 'She sounds sobered
somehow,' Vita wrote to Harold. 'I think she dreadfully minded the
collapse of France.'

Violet turned to her mother and to her mother's material preoccupations. There were problems when Mrs Keppel came to Coker Court.
'They have no modern arrangements in the kitchen,' she said. 'No
Aga stove, no gas.' Servants if found she was sure would not get on
with Dorothy. 'They might come but they would leave the next day.'
She financed Violet's move, in February 1941, to the nearby Manor
House in the village of East Coker. Its owners were spending their war
in Canada. A cook was found whom Violet coaxed to serve French
food, a housekeeper, a 'lady's maid'. Dorothy Heneage helped decorate
with Chippendale chairs, Chinese lacquer cabinets, pictures by Titian
and Van Dyck. Violet invited Vita who did not visit – she said there
was 'nothing she would like better' but they must not again depend
on each other's company. 'We should miss it too much when again
deprived of it.'

Violet made her extrovert mark on East Coker with weekend parties
and visitors from France. She and her guests attended the village
church and confused the vicar by arriving noisily and late. He then

muddled the service and she said it was because he was in love with her. She started an affair with Betty Richards who told her in French that she loved her with all her heart, called her 'my own darling foxy', lived nearby at Hamlet House, Sherborne, and had been a model in Paris.

The Princesse de Polignac stayed, Gerald Berners, Gaston Palewski, Paul Reynaud's Private Secretary, General Catroux. 'I had known him when he was Resident in Morocco which is the French equivalent to being Viceroy of India,' Violet wrote. Mrs Keppel said he was 'by far the nicest man' Violet knew. 'What a pity he is married.' Helen Terré stayed in October. She worked for the Red Cross in Vichy and had been wrongfully imprisoned in Holloway Gaol. From her Violet heard the Gestapo now occupied the tower at St Loup and had imprisoned Antoinette d'Harcourt.

Violet did book reviews for the *Observer*, articles for *Horizon*, worked at a novel in English, *Pirates at Play*, and *Prelude to Misadventure*, a memoir dedicated to the fighting French. Through Vita's contacts – Hilda Matheson and Baroness Moura Budberg who had been a lover of Maxim Gorki – she broadcast for *La France Libre* which earned her the Légion d'Honneur after the war. But she lost confidence in her worth as a writer, turned from satire to anecdote, felt no one in England cared whether she wrote or not and opted for the social round.

She and Vita wanted to meet and not to meet, felt the pain of the past like pressing a bruise. 'It upsets me to see you or hear your voice,' Vita wrote:

> I hate you for having this effect on me. I resent knowing that if
> I were suddenly to see a photograph of you it would disturb me
> for at least 24 hours. Damn you . . . you have bitten too deeply
> into my soul.

They discussed writing their story. Vita objected to the 'loathsome example' of *The Well of Loneliness*, thought she could produce a better novel, doubted she and Violet could collaborate, 'It would be a one person's book.'

I do feel that it is a great and new subject and I would like to do it. The vivid feelings that I have undergone throughout my life would make a worthwhile story of it. How much I would like to talk to you about this – quite dispassionately and with all the objective intelligence that you and I could bring to bear on it. I only wish that I could trust myself (and you) to come and stay with you.

But I don't, so I won't.

Yours, Mitya

Neither was ever overt, dispassionate or objective about this 'great and new subject'. Both were caught by it and flung to the winds. Vita fantasized about drawing her adult son Benedict into her drama of the past. In a continued compulsion to bend her own gender she saw herself reflected in him:

> Thou art thy mother's glass and she in thee
> Renews the lovely April of her prime

In 1941 he was in the army, stationed near Yeovil. She suggested he contact Violet:

She will amuse you, but you must beware of her. She is a siren (not the air raid sort). Her appearance will startle you, as she has lost her eye for make-up. She has the loveliest voice in the world; interlards her conversations with French slang so up-to-date that one doesn't understand half of it; is a mythomane as well as being profoundly untruthful; is witty; is an extravagant and fantastic personality; is a bore in the sense that she loves living in a world of intrigues and is determined to involve one in them, is in fact one of the most dangerous people I know. *You have been warned.*

To Harold she wrote 'I hope Ben won't fall in love with Violet. He might you know. But I have warned him not to.' The fantasy was projection. Ben was not going to fall in love with any woman, least of all Violet. He was twenty-seven, Violet, his godmother, was forty-six. When eighteen he confided to his mother that he was homosexual.

She told him that it would not preclude his marrying. 'Two of the happiest married people I know, whose names I must conceal for reasons of discretion are both homosexual.' She said a home, belongings, marriage, roots were the essential way to happiness.

In his thirties, in 1948, Ben told her he had fallen 'desperately in love' with the art historian David Carritt, it was 'the most overwhelming experience' he had ever had, they wanted to live together. Vita wrote to Harold calling this a muddle and a disaster: 'He is bound to fall out with D . . . and meanwhile there may have been a scandal which might involve both his jobs.' He would lose his career and reputation – he was Deputy Surveyor of the King's Pictures and editor of the *Burlington Magazine* – 'for the sake of a clever little boy who is not worth the sacrifice. I will talk to him at the weekend whether he likes it or not.' Discretion, so lauded by Mrs Keppel and her circle, spread its net wide, capturing more than social caution, tact, manners. It caught and spoiled aspirations, feelings of a quintessential kind.

Harold, asked by David Carritt for advice, replied:

If I were Plato and consulted I should say 'This can never lead to happiness therefore it must be abandoned.' But as I cannot bear to see Ben wretched I cannot give that answer.

Vita disliked David Carritt's influence on Ben (as Harold had disliked Violet's influence on Vita). She thought him cynical, hoped he would go abroad, deterred him from visiting Sissinghurst. She felt she had failed Ben, that he was too difficult for her. In his room she found a copy of Oscar Wilde's *De Profundis*, his confession about his love for 'Bosie', Lord Alfred Douglas. She thought there was wisdom in it. Perhaps it put her in mind of her own confession, locked in a Gladstone bag. 'How he paid for his follies,' she wrote.

Down the generations came the same cry from Wilde, Violet, Vita's son Ben, echoing the plea to legitimize these affairs of the heart, to view them as a valid choice, accord them social respect. For themselves Vita and Harold squared the circle and thought others could do so too. Vita was delighted when in 1955 Ben married another art historian, Luisa Vertova. The marriage lasted three years.

'Poor Mor is *out* of everything,' Mrs Keppel wrote of herself to Violet in June 1942,

> but it is such a just punishment for she had, in times past, too much. Beloved Titten please be careful & not spend anything you can avoid. After this year I shall be able to do *so* little. Personally I am not going to buy anything.
>
> All my love Sweetheart.

There was no word from the Ombrellino, telephone lines from Florence were cut. Mrs Keppel slept badly, thought this was because she went out so little, resolved not to rest in the afternoons in the hope of sleeping better at nights. Her ankles swelled up, her back ached, she suffered bouts of bronchitis from cigarettes and London fog. She saw her doctor often, drank too much gin and called the Ritz gloomy (though a typical wartime lunch menu was oeufs en cocotte, tournedo steak, meringues). 'Isn't the news awful,' she wrote to Violet on 17 June, 'Rommel gets exactly where he likes, we seem useless & only squandering lives for nothing.' She began to sign her letters to Violet 'Your old sad Mor'. 'I do hope Darling *you* will have fun & see interesting people,' she wrote.

She went to the country at weekends or when there were air raids. At Wherwell Priory, Andover, her abstracted hostess counted imaginary money in her pocket and spent much of her day in bed. Mrs Keppel played desultory bridge with Sir Randolph and Lady Baker from Blandford, Dorset, and Gracie Fields sang 'There'll Always Be an England' on the wireless.

She stayed at Sonia's house in Hampshire, but had no authority there. Sonia ruled, 'Dear Doey thinks she is the cats whiskers in everything even to growing roses on chalk,' Mrs Keppel complained to Violet. She found the place 'fearfully cold', Sonia was not getting on with her husband, the children talked and giggled at every meal, there was nothing much to eat, the last meal of the day was high tea at six 'so we sit from 6.30 to ten doing nothing, except reading'.

Life was pared down. 'Tell me what you are doing & if you miss me,' she wrote to Violet. 'I do you, every minute of the day & most of the night.' There was no bitterness between them now. Violet was the preferred daughter, loved 'more than anyone in the world'.

Like her mother Violet went to 'endless parties', teas, lunches, dinners. But though she imitated her she lacked her social ease, her effortless charm. She was too caustic, chaotic, different to be admired in the same way. She had a reputation for purloining anecdotes and jokes. Her wit subverted social certainties. At a cocktail party given by Lady Crewe she asked a group of elderly titled ladies if they were bisexual 'answering severely on being answered in the negative, "Well you miss a lot".' At a tea party of Emerald Cunard's James Lee-Milne described her as 'a large, clumsy' plain woman wearing a top-heavy hat and sitting in such a way that one could see a naked expanse of thigh'. She wished, he said, 'to enchant, astonish, alarm; but I think she seldom tried to please'. A carapace of manner hardened round her.

She again summoned courage to go to Sissinghurst and agreed the visit for 4 May 1943 but, that morning, cancelled pleading a fever. 'What a bore Violet wanting to come to Sissinghurst' Harold wrote perhaps not knowing that it was at Vita's persuasion. 'She is all very well in London but Sissinghurst is not a guest house.' Vita told him not to mention the visit,

> because her mother would disapprove and she doesn't want a row. I sympathise. Little Mrs George in a temper must be a formidable thing.

Violet arrived on 11 May and stayed one night. It was then that she said '*chacun sa tour*', with pain at the fate of hers. 'She has quite grasped Sissinghurst,' Vita wrote to Harold. 'As I knew she would.' Vita called the encounter 'extraordinarily unreal', 'rather embarrassing', 'like speaking a foreign language that one has known bilingually and not used for years'. The vocabulary was atrophied, locked in the past, not to be used again. Violet took Vita's bedroom, they did not share it. The next day she lost her belongings and missed her train from Maidstone station.

In London she dined, cautiously, once or twice with Harold — on 24 February 1943 with the former Secretary of State for War, Hore-Belisha, the Princesse de Polignac and a French general who had escaped the Gestapo. 'It was an amusing dinner,' Harold wrote to Vita. A month later at lunch at the restaurant Boulestins he introduced her to René Massigli, French Ambassador in London. 'She was at her most charming and gave me a bunch of violets for my buttonhole,' Harold said. Violet phoned Vita to say she had enjoyed lunch and liked Harold very much. 'Well the pattern of life is odd,' Vita wrote.

She was not a siren now, nor a fox, witch, seductress or squirrel. She had no power to disturb or destroy. I wish Violet would not seek always to be amusing,' Harold wrote to Vita:

> She irritates me by repeating as her own jokes which have been made a thousand times . . . Violet — I tremble to say so — might become a bore. But she is a good old sort none the less.

Vita bridled. It was a choice of words that washed away the past. 'To describe her as "a good old sort" is really the queerest choice of epithet I have ever heard.'

No one could now make Violet out. She was always on parade but eluded her audience. Marie Belloc Lowndes who in 1920 was persuasive at getting *Challenge* scrapped met her during the war at a weekend party at Trematon Castle, Saltash:

> Violet's maid unpacked for me beautifully. She said dolefully 'My lady calls me "Jones". But my name is Matilda' — so I said 'You shall be Matilda to me!' Violet is 52, looks and dresses like 28 . . .

She is a fascinating talker *and* companion. To me it is extraordinary that of the *many* women who have spoken to me of Violet Trefusis, not one gave me even the smallest inkling *of what she is like*. Even as a talker she is *extremely* individual. I expect this irritates people for she likes 'holding the floor' . . . Her love of France seems to me one of the honestly *true* things in her astonishing nature . . .

She *cried* when describing her flight from Paris with the Princess de Chimay. *Constant* heavy machine guns . . . They broke their flight at Milly Sutherland's house [widow of the Duke of Sutherland], apparently deserted. But then they found her in an upper room, dressed, and with all the jewels she could put on her person, waiting for death; as a huge ammunition dump close by was to have been blown up. It was – but not before they had forced her to leave. It was the strangest narrative to which I have ever listened, and it lasted about 2 hours.

. . . In the middle of dinner a man rang up – she was gone a good 10 minutes – only consolation of host was that she did not make the call. She makes a great many. I do wonder who her father was. She *really* has *la joie de vivre*. I suppose that quality in her mother enchanted Edward VII.

Her mother's *joie de vivre* had waned. Her back troubled her and her cough. James Lees-Milne saw her at a party of Lady Crewe's early in 1944, hobbling round the room smoking from a long cigarette holder:

She is rather shapeless, with hunched shoulders, a long white powdered face. She was gazing with mournful eyes as though in search of something.

She wanted the war to end and old customs somehow to be restored. 'Archie says I must keep my slippers by my bed so I don't tread on broken glass in case of an air raid,' she announced – this Archie being Sir Archibald Sinclair, Secretary of State for Air. She craved the sun on the terraces at the Ombrellino, the tables of Monte Carlo, to go to Aix for a cure, to be reassured by all her bank managers. England held little for her or Violet now. For them both grand romance was dead. They needed the consolation of their villas and towers under brighter skies.

On Violet's birthday in June 1944 her maid brought news of the liberation of Paris. In her mind's eye Violet saw

> the blue letter boxes of Paris, the undulating Art Nouveau letter-ing of the Métro stations . . . the blue blouses of the porters, the little girls with gold rings in their prematurely pierced ears, the concierge's crocheted shawl, her fat sated cat . . . I heard the clang of the *porte cochère*, the imprecations and hootings of the taxi drivers . . . It was too good to be true.

In October she received the necessary visa from Gaston Palewski, then Chief of Staff to General de Gaulle. 'My dear friend, naturally your presence is part of Paris. Respectfully yours,' he wrote. That same month a soldier, Hamish Sinclair-Erskine, who escaped the German army and walked through Italy to the Allied lines, called on Mrs Keppel at the Ritz. He told her the Ombrellino was intact, 'even the Chinese pagodas'.

There were restraints on the immediate resumption of pleasure. It was not discreet for a King's lady to hurry back to an enemy country. There were currency restrictions, income tax, rationing, frozen accounts. 'Please darling try & live cheaply,' she wrote to Violet.

Times were not at all what they once had been, old friends were scarce, there was rationing, egalitarianism, a servant problem. Her maid, Williams, went for a month's holiday '& I have a kind little fool who does not even wind my watches'. George's valet, Pearman, was taken to hospital with a complete breakdown. 'I don't think he will ever come back so Papa has no one'. At Sheffield Park near Uckfield, Sussex, there was no heating in Mrs Keppel's vast room and she coughed all night. At Mount Stewart, Newtownards, County Down she was horrified that Lady Londonderry dined in trousers, worked to keep the place going and had no maid. There were children staying in the house '& alas, in my passage!!' She longed to get to Aix, had nothing to do, could not walk at all she coughed so much. 'So I stay mostly in my own room which is lonely.'

Towards the end of the war Chips Channon gave a dinner party at which Mrs Keppel was the anachronistic showpiece:

> She looked magnificent in black sequins and jewels and her fine white hair and gracious manners are impressive. She is so affectionate and *grande dame* that it is a pity she tipples and then becomes garrulous and inaccurate.

It was a pity for her liver too which was not functioning properly. Neither her back pain nor the swelling in her legs would ease. Her 'nice doctor' said she would be 'all right in a few days', that her constant bronchial colds came from the dust of London. She had her hair curled in a 'permanent' which took four hours, went with beloved Archie to Bournemouth, stayed in the Palace Court Hotel, spent mornings in church and breathed a bit better in the sea air.

In the summer of 1945 Violet wrote to Vita saying she would soon be going back to France and would like to stay a weekend at Sissinghurst before she left. Her previous departure from Vita and England had been humiliating. This time she wanted to leave by choice and with self-respect. 'Oh God Oh God Oh God I *don't* want Violet here. But how on earth could I get out of it?' Vita wrote in panic to Harold. 'O *tempora mutandi* . . . how pleased I should have been once, and now just dismayed.'

Violet did not stay with her. The embers were not raked. She needed France. 'The landscape I had been starving for flowed into view.' Paris was more beautiful than she remembered. She booked in at the Ritz: 'the place looked normal enough save that there were no carpets or curtains'. Diana Cooper, whose husband Duff Cooper was now British Ambassador in Paris, held a party for her at the Embassy. Helen Terré drove her to St Loup. The butler, servants, gardener were there to greet her. Antoinette d'Harcourt and Gilone de Chimay had hidden away her valuables and these were safe. Some books had been taken, 'cherished *bibelots* were missing, German inscriptions were scrawled all over the walls, they had kicked in my Chirico and my Dufy . . .' She had, though, got off lightly, was still mistress of her mansion, *châtelaine* of her tower.

But until she renewed residency and 'stabilised' her French account she could not afford to stay. Currency restrictions meant she could only take £75 out of England. While her mother sorted out such mundane matters Violet returned to the London Ritz. Mrs Keppel worried about fitting her and her maid in over the Christmas period. 'Those Conferences on Education' were 'taking up every corner of London'. And in January 1946 there was to be the wedding of Sonia's daughter Rosalind to an army man, Bruce Shand.

Mother made many trips to Mr Williams at the Midland Bank, Pall Mall, to sort out various accounts and 'nesty eggs' for 'darling Titten'. Violet finally returned triumphant to Paris three months after that. Her mother's letters urging caution over money went unheeded. 'Except I live on capital I don't know what will happen,' Mrs Keppel wrote. She was horrified to hear that Paris was smart:

> Surely they ought not to spend money on fashions. I am not going to buy a single dress. I can't as I have no coupons, so when I do arrive in France I shall be like a char, but I would rather look like that!!!

Violet would rather not look like a char. Nancy Mitford wrote to Diana Mosley of a gala she went to in May 1946 with Duff Cooper and Jacques Février,

> suddenly Jacques seized my arm & I thought would break it & I saw the following apparition: Violet practically naked to the waist and *smothered* in birds of paradise. Oh *could* you all have seen. She also hired a regalia of jewels from Cartiers.

Violet was back, as startling as any of the bejewelled *grandes dames* she satirized in her novels. A Mr Fitzgerald couriered money from England for the refurbishment of the tower, Mrs Keppel bought her a car and was 'filled with despair' at not being able to do more. 'I could have given you a large sum to keep you for some years.' She grieved at not being able to send a cheque for her birthday,

now you are domiciled in France it is not allowed. It breaks my heart not to send you anything & I had a nice little one ready for you, but now you must either come over for it & spend it *here* or wait till I meet you in France which I hope to do on the 8th of August.

For Mrs Keppel her fifty-three-year-old daughter was now her pride and joy, a chip off the old block, always socializing, always on parade. There was usually some man in tow, an amourette, for advertisement and show: 'What did you mean' her mother asked, 'when you said to Doey in your letter to her "Alas poor Pomeroy"! so I suppose that is all off!!!' She was disconcerted to get a letter which had no ending 'except about manure for St Loup & there was no loving messages & it was not *even signed*. Darling what has happened to your letters?'

Mrs Keppel's plan for the summer was to stay with Violet in Paris, go on to Aix-en-Provence for a 'cure', meet her again there and they would travel to Florence together. She worried about how to circumvent the £75 currency restriction to pay for her trip. 'England is perfectly right of course to stop all money going out of her country. Some people manage of course.'

Somehow the Bank of England arranged a £500 transfer for her journey and she gave Betty Richards a cheque for £1000 to give to Violet. Violet travelled to Dover to meet her in the first week of August 1946. She described the visit as 'a Keppel festival' with herself 'a breathless lady-in-waiting'. She arranged a lunch party with Duff and Diana Cooper, visits to Carlos de Beistegui's chateau at Groussay and to exhibitions at the Orangerie and Musée du Trocadèro of artworks looted by the Germans.

But it was not her mother's idea of a good time. Mrs Keppel was relieved when the visit was over. From the Hôtel Splendide Royal & Excelsior at Aix she wrote to George:

> Paris was lovely to look at but I cannot like the French. Dear
> Bye [Violet] was so kind, but endless conversations in wonderful
> French which I cannot understand get thoroughly on my nerves.

She took mud baths and water dips and instructed George, Sonia and
Harry all to bring soap, tea, sugar, coffee and two hundred cigarettes
to the Ombrellino. George was to get these from the Ramadan Tobacco
Co. Ltd, 84 Piccadilly, and to go and see Mr Williams at the Bank. 'I
am writing to him today to try & get me some money for Italy.'

Money did not buy sound medical advice. The doctor at Aix said
there was nothing wrong with her, ascribed her weight loss and chronic
backache to not eating enough, said her cough did not matter in the
least, 'Isnt that odd!! for I cough all night especially in the train.'

She found the expense at Aix enormous and had to curtail her
'cure' when the hotel closed in early September. Violet with an '*ami*'
was due to join her at the end of August but wired the day before to
say '*Ami* is ill so cant come'. 'I suppose it is all over like the rest,' Mrs
Keppel wrote to George:

> I have always thought that the French think she is much richer
> than she really is, as she entertains them so lavishly at my expense,
> but I do hope she isn't too unhappy. She may have cared for
> him.

The *ami* was Prince Rodolphe de Faucigny Lucinge who was after a
rich wife. Nancy Mitford wrote to Gerald Berners saying Violet dropped
him 'because she says all his friends are dentists':

> She has now taken up with a chap called M. de Grand Guignol
> [Guido Sommi Picenardi, Marchese di Calvatore, who owned a
> 'magnificent castle' near Cremona and was recovering from a
> nervous breakdown] with whom she gave a cocktail party of great
> brilliance. Goodness I do love her.

The Keppel family reunited at the Ombrellino in early September.
There was a drought and the water pump Mrs Keppel paid 10,000 lire
for did not work properly. She supervised the restoring of the villa,

employing new servants, getting a car, planting the gardens, then returned to London for Christmas while work was done.

Back at the Ritz she was angry when presented with a large bill of Violet's. She wrote to her on 3 January 1947:

> It is nearly all made up with the following list of things you have sent out for, cars, theatre tickets etc this is very surprising. Do *you* pay for your men friends to go out with you. Far better to stay in with me. Also dearest having your maid getting cash from George & putting it down to my bill. You changed your day of leaving so that had to be paid for. You know Darling I would give you all I have if I could but if the villa has to be built up, I simply can't pay all these huge extras so I had to write all this. If I give up Italy I can quite afford your bills here. Everything has been paid don't write to anyone here about it, they will only ask you not to come back.

Violet offered to send a cheque, but Mrs K said that she would only tear it up. She could not understand why Violet was not managing her money better when she had given her £1000 as a Christmas present and an extra £1000 a year on her allowance. 'This year I must be most careful & am not buying a single thing.' She stayed at Hall Place but found it fearfully cold. Her legs were so swollen she could hardly walk. Of Sonia who was having problems with her marriage she wrote, 'I know nothing about what is happening between herself & her husband.'

She went back to Ombrellino for the spring of 1947 but not to enjoy the frescoed walls, the marble halls, imposing views of the Duomo and Palazzo Pitti, the grand dinner parties for which she was renowned. Her return was short-lived. Her Italian doctor diagnosed sclerosis of the liver and said he did not expect her to live. To Violet her mother seemed as beautiful, in control and charming as ever: 'she will even make a success of her death, was my involuntary thought'. It was a complicated involuntary thought implying that her mother had made a success of love, money, friendships, life, while she herself had not.

It implied, too, that her mother was indomitable, formidable and had set the stakes too high: 'We were the inferior daughters of a dazzling mother . . . We had to live up to her, she had to live down to us.'

Mrs Keppel died on 11 September 1947. She was buried in the Protestant cemetery near Florence. In London her death was announced on the BBC. At a memorial service in St Mark's Church, North Audley Street, those that were left of her friends – Dukes, Viscounts, Marchionesses and Earls – who defined themselves and society by their closeness to the Crown, heard tributes and prayers. Queen Mary 'was represented' though none of the royal family was there. Obituaries made discreet reference to Mrs Keppel's intimate friendship with King Edward VII and Queen Alexandra. For *The Times* 'a friend' wrote that her death more than that of any of her contemporaries put a full stop to an era. 'Discretion was perhaps her long suit,' the friend said, using a gambling term.

'In losing my mother I lost everything' Violet wrote in her memoir, *Don't Look Round*. 'Any little success I may have had is dedicated to her.' She wrote of the

> unwanted licence of loneliness. Oh to be hemmed in by frowning family obstacles . . . I can do what I like, go where I wish, there is no one to say me nay.

She was free but it had come too late. She did not now know how to choose a direction. Her one fierce attempt at flight failed. Like the bird in the glass picture her mother gave her she was lost without the cage of her mother's eyes, or without her mother's arm on which she had for so long been made to perch.

TWENTY

Mrs Keppel died without seeing her great-granddaughter Camilla, born to Sonia's daughter Rosalind in July 1947. She was too unwell to travel and Sonia said England was 'glacially cold', with no heating allowed in hotels 'or anywhere'. She had no prescience that Camilla would follow the Keppel trail and choose as her lover Bertie's great-grandson Charles, another Prince of Wales.

Mrs Keppel would have been delighted had Camilla married Charles not Captain Andrew Parker-Bowles, an army man like George. But given her respect for social appearances and discretion, her powerful intervention when her own daughter revealed a revisionist sort of love, she would have viewed with disdain the way Prince Charles, his princess and mistress made public their muddle over sex.

'Things were done much better in my day,' she said in 1936 when Edward VIII abdicated the throne to marry Mrs Simpson. She would have said so again in the 1990s when Prince Charles and his wife separated and told the nation of their loveless marriage, infidelities, breakdowns, inadequacies and family pressures.

Briefed by Mrs Keppel the Prince of Wales would have had sex with Camilla on the side, said, if asked, that of course he loved his wife and would never have used a cellular phone. She would have packed her great-granddaughter off for a tour with Captain Parker-Bowles and advised Lady Diana's entourage to send her to take the waters at Aix for her bulimia nervosa and unacceptable emotional state.

For concomitant with her notions of the divine precedence of kings, queens and royal mistresses went expectations of codes of perceived behaviour for families of the ruling class. Mrs Keppel understood that unless the semblance of royal marriage was kept alive, other undemocratic myths might in time die: the myth that love was the

291

prerogative of husband and wife, that a ruling class deserved by rights to be served and deferred to by an underclass, that jewels, tiaras, castles and vast tracts of land should by birthright go to the titled few.

Discretion was her synonym for concealment, semblance mattered not substance, the worst of fates was to be *déclassé*. It was socially acceptable to be mistress or widow, but not lesbian or divorcee. Mrs Keppel kept the social apple cart intact. Her daughter and great-granddaughter helped topple it in their way.

Violet and George Keppel went to London after Alice's death. Violet, wanting comfort, contacted Vita and hoped to go to Sissinghurst. On 20 November 1947 Harold in London heard that 'Pawpaw' was in bed at the Ritz with pneumonia. 'Blessed pneumonia great are thy mercies,' he wrote to Vita. He did not want to sleep under the same roof as Violet. 'I refuse absolutely to be left alone in our cottage with Violet. I would rather walk the fields all night.'

Pawpaw died two months after his wife, thus sparing Harold either fate. *The Times* obituarist wrote of George Keppel's splendid looks, exquisite manners and 'benign geniality':

> Admiring as we do in him so many of the characteristics of the generation which he personified, we may well question whether we have not something more to learn from its gentle courtesy and code of behaviour than in these perplexing times it is the fashion to admit.

Sonia got divorced the year her parents died. She and Violet were the main beneficiaries of their mother's will. Violet was to have use of the Ombrellino for life, then it was to pass to Sonia and her children. Its contents were to form a family fund divided on a percentage share. Violet wanted to defer the sale of the contents, to keep the villa as it was, a memorial to her mother, and to emulate her as *châtelaine*. Her mother had stamped the place with inimitable style and this she wished to preserve.

Sonia wanted her share of the capital raised. She was unsparing. She insisted on the valuation and sale of every picture, garden statue, wallpancl, doorknob, carpct or rug. Anything Violet kept she had to buy at current value from the family trust. Violet was to be left with the shell of a mansion, the spirit of her mother gone. She sent worried and unhappy letters to friends. 'I wish Violet had some responsible relation,' Vita wrote to Harold. 'But there is only uncle Archie and he is eighty.'.

Violet asked Sonia to agree to leave some of the villa furnished, pointing out she would have all of it in time. 'Darling I am terribly sorry,' Sonia replied. 'But I have *never* agreed to a "furnished bit". It just isn't on and would lead to endless complications.' She applied for export licences and pushed the sale along.

Violet listed furniture, tapestries, statues she felt were intrinsic to the Ombrellino. 'You do realise don't you,' Sonia told her, 'that the total value of these (as I think highly injudicious) eliminations wld amount to £13,760.' Violet wanted to keep her mother's bed and a picture of an Edmonstone ancestor by the Scottish portrait painter Sir Henry Raeburn. Its saleroom value, Sonia told her, was £3200.

Christie's advised against shipping to England large items like wall panels:

6 Dutch panels (value £800)
3 Chinese panels from the Dining Room (value £400)
4 Tempora panels from the Music Room (value £320)
6 Chinese silk panels from Mama's bedroom (value £240)

These were to be sold in the villa along with all carpets and rugs. Sonia recommended two auctioneers in Florence – Galleria Ciardello and Cesáre Falardelli.

Whichever we decide on should start his catalogue soon. Rosalind had another sweet little daughter, Annabel, on Feb 2nd & both are v. well.
    Camilla is lovely.

Violet tried to raise capital to buy some of the furniture back. But all her inherited money was tied up in dividends and trust funds. 'I'm afraid no one can make you understand the legal aspects involved

here in your wish to break Mama's Italian will so that you get capital,'
Sonia wrote to her:

> As British subjects we *must* disclose to the Bank of England any
> monetary transactions made in foreign currencies and the
> amount involved. If we *don't* we run the risk of going to jail!

It was all ghastly: a scene from one of Violet's novels but without
her brittle humour, a parable of the vanity of riches, the conflict
between possessions and love, the inheritance of a vast stone mansion
stripped of its treasures, warring sisters competing for their dead
mother's affection, squabbling over the spoils accrued from her illicit
relationship with an indulgent king. Family, the root relationship of
society, had degenerated into a wrangling over things and money
between two women who had much more than enough.

As Violet saw it her sister was now destroying what bombs had
spared and the German army left unplundered. It was never her
mother's intention that she should inherit an empty house. Violet
perceived possessions as metaphors and did not care about their saleroom worth. Friends spoke of her bizarre generosity. How she would
give away an emerald, an amber paperweight, a brooch, a tie, a souvenir
ashtray. Her generosity perturbed or annoyed depending on what she
gave. 'One doesn't need things,' she had written to Vita. 'What one
needs is the sun, the person one loves, to be free.'

Denied freedom in love she aspired to be like her mother, who was
defined by what she had, for whom a palace was home. She wanted
to be her mother's daughter for no other relationship endured, to live
in her mother's mansion, emulate her social parade. Without her
presence and control she felt chaotic and adrift. Her childhood chant
'*de Madame Keppel je suis la fille*' became her way of life.

Sonia wanted to have what was hers, a compensatory justice for
not having been loved enough. For her, too, possessions had been
rivals. She stayed as rooted in the family drama as Violet, identified
with her father who was rendered inconsequential by Mrs Keppel and
the King, detested Violet for her childhood cruelty, her flamboyant

life, for eclipsing her as a writer. Her own biography of her Keppel antecedents *Three Brothers in Havana* was not more readable than her father's manuals on Renaissance art. Her memoir *Edwardian Daughter* gave an equivocal picture of her mother. Her one novel she called without irony, *Sister of the Sun*. Its heroine studies art in Paris, is 'the symbol of emancipation for her sex and generation'. She marries a man she does not love because she is hopelessly in love with her brother-in-law, an artist. (In later years Sonia spoke admiringly of Denys Trefusis.) She has jewels, furs, cars, is 'about as happy as a caged skylark' and after the wedding ceremony she tells her husband, 'I felt as if I were deputising for someone else.'

Violet thought Sonia's response to their mother's will was because she was jealous that she, Violet, was Edward VII's daughter. In a letter to John Phillips six years before she died she wrote of Sonia:

> We had a curious conversation: she simply cannot accept my being who I am, clearly a childhood inferiority complex, which has, in a way poisoned her life. I told her to believe what she liked, and whatever gave her most comfort. I can both understand and sympathize because if anyone was ever given a '*traitment de faveur*' it was I.

At first Violet was forced to close many of the villa's empty rooms. She could not afford to furnish both it and St Loup. She then slowly recreated the Ombrellino as a monument to her mother. She resorted to her own parodic style, filled the vast frescoed rooms with indifferent furniture and quantities of bad pictures, bought plagiarisms and fakes and accorded them romantic provenance. She chose baroque statues, ornate mirrors, said a painting of a doge was a Tintoretto, a painting of a Medici was a relative, a huge silver sturgeon was a gift to Peter the Great from the people of Holland, a Chinese lacquer writing desk was given by Queen Anne to the 2nd Earl of Albemarle. Objects had an attribution linking her in royal line. On a lavatory wall she hung group photographs of Edward VII at country house picnics.

She took to saying, 'I am the daughter of Edward VII *but don't tell anybody*.' Guests were cautious and thought the fantasy 'dangerously dotty'. To hedge her bets she drew up convoluted genealogical trees purporting to show how the Keppels descended from Giovanni de Medici via Henri VI of France and Charles I of England. She spent a good deal of time investigating whether, as a member of the Edmonstone family, she was entitled to wear the Royal Tartan:

> Dear Mrs Trefusis
>
>   . . . Several members of the Edmonstone Family held High Offices which would have entitled these, and doubtless at such junctures, their children in the home, to wear the Royal Tartan, but I cannot see any principle for a doctrine that the Edmonstones, as a family, would have a right to wear the Royal Tartan, and I fancy it originated from certain of the Lairds of Duntreath having worn it *ex officio* for the above reason . . .
>
>   Descent from Robert II and/or a Crown charter of Duntreath are things which, if one thinks of it, could not be a foundation for wearing Royal tartan, for the result when applied in other instances would be to supersede Douglas, Boyd, Hamilton, Macdonald and quite a number of other tartans.

Her preoccupations were strange, her obsessions mocked, her claims neither believed nor entirely disbelieved. For herself Violet was as much Edward VII's daughter as anyone's. She had no other proof of paternity. When George VI died in 1952 Nancy Mitford wrote to a friend, 'Violet has plunged into a *deuil d'Andromaque** but then she is one of the family'.

In life as well as writing she dealt in metaphors, games, conundrums. After her mother's death she employed a French servant called Alice. This Alice, she said, was Proust's cousin and the mistress of a Russian grand duke. Violet behaved toward her like a needy, demanding, deprived child. Alice dressed her, looked after her money, instructed

---

* The mourning of Andromache, heroine of Homer's *Iliad*, whose husband Hector was killed by Achilles.

the other servants, was her surrogate mother, nursemaid, confidante
and lady-in-waiting. Vita visited St Loup in March 1949 on her way to
Spain to see the birthplace of her grandmother Pepita. She was alarmed
at Violet's behaviour:

> It reminds me of BM. It's really more than a little mad. She
> curses her [Alice] *all* the time. If I spoke to Rollo [her Alsatian
> dog] like that he would run away and never come back. She
> (Alice the maid) poured it all out to me this morning, says her
> health is breaking down (V even wakes her up at all hours of
> the night) and that she will have to leave. Of course V doesn't
> believe it but the day will come when Alice will really go, and I
> don't know what V will do without her. It's a sort of lust for
> power I think: she must have someone to bully.

Alice did not leave, though her job went beyond any rational concept of service. She wore the mantle of the other Alice who was at a
king's beck and call. She was chic and charming in a way that Violet
was not, humoured her mistress as if she was ersatz royalty, and in a
paradox of who was servant and who was served, ruled at St Loup and
the Ombrellino.

For Violet had, as Vita knew, behind the neediness, bad behaviour,
display and parade, an abundance of heart, a compensatory generosity.
'I don't want to go, I don't, I don't, I don't,' Vita said to Harold of her
visit to Violet's tower, a reciprocal visit which she felt obliged to make.
But Violet met her at the Gare du Nord, made her chauffeur Henri
drive slowly because Vita was afraid of speed, filled her bedroom at
St Loup with flowers from Florence: anemones, ranunculi, gardenias,
carnations. 'She is,' Vita wrote, 'surprisingly kind'.

St Loup gave her a feeling of recognition, a sense of home. She was
surprised Violet was such a 'good hausfrau' though the atmosphere
was chaotic: random instructions to servants, the sudden sacking of
the chauffeur, various helpers from the village floating in and out.
She drank champagne in Violet's garden room painted with murals
of Scotland. The chef cooked a delicious meal. There were wild violets

and cowslips in the woods. She went with Violet to Provins. 'It is her Cranbrook' — Sissinghurst's town — she told Harold. 'You would be amused to see her calling first at the butcher and then at the charcutier and then at the patissier.' In Paris at the flower market Violet bought her primrose roots to smuggle home. They walked to a little restaurant and the food was divine.

Mindful of the past they shared, the home they never had and her quarrels with Sonia, Violet said she would like Vita to have St Loup when she died. Vita was pleased and flattered: 'my love of St Loup is genuinely *for its own sake* — as well as yours' but apprehensive that it ought to go to Sonia and her children. Violet said they would neither want it nor appreciate it. Beyond her desire to disinherit her sister, the legacy of her tower at St Loup was a way of manifesting her love of Vita and France, the true aspects of her life.

Vita visited again with Harold the following year. Violet did everything to make their stay pleasurable: tuberoses and writing tables in their bedrooms, zabaglione and delicacies to eat, a wallet for Harold, a bag for Vita. From her own tower and in the safety of letters, Vita thanked her. She wrote of the bonds of childhood and passion 'such as neither of us will ever share with anyone else'.

> Oh, you sent me a book about Elizabeth Barrett Browning. Thank you darling, generous Lushka and you gave me a coal-black briquet. It lights up into the flame of love which always burns in my heart whenever I think of you.

Their talisman ring was she said on her table on its customary piece of lapis lazuli

> which reminds me to remind you of the promise you made as you held it in your hand. I should be really bitterly hurt if you didn't tell me — you know what — in advance, and if I were to learn it accidentally from somebody else.

The 'you know what' was presumably about not falling in love with anyone else.

Violet was fifty six and there was no danger of it. But though love was a past secret, a private pain, there was still a need for present displays. She trailed as fiancés sundry princes, marquises and counts. Betty Richards, her lover at East Coker during the war years, advised against Prince Rolphe de Faucigny Lucinge as a spouse:

> I do hope that you will *not* have a change of heart and marry Rolphe . . . I feel sure that marriage would be fatal; no darling, you deserve something better than R. and I don't say this just because he hasn't got any money; were I well off I should never mind the idea of someone marrying me *with* my money.

Violet flirted awesomely, particularly with young gay men. James Pope-Hennessy (murdered in 1974), an erstwhile lover of Harold's, said she had Paris manners and resembled Madame de Staël. At a dinner party in London in June 1950 she looked at him across the table 'in a romantic manner' and said 'You look too young to be dining downstairs; you should be upstairs having your bread and milk.'

She described the Lascaux caves, begged him to go there with her in August which he 'wouldn't think of', and said Vita was so impressed by the comfort of St Loup she was thinking of making Sissinghurst habitable.

He saw her again three days later at a party at Hertford House to commemorate the fiftieth anniversary of the Wallace Collection. The King and Queen were there, Massigli the French Ambassador, and Vita 'looking very blue and ill' wearing a borrowed black dress and shawl. Afterwards Harold wrote to Vita that she looked splendid 'with her dingle dangles' and he wished she would go oftener to parties and 'not have to scrounge round for dresses'. But it was Rollo, retreat and Sissinghurst that suited her, she did not want parties, dresses, social occasions.

Parties, dressses, social occasions filled Violet's days and nights. Society of a parodic kind became her way of life. She was an entertainer who played bitter games, their meaning only guessed at by a few. Tony Gandarillas, the Chilean Ambassador, small, witty and addicted to

opium, told James Pope-Hennessy that Violet was now in love with
him. Nancy Mitford said she claimed 'she has a lover in the bullfighting
trade. Carmen Trefusis.'

Violet's writing career came to an end. Vita accused her of scribbling
for an hour or so in bed in the mornings between shouting at Alice
and effecting the day. A postwar novel *Pirates at Play* was a farce about
the English in Florence. A memoir, *Don't Look Round*, published in 1952
she called a collage. Dedicated to her mother it was an exercise in
concealment, a witty façade, an exemplar of Edwardian discretion,
revealing nothing but loyalty, wit and charm. From it, no one would
know who Violet was, whether she was happy or unhappy, cared a
lot or not at all. Nancy Mitford suggested the title *Here Lies Madame
Trefusis*. There were no echoes of passion or pain, no statements of
commitment, no revelations of feeling. Her only confession was of
chronic insomnia.

Managing her homes took her time. She would drive between
St Loup and Florence her big Mercedes filled with servants, packages,
provisions. At the Ombrellino she employed a lugubrious butler called
Terzilio, Giovanni a cordon-bleu chef, a clutch of other servants, a
series of chauffeurs whom she sacked or who left because she was
always an hour late or muddled about when she wanted to be where.
She considered herself a gourmet. If she thought a meal good Giovanni
was summoned and congratulated, if not he was berated for all to
hear.

In the late 1950s she acquired the wing of a mansion in the rue du
Cherche Midi which had once belonged to the Duc de Saint-Simon.
She decorated it with marble busts on gilt consoles, Louis XV chairs,
Aubusson rugs, eighteenth-century portraits, *trompe-l'oeil* paintings. She
called herself aptly 'a *déclassée* woman who lives only in *classé* houses'.
She flaunted the trappings that when young she had professed to
despise.

Asked to do an entry for *Figaro Littéraire* she wrote of her vast salon
in the rue du Cherche Midi, her marvellous cuisine, her beautiful jewels. Against her name in the telephone directory was inserted

'*femme de lettres*'. She began to say she was thirtieth in succession to the throne.

In 1952 the writer Susan Mary Alsop and her mother sometimes lunched at the Ombrellino. They thought it underfurnished, sprawling and Violet quirky and a bit of a fraud. There was a sense of 'hanger-on beaux from Paris' and servants using her for her money. Violet went on about being Edward VII's daughter, she wore full skirts and was a messy eater:

> When she rose majestically at the end of a meal a cascade of crumbs and odd bits of food would fall to the floor. I was revolted. We were rather ashamed of going there and didn't very often. Reading *Portrait of a Marriage* I feel an obtuse fool; there must have been poetry and fascination there.

Guests at the Ombrellino and St Loup came and went. Violet was inordinately insistent to those who refused an invitation. She wheedled, cajoled and even cried. Rejections were more than forcefully made for she took little notice of them. Nancy Mitford said Violet tortured her by phoning her all the time when she was trying to work. 'As she can write books without working she doesn't understand the necessity for those less gifted of doing so.' She had to leave the telephone on 'because of various matters to do with the lease – nobody else telephones and I've begged her not to, she doesn't pay the least attention.' Betty Richards had some abdominal operation in July 1951 and dreaded Violet coming to stay:

> much as I love you & long to see you darling *you would only be doing me a very great disservice, retarding a convalescence it will take me all my physical strength and strength of will to cope with* were you to come over here now. *Please* darling.

Violet became unaware of the figure she cut. Vita, visiting the Ombrellino in September 1952, could not understand why servants stayed. Violet did not give them instructions then cursed them for not having done what they did not know she wanted. She never told them how many there were for lunch or dinner, failed to order the car then was angry when it was not there, or ordered it for eleven and then was not ready until twelve. Alice, her slave, took every opportunity to complain to Vita about Violet without her overhearing. She had a 'second-in-command' called Rita and whenever cries of 'Rita, Rita' echoed through the villa, Vita thought they were for her.

'Today is the anniversary of her mother and she minds' Vita wrote to Harold on 11 September. She did not like the climate created by Violet's gay friends, Jean de Gaigneron — Harold's lover in 1919 — 'who is so waspish', 'Princey' — Prince Rodolphe de Faucigny Lucinge — and Philippe Jullian. 'I feel they all dislike each other.' She was hauled off to an 'incredibly boring' cocktail party given for a youth congress at the French consulate. There were ten guests for lunch at the Ombrellino, more for dinner. The next day they were supposed to lunch at the villa of the Marchese Torrigiani near Lucca. At the last minute Violet said she was not coming, Vita and the three men were late setting off, they had difficulty finding the place and had been expected for tea, not lunch. It was all chaotic. The Marchese coped and was unsurprised but Vita wanted desperately to go home to Sissinghurst and never to visit again.

Violet was brittle in body and mind. Osteoporosis led to painful breaking of bones. She broke a femur tripping on a step at the theatre, a shin when she fell from a chair. She had her hip pinned with a perspex plate. It left her with a limp and she walked with a stick. She began to resemble a dowager duchess, plumes waving, tapping her cane. She had her hair permed into girlish curls, took strong painkillers, the occasional barbiturate.

She passed on everything she heard with rococo embellishments of her own, claimed her novels were coast-to-coast bestsellers, that she knew everyone of importance, had been courted by the world's leading statesmen, poets, musicians. The Swedish ambassador told James Pope-Hennessy she was a war heroine who had been parachuted into France every week, which was how she broke her bones and why she was given the Légion d'Honneur.

Her messiness and chaos, her constant painting of her face, seemed to signal inner distress. Nancy Mitford called her Auntie Vi, said she was 'the ruin of a small evening. She made up her face ten times at dinner. I counted.' The photographer Cecil Beaton found she had retouched his photos of her with the same impatient approximation she gave to painting her face. Parting from Vita at a station in July 1952 aged fifty-eight she said, 'Oh now in five minutes time you will have disappeared and I shan't feel safe any more. No sanctuary left.'

Many of her traits went into the haughty egocentricity of Lady Montdore in Mitford's *Love in a Cold Climate*. Harold Acton said:

> One can almost hear Violet remarking like Lady Montdore 'I think I may say we put India on the map. Hardly any of one's friends in England had even heard of India before we went there you know.'

At the Ombrellino after her mother's death Violet took centre stage. Always her mother's understudy, she had learned the script, knew the moves and attitudes but her performance was caricature. She was too intelligent, too caustic and disappointed for it to be otherwise. The true spirit of Edwardian hypocrisy eluded her. At heart she grieved the price it made her pay. Hers was anachronistic impersonation, disconcerting parody. Like her mother she tended to take ambassadors to one side to say she was worried about China or Japan but she delivered the lines like a spoof.

The Duc d'Harcourt in his memoirs included a Proustian pastiche of Violet at her mother's villa, rejuvenating when royalty was among her guests, forgetting her cane and her limp, pushing her way to their side and executing curtsies to uncertain kings and princes. The laugh was on them and on her. Her childhood question, 'Mama why do we call Grandpapa "Majesty"?' had never been answered. It held resonance of sexual duplicity, concealment and the absurdity of pomp. She had wanted something quite other for herself. 'I have crushed down the vision of life with you,' she had written to Vita, 'but always it remained at the back of my mind, so wide, so open, a life so free.'

Unloved and unloving in her mother's grand mansion she made her own risible majestic display of majesty. She contrived outlandish protocol whereby she would come into dinner on the arm of some Pretender only when all her guests were assembled, like Edward VII in his day. She sat at the head of table, on her right the French Ambassador, some duke on her left:

> The magnificent vermeil plate was massively displayed . . . Lady Enid Browne sat on the main table because she was descended from the Earls of Chesterfield and Stanhope. Her neighbour, the Marchese Valdamara Fioravanti, who sold his honey to everyone in Bellosguardo, had his place there too. He used to keep an enormous pet crocodile in the bath. His mother had it murdered, stuffed and encrusted with jewels then kept it in a state bed in a guest room. The Marchese was eccentric but a Knight of Malta . . .

Once when she noticed there were thirteen at table she thought it unlucky and peremptorily sent the French Consul home. After dinner she summoned her guests in order of rank to sit and amuse her, dismissing them if they palled. Egocentric, pretentious and artificial she seemed like an exiled Queen in Wonderland, a parody of her own parodies of materialism and loss. Her visitors were cast in roles she contrived, walk-ons in some glittering comedy of manners, perfected by her mother, travestied by herself.

She drew God into her games. At the church of St Mark's in the Via Maggio she inherited her mother's roped-off pew and embroidered cushions — front row, right of centre aisle. In church, bronze plaques commemorated her mother and George Keppel. Like Mrs Keppel approving the day's menus, in advance of Sunday worship Violet would summon the vicar, the Reverend Church, to the Ombrellino to consider hymns and prayers. He waited in her salon drinking her whisky until she made her entrance.

~'

On 14 December 1961 Vita mentioned in her daily letter to Harold 'a slight touch of that gastric flu'. She thought it would last twenty-four hours. It lingered. She wrote of 'tiresome tirednesses', her tower room was cold. She was operated on for cancer but without success. Harold kept to his schedule and went down to Sissinghurst on the weekend train. In too much pain to move, she went on with their ritual of daily letters but in a faint illegible scrawl. His replies – about daily events and who he had lunch with at the Beefsteak – compounded the virtues of fortitude and loyalty and the fatal omission of a vocabulary for suffering or desire.

She died on 2 June 1962. Her body was taken to the vaults of the chapel at Knole. Harold returned the doge's lava ring to Violet as Vita asked in her will.

'Do you know Mitya,' Violet had written to her in 1920,

> that my only really solid and unseverable lien with the world is *you*, my love for you? I believe if there weren't you I should live more and more in my own world until finally I withdrew myself inwardly altogether. I'm sure it would happen.

She found no workable alternative to that lien. She lived alone without it in her mother's house and her fantasy castle, the terraces, statues and daunting rooms all hers. When she travelled to London she stayed at the Ritz in her mother's world.

As she became more frail her fiancés gave way to nephews, gay young men without much money, impressed by her theatre, status and display. The writer and artist Philippe Jullian was 'in favour and out, then in again'. Then a playwright friend of his, Jean Pierre Grédy, then an English writer, Quentin Crewe. She kept her escorts, admirers, her pretenders to the throne. Frank Ashton-Gwatkin, a retired diplomat, travelled with her and tried to please. John Phillips, a young American in Florence, was intrigued by her, cared for her, played her quasi-romantic flirtatious games.

Her health declined from 1963 on. In summer that year she again broke her hip. 'Approaching seventy, Violet looked eighty.' Sleep eluded her so she took barbiturates, broken bones pained her so she took analgesics. 'With a single glass of champagne she could appear completely befuddled.' At a New Year's party at the Ombrellino in 1967 when the guests were assembled and the table laid with the silver-gilt sturgeon at its centrepiece, the gold-plated cutlery with the monogram of Catherine the Great, the Venetian crystal, the Meissen china, she made her entrance on the arm of her butler. Brightly rouged, glittering with diamonds, vague with drugs, she sat at the head of the table 'on a sort of bishop's throne', ate nothing and said to everyone and no one, 'I'm alone, so alone.'

She died at the Ombrellino of a malabsorption disease in March 1972. She wasted away in her mother's bed. The funeral gathering included 'the Florentine aristocracy and Queen Helen of Romania'. Some of her ashes were scattered on her mother's grave in the cemetery, I Allori, near Florence. The rest were scattered below her tower at St Loup.

In her will she dispersed all the worldly goods acquired by her mother with the King's help — an emerald here, a picture there. She gave grandly to those who were kind to her in the last years of her life: St Loup and its contents went to John Phillips, her apartment at the rue de Cherche-Midi went to her nurse who sold it to Andy Warhol. Ombrellino reverted to her sister who sold it. It became a trade centre used for official and civic functions.

As for Violet's heart, the struggle it made, the denial it endured, she asked that it be sealed in the medieval wall of the monks' refectory at St Loup. On the wall is a plaque, a valediction in French: 'Violet Trefusis 1894—1972, English by birth, French at heart.' Before she died she wrote the lines

> My heart was more disgraceful, more alone
> And more courageous than the world has known.
> O passer-by my heart was like your own.

She chose as her epitaph, 'She Withdrew'.

Sources and Bibliography

Most of Violet Trefusis's papers are at the Beinecke Library, Yale University. Some, including letters from Alice Keppel and Sonia Cubitt, are with Violet's executor, John Phillips. The Sackville/Nicolson archive is at the Lilly Library, Indiana University; other papers, including letters from Pat Dansey to Vita Sackville-West, are with Nigel Nicolson. Letters from Denys Trefusis to his sister Betty and to his uncle the Honourable John Schomberg Trefusis are with his niece, Phyllida Ellis. Published collections of letters from Violet Trefusis, Vita Sackville-West, Harold Nicolson and Virginia Woolf, are acknowledged below.

ix	Most are collected	*Violet to Vita: The Letters of Violet Trefusis to Vita Sackville-West*, ed. Mitchell A. Leaska & John Phillips, (Methuen 1989)
x	One thing I did	Pat Dansey to Vita, August 1921 (Nigel Nicolson)
	You are going to tell	quoted in Jeffrey Weeks, *Sex, Politics and Society* (Longman 1981)
	I am bold enough	ibid
xi	It is a love story	Nigel Nicolson, *Portrait of a Marriage* (Orion Books 1992)
	pernicious influence	*Vita and Harold: the Letters of Vita Sackville-West and Harold Nicolson*, ed. Nigel Nicolson (Weidenfeld & Nicolson 1992)
	intolerable conduct	Nigel Nicolson to John Phillips, 31 August 1976
	I wish Violet was dead	Harold to Vita, 9 September 1918, *Vita and Harold*
xii	I cannot help that	Nigel Nicolson to John Phillips, 18 December 1972
	I HATE the furtiveness	Violet to Vita, undated 1920 (Beinecke Library)

Sources and Bibliography

Part One: Queens and Heirs Apparent

ONE

3	There were three	The Princess of Wales, BBC Panorama, November 1995
	rampant bulimia	ibid
5	I have it now	*Portrait of a Marriage*
	Money was freely	G. Cornwallis-West *Edwardian Hey-Days* (Hogarth Press, 1930)
6	It was so necessary	Vita Sackville-West, *The Edwardians* (Hogarth Press 1930)
	how to choose her friends	Consuelo Vanderbilt Balsan, *The Glitter and the Gold* (Heinemann, 1953)
7	Dear Mrs Keppel	Queen Alexandra to Mrs Keppel (undated)
	What a pity	quoted in Georgina Battiscombe, *Queen Alexandra* (Constable 1969)
	As a child	Violet Trefusis, *Triple Violette*, unpublished memoir in French (Beinecke Library)
8	I adore the unparalleled	*Violet to Vita*, 27 August 1918
	We are not as lovable	*Triple Violette*
	From my earliest childhood	Sonia Keppel, *Edwardian Daughter* (Hamish Hamilton 1958)
	and a certain elusive smell	ibid
	My mother began	Violet Trefusis, *Don't Look Round* (Hutchinson 1952)
	The Prince had wanted	Victoria Sackville, unpublished diaries, July 1898 (Lilly Library, Indiana)
10	We heard a fine	Margot Asquith, *Autobiography* (Eyre & Spottiswoode 1962)
	excellent influence	quoted in Philip Magnus, *King Edward VII* (John Murray 1962)
11	he would never have done	quoted in Christopher Hibbert, *Edward VII: A Portrait* (Allen Lane 1976)
	Dear Mrs Keppel	William II to Mrs Keppel December 1907 (John Phillips)
12	She was convinced	Frederick Ponsonby, *Recollections of Three Reigns* (Eyre & Spottiswoode 1951)
	I want you to try	quoted in Gordon Brook-Shepherd, *Uncle of Europe* (Harcourt Brace Jovanovich 1975)
13	Oh dear	*The Diary of Virginia Woolf: Volume 4 1931–35*, ed. Anne Olivier Bell (Hogarth Press 1982) 10 March 1932

| How can one make the best | *Violet to Vita*, 1 May 1920 |
| We love only once | Cyril Connolly (Palinarus), *The Unquiet Grave* (Horizon, 1944) |

TWO

15	Who was my father?	Violet to Vita, October 1919 (Beinecke Library)
16	Here I can breathe	ibid, 25 August 1920
	The atmosphere	*Don't Look Round*
	From Ithaca	ibid
17	At last in 1868	ibid
	They seemed to complete	ibid
18	One could picture	Harold Acton, *More Memoirs of an Aesthete* (Methuen 1970)
19	A frightful bounder	ibid
20	I feel that in entrusting	John Stephenson *A Royal Correspondence. Letters of King Edward VII and King George V to Admiral Sir Henry F. Stephenson* (Macmillan 1938)
21	From a really great	Rebecca West, *1900* (Weidenfeld and Nicolson, 1982)
	Throughout her life	*Edwardian Daughter*
	My mother	*Don't Look Round*
22	several lovers	Daisy, Princess of Pless *From My Private Diary* (John Murray 1931)
	rich and influential	Mary Soames, *Clementine Churchill* (Cassell 1979)
	Mrs Favourite Keppel	11 September 1901. Mary Curzon, *Lady Curzon's India: Letters of a Vicereine*, ed. John Bradley (Weidenfeld & Nicolson 1985)
	which rather shocked	Victoria Sackville, unpublished diaries (Lilly Library)
23	The Alington household	*Edwardian Daughter*
	it was charming	ibid
24	The parties	Philip Magnus, *King Edward VII*
	At times I was	*Recollections of Three Reigns*
	His angry bellow	Magnus, *King Edward VII*

THREE

| 25 | no one can represent | 9 July 1864, quoted in Philip Magnus, *King Edward VII* |

I don't know what   Magnus, *King Edward VII*

my father, my protector   19 June 1858, quoted in Giles St Aubyn, *Queen Victoria* (Sinclair Stevenson 1991)

26   None of you   26 August 1857, Magnus, *King Edward VII*

27   peculiarities arise   ibid

A very bad day   Frederick Waymouth Gibbs 'The Education of a Prince'. Extracts from diaries 1851–6 (*Cornhill Magazine* 986)

28   I am in utter despair   4 March 1858, *Dearest Child: Letters Between Queen Victoria and the Crown Princess of Prussia 1858–1861*, ed. Roger Fulford (Evans Brothers 1964)

His only safety   9 April 1859, ibid

learn the duties   Magnus, *King Edward VII*

The agony and misery   12 November 1862, Giles St Aubyn, *Edward VII Prince and King* (Collins 1979)

29   If you were to try   ibid

for there must be   January 1862, *Queen Victoria*

future reunion   Victoria to Queen Augusta, *Edward VII Prince and King*

Why should we go   ibid

too weak to keep   13 January 1862, *Dearest Mama: Private Correspondence of Queen Victoria and the Crown Princess of Prussia 1861–1864*, ed. Roger Fulford (Evans Brothers 1968)

31   her walk, manner   4 June 1861, *Dearest Child*

I don't think he can be   1 October 1861, ibid

What you say   12 October 1861, ibid

I frankly avow   11 September 1862, Magnus, *King Edward VII*

32   far worse than a funeral   4 February 1863

I opened the shrine   7 March 1863, *Edward VII Prince and King*

33   I could not remain   Louise Cresswell, *The Lady Farmer: Eighteen Years on the Sandringham Estate* (Temple Co. 1887)

Alix looked very ill   12 March 1864, *Dearest Mama*

The princess had another   *Queen Alexandra*

34   very forcibly   Magnus, *King Edward VII*

she will be quite bored   Filmer MSS U120 C77 Kent County Record Office

very unsatisfactory   *Edward VII: A Portrait*

Then the torrent   *1900*

FOUR

36	If ever you become	18 January 1868, Magnus, *King Edward VII*
	a very dissolute	Magnus, *King Edward VII*
37	I am sorry	February 1870, quoted in Graham and Heather Fisher, *Bertie and Alix: Anatomy of a Royal Marriage* (Robert Hale 1974)
	I am so looking	Edward VII to Mrs Keppel, New Year's Day 1910. ADD A5 475 (Royal Archive, Windsor)
	the public may suppose	*Edward VII, Prince and King* (Collins 1979)
	The matter appears	ibid
38	I trust by what	*Bertie and Alix: Anatomy of a Royal Marriage*
39	Why should a young	Hibbert, *Edward VII*
	the people of England	ibid
	there are not wanting	ibid
	The Government really	*Royal Victorians*
	I am over 28	*Bertie and Alix: Anatomy of a Royal Marriage*
40	It is the custom	Alfred E. Watson, *King Edward VII as a Sportsman* (Longmans 1911)
	if made public	Magnus, *King Edward VII*
	anticipated the danger	ibid
	held the crown	ibid
	being aware of peculiar	ibid
41	Blandford, I always	ibid
	arrange his matters	ibid
	How can one make	*Violet to Vita*, 1 May 1920
42	It would be difficult	Lillie Langtry, *The Days I Knew* (Hutchinson 1925)
	My only purpose	ibid
	etiquette demanded	ibid
43	A petition has been filed	Ernest Dudley, *The Gilded Lily* (Odhams Press 1958)
44	a very distinguished	*Edward VII: A Portrait*
	unfortunate lunatic	*Royal Victorians*
	It is one of God's mercies	Harold to Vita, 17 February 1949 (Lilly Library)
45	He was more than kind	Countess of Warwick, *Life's Ebb and Flow* (Cassell 1920)
	you have systematically	Lord Beresford to the Prince of Wales, 12 July 1891 (Salisbury papers, quoted in Hibbert, *Edward VII: A Portrait*)
46	His signing	Magnus, *King Edward VII*

	We profoundly regret	*The Times*, 10 June 1891 (quoted in Hibbert, *Edward VII: A Portrait*)
47	Those who revealed	Countess of Warwick, *Afterthoughts* (Cassel, 1931)

FIVE

48	Once upon a time	*Triple Violette*
49	With one terrifying	*Edwardian Daughter*
50	When Mamma	ibid
	very ugly	Osbert Sitwell, *Laughter in the Next Room* (Macmillan 1949)
	You are drunk	*'Chips' The Diaries of Sir Henry Channon*, ed. Robert Rhodes James (Weidenfeld 1993)
	I am curious to know	Winston Churchill to his mother, 22 January 1902, quoted in Randolph Churchill, *Young Statesman, Winston Churchill, 1901–1914* (Minerva 1991)
51	My dear Mrs George	The Prince of Wales to Mrs Keppel, May 1901 (Royal Archive, Windsor)
52	a number of other	*Edward VII: A Portrait*
	The Queen has taken	*The Glitter and the Gold*
53	the complete supremacy	8 April 1901, *Lady Curzon's India: Letters of a Vicereine*
	Dear Soveral	quoted in *Uncle of Europe*
	I came to rely	*Edwardian Daughter*
54	one of whom	*Edward VII and his Jewish Court*
	I hereby acknowledge	7 March 1901, (Cassel papers, Hartley Library, Southampton University)
	Referring to our	5 March 1903, ibid
55	My dear Cassel	Edward VII to Ernest Cassel, September 1901. ibid
	The drawing room	Lord Esher to his son Maurice, April 1908. *Journals and Letters of Reginald Esher*. Ed. Maurice Brett (Nicholson and Watson 1934–8)
56	Israel in force	July 1900, Lincolnshire papers Bodleian Library Oxford
	I quite made up	*The Diary of Sir Edward Hamilton*, ed. Dudley Bahlman (University of Hull 1993)
57	one of a new breed	*Edward VII and his Jewish Court*
	When she came	*The Enigmatic Edwardian*

58 The poorer classes   Ernest Cassel to Edward VII, 1902 (Cassel
                             papers, Southampton)

    You will have doubtless heard   Edward VII to Ernest Cassel, 1 June 1902
                             (Cassel papers, Southampton)

59 The party is like   Ernest Cassel to his daughter, 1906 (Cassel
                             papers, Southampton)

    The King is rather pleased   ibid, April 1902

    a stout Teutonic   *Edward VII and his Jewish Court*

60 I have had   ibid

    Levee dress   (Cassel papers, Southampton)

    greatest wish   *Recollections of Three Reigns*

61 The King is perfectly   Lord Esher to his son Maurice, July 1905.
                             Journals and Letters of Reginald Esher

    She sits next to him   ibid

    HM was in capital   Lincolnshire papers

62 wonder dully what relation   *Violet to Vita* (undated 1918)

SIX

63 Studded wardrobe-trunks *Edwardian Daughter*

64 Out of a square   ibid

    Sir Ernest was fervently ibid

    At Biarritz   *Uncle of Europe*

65 We are his servants   Janet Morgan, *Edwina Mountbatten: A Life of Her
                             Own* (HarperCollins, 1992)

    lovely little jewelled   *Edwardian Daughter*

66 Mama was waiting   *Triple Violette*

    Mrs George Keppel   *Uncle of Europe*

67 I put on a frock   ibid

    Before leaving   Asquith to Mrs Keppel, 9 May 1908 (John
                             Phillips)

    Monsieur Jean   *Don't Look Round*

68 Every year   *Violet to Vita*, 16 September 1910

    We used to come   *Don't Look Round*

69 her tapering   ibid

    in the category   *Edwardian Daughter*

    When roused to anger   *Don't Look Round*

    Persuasion   unpublished note (Beinecke Library, Yale)

70 suspicious, introspective   *Don't Look Round*

    This book Mama   *Edwardian Daughter*

71 My first (and salutary) *Don't Look Round*

72 The great lost the power ibid

	of a sudden	ibid
	to be dragged	*Don't Look Round*
	It seems to me	*Portrait of a Marriage*

SEVEN

74	One never loves	Violet Trefusis, *Hunt the Slipper* (Virago 1983)
	which became more	*Don't Look Round*
	I who was the worst	*Portrait of a Marriage*
	Vita belonged to Knole	*Don't Look Round*
	It was necessary	ibid
75	It is above all	Vita Sackville-West, *Knole and the Sackvilles* (Heinemann 1922)
	But you require	*Knole and the Sackvilles*
76	Had you been a man	*Violet to Vita*
	Violet is *mine*	*Portrait of a Marriage*
	as floppy as	Vita to Harold, 19 May 1943 (Lilly Library)
77	There he stands	Vita to Harold, 8 September 1941 (Lilly Library)
	intermittent yet	*Don't Look Round*
	In her too	ibid
79	All the fast	Victoria Sackville, unpublished diary
	He made me sit	Vita Sackville-West, *Pepita* (Hogarth Press 1937)
	He put me at	ibid
	mais pourtant	ibid
80	I wonder whether	Victoria Sackville, unpublished diary
	Baby very naughty	ibid
	Everybody says	Victoria Sackville, *Book of Reminiscences* (Lilly Library)
81	the figure of	23 January 1927, *The Diary of Virginia Woolf: volume 3 1925–30*. Ed. Anne Olivier Bell (The Hogarth Press 1980)
	L says that I talk	Victoria Sackville, unpublished diary
	those lovely, lovely	*Portrait of a Marriage*
82	Often when I went	ibid
	She loved me as a baby	*Pepita*
83	one moment	ibid
	it has been rather	*Portrait of a Marriage*
	I thought they would	quoted in Victoria Glendinning, *Vita* (Weidenfeld and Nicolson 1983)
84	I think she touched	*Pepita*

	annual, biennial	ibid
85	she possessed	ibid
	Do you know	*Violet to Vita*, 7 May 1920
	Genealogies	*Vita*
86	Mr Keppel is really	Vita's diary, 4 April 1908 (Lilly Library)
	It speaks highly	*Don't Look Round*
	If I'd read	Violet Trefusis, *Broderie Anglaise* (Paris 1935. English translation by Barbara Bray, Harcourt Brace Jovanovich 1985)
	stumbled out	*Portrait of a Marriage*
87	I can't hear	ibid
	How I loved you	*Violet to Vita*, August 1920
88	Darling, how dreadfully	ibid, 14 August 1920

EIGHT

89	full justice	Magnus, *King Edward VII*
	Mrs Keppel and the affront	ibid
	The King's cold	Mrs Keppel to the Marquis de Soveral, quoted in *Uncle of Europe*
90	the matter you	*Edward VII and his Jewish Court*
	I shall be sorry	Magnus, *King Edward VII*
	Poor Alice	Ernest Cassel to his daughter, May 1910 (Cassel papers, Southampton)
91	looked as if	ibid, 6 May 1910
	Yes I have heard	*Uncle of Europe*
	I never did any harm	Lord Esher's journal, 12 June 1910. Quoted in James Lees-Milne, *The Enigmatic Edwardian* (Sidgwick & Jackson, 1986)
92	interest I gave	*Edward VII and his Jewish Court*
	It was the fruit of a quite	ibid
	Mrs Keppel had lied	quoted in James Lees-Milne, *The Enigmatic Edwardian: The Life of Reginald 2nd Viscount Esher* (Sidgwick & Jackson 1976)
93	We went up	*Edwardian Daughter*
	Why does it matter	ibid
	Today the King	Wilfrid Scawen Blunt, *My Diaries* (Secker 1919)
95	regular sweep	ibid
96	surely one	Osbert Sitwell, *Great Morning* (Macmillan 1948)
	My dear Lady Knollys	*Uncle of Europe*

97 No young lady's — *Don't Look Round*
   I want you to come — *Violet to Vita*, 8 October 1910 (written in French)
   you ask me pointblank — ibid
   O my dears — *Vita*
98 wife of a gentleman — *Violet to Vita*, 12 December 1910
   I didn't think — *Portrait of a Marriage*
   Your speech impressed — *Violet to Vita*, 31 October 1910 (written in French)
   The chauffeur sounded — *Edwardian Daughter*
99 My dear Harold — *Vita and Harold*, 5 November 1910
100 For the first time — *Violet to Vita*, 12 December 1910 (written in French)
101 I hope terribly — ibid 12 December 1910
   The parting with Mama — *Edwardian Daughter*
   I remember admiring — *Portrait of a Marriage*
   O Vita — *Violet to Vita*, undated 1911 (written in French)
102 I knew it then — *Portrait of a Marriage*
   like the Babes — *Don't Look Round*
103 I liked the two — *Edwardian Daughter*
   No I am not angry — 31 July 1911 (Beinecke Library, Yale)
104 A lady caught — *Edwardian Daughter*
   In these spacious — ibid
   Not only were the rooms — *Great Morning*
105 masses of beautiful — *Edwardian Daughter*
   After a month — *Don't Look Round*

NINE

106 exquisite beauties — *Edwardian Daughter*
   their conversation — Vita Sackville-West, *The Edwardians*
107 The house was full
108 She was tall — *Don't Look Round*
   This is a rather nice — Violet to Vita, 8 June 1912 (Beinecke Library)
109 He lays down — Vita to Harold, 6 June 1913 (Lilly Library)
110 Isn't it funny — Harold to Vita, 28 July 1913 (Lilly Library)
   Accepté mes félicitations — Violet to Vita, 5 August 1913 (Beinecke Library)
111 Dear Mr Smith — quoted in Susan Mary Alsop, *Lady Sackville* (Weidenfeld and Nicolson 1978)
112 How she flung — *Portrait of a Marriage*
   I remember — ibid

113 Everything in me   Harold to Vita, 11 September 1914 (Lilly
         Library)
114 not very attractive   *Edwardian Daughter*
115 It required   *Don't Look Round*
     He would arrive   *Edwardian Daughter*
     His courtship was too   *Don't Look Round*
116 It was tacitly   ibid
     Even Mama   *Edwardian Daughter*
117 You and your dog   ibid
118 There's a war   ibid
     Poor Archie   ibid
     The idea of matrimony   *Don't Look Round*
119 I think perhaps   *Pepita*
120 Damn that little too too   Harold to Vita, 7 June 1917 (Lilly Library)
121 I used to invent   Pat Dansey to Vita, 4 September 1922 (Nigel
         Nicolson)

Part Two: Portrait of a Lesbian Affair

TEN

125 I simply cant   *Violet to Vita*, 29 October 1917
126 bloody time   Harold to Vita, 6 November 1917 (Lilly
         Library)
     untidy or crawly   ibid, 6 November 1917
     like a searchlight   ibid, 7 November 1917
     And I shall be   ibid, 7 November 1917
     my whole soul   ibid, 7 November 1917
     frightfully opty   ibid, 15 March 1918
     We were in fact   *Portrait of a Marriage*
127 in the unaccustomed   ibid
     I was infinitely   ibid
128 I am young   Violet to Vita, undated 1918
     I felt like a person   *Portrait of a Marriage*
129 How triumphant we were   *Violet to Vita*, 20 July 1919
     I wish I was more   Harold to Vita, 9 May 1918 (Lilly Library)
130 where no one will want me   Vita to Harold, 11 May 1918 *Vita and Harold*
     Darling one day   ibid
     God Mitya do you wonder   Violet to Vita, undated May 1918 (Beinecke
         Library)
131 I am drunk with the beauty   *Violet to Vita*, undated 1918
     she looks so charming   Victoria Sackville, unpublished diary, 18 May

		1918 (Lilly Library)
132	God knows it is	*Violet to Vita*, 23 January 1918
	O Mitya come	ibid, 14 August 1918
	How happy we were	ibid, 20 July 1919
133	I adore you	ibid, 22 July 1919
	Married life under	Victoria Sackville, *Lady Sackville*
134	What sort of life	*Violet to Vita*, 22 July 1918
135	all things seductive	Vita Sackville-West, *Challenge* (Collins 1974)
	Her humour	ibid
136	so marvellously	*Violet to Vita*, 27 August 1918
	God knows	ibid, 19 August 1918
	I hate lies	ibid, 26 August 1918
	How right you were	ibid, 23 July 1918
137	I want you for	ibid, 25 August 1918
	I have greatly dared	ibid, 26 August 1918
138	O Vita get away	Violet to Vita, 15 September 1918 (Beinecke Library)
139	What *is* the good	*Violet to Vita*, 23 September 1918
140	Mitya, even you	ibid
	This is *the best*	*Vita* and *Portrait of a Marriage*
141	It does seem unfair	Violet to Vita, October 1918 (Beinecke Library)
142	Chinday was at her worst	*Violet to Vita*, October 1918
	As Mrs Nicolson	Sidney Russell Cooke to Violet, 31 October 1918 (Lilly Library)

ELEVEN

146	Mitya will never leave	*Violet to Vita*, 21 March 1919
147	that swine Violet	Harold to Vita, 5 December 1918 *Vita and Harold*
	She flatters you	*Vita*
148	It is nobody's business	Victoria Sackville, *Book of Reminiscences*, 1922, published in Susan Mary Alsop, *Lady Sackville*
	You say Violet	Harold to Vita, 14 February 1919 (Lilly Library)
149	I have destroyed	Harold to Vita, February 1919 (Lilly Library)
	I'm glad	Violet to Vita, 16 March 1919 (Beinecke Library)
150	She talks in a voice	Vita to Harold, 20 March 1919 (Lilly Library)
	Mitya I can't face	*Violet to Vita*, March 1919
151	You know how I loathe	ibid, 21 March 1919

	hell of having to endure	Violet to Vita, March 1919 (Beinecke Library)
	What's going to happen?	*Violet to Vita*, March 1919
152	I feel really	Harold to Vita, 29 March 1919 (Lilly Library)
	Poor Denys	Vita to Harold, ibid, 30 March 1919
	I certainly told	*Violet to Vita*, 8 May 1919
153	his word of honour	ibid, 30 March 1919
154	specialise in Russian	Denys to John Schomberg Trefusis, 1910 (Phyllida Ellis)
	You look as though	ibid, April 1919
	very county	Phyllida Ellis to author, April 1994
	caged up	Denys to his sister Betty, 1911 (Phyllida Ellis)
	I *hate* them, Mitya	*Violet to Vita*, 2 May 1919
155	Living permanently	*Portrait of a Marriage*
	You simply can't	Harold to Vita, 29 March 1919 *Vita and Harold* (Lilly Library)
156	he will say	*Violet to Vita*, undated March 1919
	Hadji this	ibid, 19 April 1919
	O darling	
	All I can do	Harold to Vita, 22 May 1919 (Lilly Library)
	She says I would	Violet to Vita, 29 April 1919 (Beinecke Library)
157	I don't absolutely	*Portrait of a Marriage*
	My dear Vita	Denys Trefusis to Vita Sackville-West, 3 May 1919 (Lilly Library)
158	rigidly suppressed	Denys Trefusis to his sister Betty, 1911 (Pyllida Ellis)
	ought to be confined	*Violet to Vita*, 5 May 1919
	Really, how nice	ibid, 6 May 1919
159	I don't think any	Pat Dansey, to Vita, May 1919
	We are making	*Violet to Vita*, undated 1919
160	When I say care	ibid, 23 September 1918
	I nearly struck	ibid, 6 May 1919
	I can't, *can't* have one	ibid, 9 May 1919
	Unless you make	Pat Dansey to Vita, undated 1919
161	I should like to	Harold to Vita, 24 May 1919 (Lilly Library)
	I think he will	*Violet to Vita*, June 1919
	V's wedding	Vita to Harold, 1 June 1919 (Lilly Library)
	you must come	Harold to Vita, 3 June 1919 (Lilly Library)
	Violet thinks I will	Vita to Harold, 9 June 1919 (Lilly Library)
163	All that time	*Portrait of a Marriage*

TWELVE

164 I treated her savagely   *Portrait of a Marriage*
     Don't you know   ibid
165 What are you thinking   *Violet to Vita*, July 1919
166 If only I knew   ibid, 26 June 1919
     O God another   ibid, 8 July 1919
167 All this will   ibid, 21 July 1919
168 Will the young   *Edwardian Daughter*
     I see no one   Violet to Vita, September 1919 (Beinecke
                                  Library)
169 when you are not with me   Vita to Violet, fragment, 1919 (Beinecke
                                  Library)

     Tomorrow you will go   Violet to Vita, September 1919 (Beinecke
                                  Library)
170 I had another frightful   ibid
171 I can't impress   *Violet to Vita*, 17 October 1919
172 I said nothing   Victoria Sackville, unpublished diary, 18
                                  December 1919 (Lilly Library)

     I feel I ought   *Violet to Vita*, 6 January 1920
173 I felt blackened   *Portrait of a Marriage*
     I know you can   Vita to Harold, 1 February 1920, *Vita and Harold*
174 It was a sort   Violet to Vita, 16 February, 1920 (Beinecke
                                  Library)

     she refused so positively   Vita to Harold, 9 February 1920. *Vita and
                                  Harold*

176 He was pompous   *Portrait of a Marriage*
     Denys was very cool   Victoria Sackville, unpublished diary,
                                  February 1920 (Lilly Library)

177 This must never go   *Portrait of a Marriage*
     She calls it banishment   Vita to Harold, 14 February 1920 (Lilly
                                  Library)

178 I am simply dazed   *Violet to Vita*, 14 February 1920
     Every day L telephones   Vita to Harold, 18 February 1920 (Lilly
                                  Library)

     O my darling   Violet to Vita, 16 February 1920 (Beinecke
                                  Library)

179 You can't seriously   *Violet to Vita*, 29 January 1920

THIRTEEN

180 Pat is a powerful   *Violet to Vita*, February 1920
     he does nothing but   ibid, 16 February 1920

181	he yelled	ibid, 20 February 1920
183	I only called	*Edwardian Daughter*
	'My dear Lord'	ibid
	I know that just	Denys Trefusis to Violet, 24 February 1920 (Beinecke Library)
184	I am afraid	Pat Dansey to Vita Sackville-West, 2 March 1920. *Violet to Vita*
	I could not be	*Violet to Vita*, 9 March 1920
185	Darling, I saw	Pat Dansey to Violet, 15 March 1920. *Violet to Vita*
186	a debased crippled	*Violet to Vita*, 1 May 1920
	I am singularly pure	ibid, 7 May 1920
	Before I had always	*Portrait of a Marriage*
187	You have told me	Violet to Vita, 12 March 1920 (Beinecke Library)
188	My dear I worry	Pat Dansey to Vita, 8 May 1920 (Nigel Nicolson)
	I saw the sort	*Portrait of a Marriage*
	In the Middle	*Violet to Vita*, 8 May 1920
189	How can you expect	ibid, 19 March 1920
	What a dreadful	ibid, 11 May 1920
	Hate seeing her	Vita Sackville-West, unpublished diary, 22 April 1920 (Lilly Library)
190	I can't bear	*Violet to Vita*, 22 May 1920
	I am twenty-six	ibid, 5 June 1920
191	O Mitya, you can	ibid, 7 July 1920
	I fear the scandal	Mrs Keppel to Violet, undated (Beinecke Library)
	I could not live	*Violet to Vita*, 21 July 1920
192	Jean is a nice	Harold to Vita, 17 January 1919 (Lilly Library)
	Can you arrange	ibid, 19 July 1920
	Having written it	*Portrait of a Marriage*
193	Darling it's true	*Violet to Vita*, 24 August 1920
	three dozen nightgowns	*Edwardian Daughter*
194	She has been gardening	*Violet to Vita*, August 1920 (Beinecke Library)
	You haunt this place	*Violet to Vita*, August 1920
195	She fusses	ibid, October 1920
	She is diabolical	ibid
196	If I can't be	ibid, 19 September 1920
	This time last year	ibid, 17 September 1920
	I can only feel	ibid, 2 October 1920
	I love nothing	ibid, 14 October 1920

197 It was like two   *Portrait of a Marriage*
    she seems absolutely   *Book of Reminiscences*

FOURTEEN

200 On Saturday we shall   Harold to Vita, 8 February 1921. *Vita and Harold.*

201 M'elle never leaves   Violet to Vita, 14 March 1921
    Another letter   *Violet to Vita*, 9 March 1921
202 My poor mother   ibid, 18 March 1921
203 And what should I   ibid
    If only you would   ibid, 29 March 1921
204 It is possible   *Portrait of a Marriage*
    blazing blue eyes   *Dictionary of National Biography*, 1921 entry by Vita
205 Tell Dottie she is   Harold to Vita, March 1921, quoted in Victoria Glendinning, *Vita* (Weidenfeld & Nicolson, 1983)

    the most corrupt   *Violet to Vita*, 1 May 1921
    It seems so odd   ibid
206 Men chinday now completely ibid, 27 May 1921
    everything to me   ibid, 19 July 1921
207 I would gladly do   Pat Dansey to Vita, 15 August 1921 (Nigel Nicolson)

208 Her mother *refuses*   ibid, 1 September 1921
209 Beyond that I have   ibid, 10 November 1921
    I do wish, Vita   ibid, 23 December 1921
    I only feel   Harold to Vita, 8 January 1926. *Vita and Harold*

210 I do not remember   Raymond Mortimer to Vita, 29 December 1925 (Lilly Library)

    It is only very
    I curse myself   Vita to Harold, 8 December 1922. *Vita and Harold*

211 And with it all   ibid, 16 November 1922

FIFTEEN

212 How black is my future   Violet to Pat Dansey, March 1921 (Beinecke Library)

    Denys would frequently   *Don't Look Round*
213 I have to go and see   Pat Dansey to Vita, 1 August 1922 (Nigel Nicolson)

	I *do* hate	ibid, 10 March 1922
214	I will go as	Violet to Pat Dansey, 15 March 1922. *Violet to Vita*
	Well! I'm damned	Pat Dansey to Vita, March 1922 (Nigel Nicolson)
215	Darling if V	ibid, 6 May 1922
	Surely from old	ibid, 17 August 1922
216	I was fearful	ibid, 8 April 1922
217	Apparently her mother	ibid, 4 December 1922
218	I loathe being	ibid, 17 July 1923
	Would it be easier	ibid, 30 August 1923
	Three perfect days	ibid, 11 November 1923
	I centralized on	ibid, 24 November 1923
219	I would sooner die	ibid, 3 August 1924
	I do apologise	ibid, undated 1924
	I am going to tell	ibid, 26 June 1924
220	in a very amorous	ibid, 27 May 1926
	She never bought	Lord Northumberland to Vita Sackville-West, 3 February 1924 (Lilly Library)
	I do *not* want	Vita to Harold, 12 February 1923 (Lilly Library)
221	I surrendered	*Don't Look Round*
222	Every night	*The Hook in the Heart*, unpublished manuscript (Beinecke Library)
	How could she make	ibid
	Her love of love	ibid
223	Disowned by	ibid
	People quailed	*Don't Look Round*

Part Three: Chacun Sa Tour

SIXTEEN

227	a cold beauty	quoted in Michael de Cossart, *Food of Love: Princesse Edmond de Polignac and her Salon* (Hamish Hamilton, 1978)
228	the hideous Hotel	*Horizon Review of Literature*, 1941–50
229	constantly heard	ibid
	Together they would	*Don't Look Round*
231	It represented	ibid
232	I am always - being	Violet to Vita, undated 1920 (Beinecke Library)
	Sometimes Mrs Keppel	quoted in Philippe Jullian & John Phillips,

	Violet Trefusis: Life and Letters (Hamish Hamilton 1976)
She went round	Duff Cooper to Diana Cooper, 6 February 1927. Quoted in *A Durable Fire: the letters of Duff and Diana Cooper*, ed. Artemis Cooper (Collins 1983)
233 In love there is	quoted in Charlotte Wolff, *Hindsight: An Autobiography*. (Quartet 1980)
a mediocre little	*Don't Look Round*
self-love in all	Violet Trefusis, *Sortie de Secours* (Editions Argo, 1929)
234 In London she had	Harold Acton, *More Memoirs of an Aesthete* (Methuen 1970)
235 quality, beauty	*Don't Look Round*
A fine figure	*More Memoirs of an Aesthete*
236 Winston was so happy	Clementine Churchill to Violet, 10 July 1952 (John Phillips)
237 Oh my God	Vita to Harold, 2 December 1924 (Lilly Library)
You are always so opty	Harold to Vita, 2 December 1924 (Lilly Library)
238 disastrous European	Denys Trefusis, *The Stones of Emptiness.* Unpublished manuscript (Phyllida Ellis)
Above all I have	ibid
239 For 1½ roubles	ibid
Lord bless me	Virginia Woolf to Vita, 7 February 1927. *A Change of Perspective: The Letters of Virginia Woolf, Volume III: 1923–1928.* Ed. Nigel Nicolson (The Hogarth Press 1977)
He went there	*Don't Look Round*
240 he continued to go	ibid
I can only suppose	ibid
put her head round	Phyllida Ellis to author August 1994
241 By now you doubtless	Violet to Cyril Connolly, 20 September 1929. Quoted in *Violet Trefusis: Life and Letters*

SEVENTEEN

242 one steep Utrillo-like	*Don't Look Round*
243 The subtlety of *Challenge*	Vita Sackville-West, *Challenge*. Foreword by Nigel Nicolson (Collins 1974)

	In the end	*Pictureqoer*, May 1927
244	I ache with the sense	*Violet to Vita*, 18 March 1921
	so enchantingly	Virginia Woolf, *Orlando: A Biography* (The Hogarth Press 1928)
245	was a terrible failure	Vita to Harold, 17 August 1926. *Vita and Harold*
	soul friendship	ibid, 26 December 1925
	She lives too much	ibid, 9 November 1926
	Probably I would	ibid, 17 August 1926
	It is incredible	Vita to Virginia Woolf, 21 January 1926. Quoted in *The Letters of Vita Sackville-West to Virginia Woolf*. Ed. Louise De Salvo & Mitchell A. Leaska (Hutchinson 1984)
	she shines	*The Diary of Virginia Woolf: volume 3 1925–30.*
246	opulence and freedom	ibid, 4 July 1927
	Vita stalking	ibid, 23 January 1927
247	Do you know	Vita to Virginia 11 June 1927. *The Letters of Vita Sackville-West to Virginia Woolf*
	You see I was reading	Virginia to Vita, 14 June 1927. *A Change of Perspective*
248	was like a cloak	Vita to Virginia, 11 October 1928. *The Letters of Vita Sackville-West to Virginia Woolf*
	the longest	*Portrait of a Marriage*
249	I know what a flawless	Violet to Vita, January 1928. Quoted in Victoria Glendinning, *Vita*
	I kept thinking	Vita to Harold, 17 May 1928 (Lilly Library)
	I must try	ibid, 10 October 1928
251	Would he never manage	*Broderie Anglaise*
252	consists of nothing	ibid
	Her exclusive	ibid
253	fainting with pleasure	ibid
255	why make her into	ibid
	a brilliant, volatile	ibid
256	Were you or weren't you	ibid
	Who d'you think	Virginia to Vita, 8 November 1932. *The Sickle Side of the Moon: the Letters of Virginia Woolf: Volume V, 1932–35*, ed. Nigel Nicolson (The Hogarth Press 1979)
257	No, I'm not	ibid, 7 January 1933
	Not with a quarrel	*The Diary of Virginia Woolf: Volume 4 1931–35,* 11 March 1935

EIGHTEEN

258 The tallest feather   *Don't Look Round*
259 the relationship between   Peter Quennell, *Customs and Characters* (Little Brown & Co. 1982)
260 still, you'll be able   Violet Trefusis, *Hunt the Slipper* (Virago 1983)
    but she cannot   21 April 1934, *'Chips' The Diaries of Sir Henry Channon*
    If I speak   *Don't Look Round*
261 Little love   Violet to Mrs Keppel, undated (John Phillips)
262 During the evening   *Violet Trefusis: Life and Letters*
    She had none   *Hunt the Slipper*
263 I wish we could have   ibid
    I will not pretend   *Don't Look Round*
264 He called on me   ibid
265 Lord B. is marrying   Virginia to Vita, 22 November 1933. *The Sickle Side of the Moon*
    Happiness for me   *Sortie de Secours*
    I wonder how much   *Violet Trefusis: Life and Letters*
266 My mother chaffed   *Don't Look Round*
    No wonder I fell   ibid
    une ame damnée   *Vita*
267 People arrived   *Don't Look Round*
    I had poise   ibid
268 We were dancing   Lady Cecilia McKenna to author, September 1994
    I am here till   Alice Keppel to Violet, 29 August 1939 (John Phillips)
    Harry I consider   ibid, 29 August 1939
269 I must know   ibid, 19 September 1939
270 Would I be happy   Vita to Harold, 8 June 1939 (Lilly Library)
    gave one long gasp   Harold to Vita, 28 September 1939 (Lilly Library)
    Papa's temper   Alice Keppel to Violet, 11 April 1939 (John Phillips)
271 Never shall I forget   *Don't Look Round*
    This hotel   Alice Keppel to Violet, 20 April 1939 (John Phillips)
272 To hear Alice   23 September 1942, *'Chips' The Diaries of Sir Henry Channon*

NINETEEN

273 People were very   *Don't Look Round*
     Curious how war   Vita to Violet, 12 September 1940 (Beinecke Library)

274 The very sound   ibid, 31 August 1940

275 I mind for you   ibid, 14 October 1940
     wings of the past   ibid, 15 December 1940

277 It upsets me   ibid, 16 March 1941

278 I do feel   ibid
     She will amuse you   Vita to Ben Nicolson, July 1941 (Lilly Library)
     I hope Ben won't   Vita to Harold, July 1941 (Lilly Library)

279 Two of the happiest   Vita to Ben Nicolson, May 1948 (Lilly Library)
     He is bound   Vita to Harold, September 1948 (Lilly Library)
     If I were   Harold to David Carritt, 13 January 1949 (Lilly Library)

280 Poor Mor   Alice Keppel to Violet June 1942 (John Phillips)

281 A large clumsy   quoted in James Lees-Milne, *Prophesying Peace* (Chatto & Windus, 1977)

282 I wish Violet   Harold to Vita, 8 February 1944 (Lilly Library)

     To describe her as   Vita to Harold, 8–9 February 1944 (Lilly Library)

     Violet's maid unpacked   25 September 1945, Marie Belloc Lowndes *Diaries and Letters 1911–47* Ed. Susan Lowndes (Chatto & Windus 1971)

283 She is rather   *Prophesying Peace*

284 the blue letter   *Don't Look Round*

285 She looked magnificent   19 November 1943, *'Chips' The Diaries of Sir Henry Channon*

     Oh God Oh God   Vita to Harold, 21 June 1945 (Lilly Library)

286 cherished *bibelots*   *Don't Look Round*
     Except I live on capital   Alice Keppel to Violet, 23 March 1946 (John Phillips)

     suddenly Jacques   Nancy Mitford to Diana Mosley, 25 May 1946. *Love from Nancy: the Letters of Nancy Mitford.* Ed. Charlotte Mosley (Hodder & Stoughton 1993)

287 now you are domiciled   Alice Keppel to Violet, 1 June 1946 (John Phillips)

     England is perfectly   ibid, 9 June 1946)

288 Paris was lovely   Alice Keppel to her husband George, 12 August 1946 (John Phillips)

    I have always thought   ibid, 27 August 1946 (John Phillips)

    because she says   Nancy Mitford to Gerald Berners, 11 November 1946. *Love from Nancy: the Letters of Nancy Mitford*

289 It is nearly   Alice Keppel to Violet, 3 January 1947 (John Phillips)

    she will even   *Don't Look Round*

290 We were the inferior   unpublished fragment (Beinecke Library)

TWENTY

292 Admiring as we do   *The Times*, 27 November 1947

293 I wish Violet   Vita to Harold, 19 April 1949 (Lilly Library)

    Darling I am terribly   Sonia Cubitt to Violet, 6 (John Phillips) February 1949

    Whichever we decide   ibid

    I'm afraid   ibid, 30 July 1949

295 We had a curious conversation   Violet Trefusis to John Phillips, September 1966

296 Dear Mrs Trefusis   Lord Learney to Violet, 24 November 1959

297 It reminds me of BM   Vita to Harold, March 1949 (Lilly Library)

298 It is her Cranbrook   ibid

    my love of St Loup   Vita to Violet, 4 October 1949 (Beinecke Library)

    Oh you sent me a book   ibid, 1 October 1950

299 I do hope that   Betty Richards to Violet, 18 February 1949 (John Phillips)

    At a dinner party   14 June 1950, diary of James Pope-Hennessy. *A Lonely Business: A Self-portrait of James Pope-Hennessy*. Ed. Peter Quennell (Weidenfeld & Nicolson 1981)

301 When she rose   Susan Mary Alsop, *To Marietta from Paris* (Weidenfeld & Nicolson 1976)

    As she can write   Harold Acton, *Nancy Mitford: A Memoir* (Hamish Hamilton 1975)

    much as I love   Betty Richards to Violet, July 1951 (John Phillips)

303 the ruin of   *Nancy Mitford: A Memoir*

    One can almost   ibid

    The magnificent   *Violet Trefusis: Life and Letters*

305 Do you know Mitya   *Violet to Vita*, 7 May 1920

Index